STYLE AND PROPORTION
The Language of Prose and Poetry

STYLE AND PROPORTION
The Language of Prose and Poetry

JOSEPHINE MILES

University of California, Berkeley

Little, Brown and Company   BOSTON

PREFACE

How do the words and structures of language in literature differ from era to era, from place to place, from kind to kind? This is the question I undertake to ask in this book. In previous work I have asked chiefly about words in poetry. Now I hope to extend this question from words to their proportions in sentence structures, and from poetry to prose, in order to gain a more general view of literary styles in language. In widening the question, I have narrowed the range from the two hundred poetic texts considered in *Eras and Modes in English Poetry* to sixty texts in poetry and another sixty in prose — ten for each of five centuries in Britain and ten for somewhat more than a century in America. The proportions abstracted from these texts are presented at the end of the book, along with details of method by which they have been derived. Here let me suggest the line of thought that makes the questions and the resultant abstractions useful to literary study.

I think that an art gives shape and stability to valued materials of life, in order that they be stressed, attended, preserved. I think that their shapes and emphases are limited and intensified not only by valued materials but also by the habitual forms in which they are conveyed; in language, by the standard structures within the language itself. I think that among the possibilities offered by the medium, each artist chooses certain ones to stress characteristically, so that he develops, in selecting and arranging his materials, recognizable habits, a style, which is one special variation upon one among the more general styles established by certain lines of choice. I think that individual readers and those who write works of art in language can profitably discern forms not only in the experiences embodied in the work, and not only in the aesthetic forms of the

v

work as art, but also in the medium, the language, in its elements and proportions, as they provide both limitations and potentialities. A reader may appreciate, a writer may practice, the forms which best serve his own sense of values.

Of the many studies that have illuminated how forms of art are related to values of life, few, with the pre-eminent exceptions of Erich Auerbach's *Mimesis*, Erwin Panofsky's *Iconology*, and Heinrich Wölfflin's *Principles of Art History*, have dealt with the mediating forces in the traditional structures of the medium. In language, perhaps Owen Barfield, Donald Davie, William Empson, Leo Spitzer, W. K. Wimsatt are most noteworthy, along with such early treasurers of gems as George Puttenham and Edward Bysshe. Of the many who write of language as a cultural phenomenon, on the other hand, few except Edward Sapir and Otto Jespersen even hint at art's intensifying patterns, though sociologists recently have become interested in discovering intensifying patterns in general. As for prose patterns in particular, they have been remarked mostly in the small units — word, cadence, or sentence-length — by such minutely observant scholars as Sherman, Lee, Croll, Williamson, and Ohmann. Now for cross-references: for practical reasons as well as theoretical, for immediate reasons as well as historical, we can afford a great deal of new speculation about how language functions in literature, how literature functions in language.

The manner or art of the message rests not only upon the character of the message and that of the author, *l'homme même*, but also upon that of the medium, the language, which may change in emphasis from time to time, place to place, and type to type. Therefore I attempt first a general chapter on the articulations of language; then three historical and comparative chapters considering differences evident in time, place, type; and then a final, general chapter, which relates the grammatical elements to logical and rhetorical elements in language in sound and sense, in order to suggest the complex choices that make up an individual style within a general style.

My purposes are understanding, use, and enjoyment. Students and scholars, no less than artists, enjoy knowing how things work, and perform the better for the knowledge. I have tried looking at literary styles as habitual uses of material and manners that may be discriminated in ways relevant not only to literary textures but also to the needs and feelings of everyday writing. How our language, how our literature has worked, how our writing may work — these are my primary interests.

My thanks are due for sustaining if not approving argument and advice to Paul Alkon, Paul Alpers, Stephen Booth, Y. R. Chao, Noam Chomsky, Phillip Damon, Elizabeth Closs, Dell Hymes, Yakov Malkiel, Leo Ruth, Julian Boyd, Sheldon Sacks, William Shipley, Karl Uitti, Richard Worthen; for sustaining aid to Michael Cooke, John Paul Graff, Carol Mabon, Janet Nathanson, Diana Smith; for aid, also, to the American Council of Learned Societies and the University of California Committee on Research. Some of these pages have appeared in different form in *The Minnesota Review*, *The English Journal*, *College Composition and Communication*, and the pamphlet *Emerson* (University of Minnesota Press, 1964). The variety of my debts only begins to suggest the vitality of the field.

J. M.

TABLE OF CONTENTS

STYLE AND PROPORTION
The Language of Prose and Poetry

◀◀ ONE ▶▶

Language and Proportion

Prose proceeds forward in time by steps less closely measured, but not less propelling, than the steps of verse. While every few feet, verse reverses, repeats, reassesses the pattern of its progression, prose picks up momentum toward its forward goal in strides variably adapted to its burdens and purposes. Both use steps; neither merely flows; each may be perceived and followed by its own stages of articulation. A printed text indicates such stages graphically by white spaces, the graphic representation of pauses in utterance, between words, between sentences, and between paragraphs, the spaces of increasing size representing increasing durational emphasis. Prose does not, however, make use of the additional white space of margins which represent the more regular rhythmic and thus typographical reversals of verse. Is this why a page of prose does not seem for the usual reader adequately posted, but rather a maze of print into which he must cast himself without such guidelines as verse supplies? And do many readers enjoy prose dialogue because the back and forth breaks in the print serve to provide the sort of pauses they need for recognition of emphasis? It is true that modern print especially provides additional guides in the form of punctuation: capital letters to begin steps, period marks to end them, with various lighter pauses in between. But verse makes use of all these and then, in addition, marks off its linear units as they coincide with, and cross over, its units of statement. Has prose no comparable guides?

I think it has, and I think the reason we have not recognized and used them as fully as we might in reading the sense of a page is that they are not external measures like line length but rather internalized, built into the content, the guideposts of explicit connective terms. Rather than milestones, they are road signs of varying content, indicating the contexts

1

of statement by junctures like *on one hand* and *on the other; either, or; behind, ahead; now, then; to, from;* related less to recurrent measures than to the occurrent locuses of significance along the way. Poetry, while it works with these same explicit materials, using these same signs, has somewhat less frequent need for them because of the guidances given by measure; therefore, it uses consistently fewer explicit connectives than prose — by one in every two or three lines.

Suppose that printers shared my belief in the lively function of connective units to locate the steps by which prose moves forward: then they might well use their white spaces to aid in recognition, as in the following sentence.

> Early in the morning,   in a small town   near the highway,   because he was hungry   and though he was   in danger,   the young boy, looking   neither to left   nor to right,   climbed the path   to the city hall.

The sentence takes a step: its verb locates itself in time and relation, *The boy climbed the path;* subject acts upon object, in past tense. The rest of the material of the sentence is additional: specifically linked by the links *in, near, because, though, neither, nor, to.* The only other terms not so linked are the words of modification, the single adverbs and adjectives *early, small, happy, looking, young.* First we get one of these, the single word *early,* then a phrase of time; then two phrases of place; then two contrasting clauses of consequence; then the subject qualified, first by an adjective and then by a participle controlling two disjunctive alternative phrases; finally, the verb, and its object with a qualifying phrase of location. All this variety can be ordered into three parts: the basic section, the predication of subject, *the boy climbed the path;* the qualifying phrases and clauses signalized by connectives *in, near, because,* and so on; and the adjectives that assume rather than predicate.

This is a moderately long sentence, about average for modern English; but note how much longer the wordage, though shorter the sentences, if it were to be transformed back to its root statements, from qualifiers and connectives back to their basic predications, from *a small town near the highway* to *the town was small, the town was near the highway.*

> The time was early. The time was morning. The place was a town. The town was small. The town was   near the highway. The boy was young. The boy was hungry. The boy was   in danger. The boy did not look   to the left. The boy did not look   to the right. The boy climbed the path. The path belonged   to the city hall.

2

Even without the further divisions possible, the text is half again as long. On the other hand, it can be shortened by the reduction of phrases and clauses to qualifiers.

Early this morning   in a small highway town,   hungry   and in danger, the young boy, looking   neither left   nor right, climbed the city-hall path.

While the alternatives of qualifying and connective forms are plain, it is also plain that some alternatives are better suited to one purpose than to another. The sentence just varied seems to take to localizing subordinations better than it does to itemizations of process or of quality. More seriously, characteristic passages by admirable writers of prose exemplify the same sort of possible differences in choice of grammatical method for different purposes. In other words, the reader who can recognize the signifying sections of a prose passage and how they work together can recognize also what their alternatives may be, in structure as well as in content, and so can then more fully appreciate their purpose in their character. It is possible to recognize alternative modes of progression just because the alternatives are limited by grammatical possibility. In the roots of grammar, the stems of logic and the flowers of rhetoric take their being.

In statements small or large, from word to paragraph, the root of potentiality is the verb, as in "The boy climbed the path," the establishing of a relation in time by the verb root and its suffix of time and person. Verb implies noun, predicate implies subject, in a way that subject cannot in turn imply predicate, so the relation of the two is not isometric, not binary, not susceptible of two-part analysis. Topic is subsumed by theme. Even minimal statements like *He speaks,* where pronoun-substitute works with verb alone, establish the specific time of the suffix in relation to personal action, so that *speaks* is more grammatically complex than *he,* implying *he* as *he* does not imply *speaks,* and so establishing the sentence in a way that *he* cannot.

The augmentation of subject-verb into more amply loaded sentences is made by the addition of attributive words, like adjectives, adverbs, and nouns in apposition; or, more complexly, by the substitution of larger forms for these smaller. This is how prepositions and conjunctions function as connectives: to introduce the substantive forms that in phrasal or clausal structure serve in the place of adjectives, adverbs, and nouns. Only verbs cannot be substituted for. So a subject or nominative may be *The man* or *He* or *Whoever you think he is,* and a qualifier may be *The man is honest* or *The honest man speaks* or *The man who is honest speaks* or *The man in honesty speaks*. Both implicitness in order and explicitness in connective labels like *who* and *in* serve to signal the substitutions or transformations. Noam Chomsky has drawn upon examples used by the Port-Royal grammarians of the seventeenth century to illustrate how lucidly these various modes of structure have been recognized as substitutive or transformative. Three short sentences are *Dieu est invisible, Le monde est visible, Dieu a créé le monde. God is invisible, The world is visible, God has created the world.* From the first two, parts can be drawn to amplify the third, in substitutive phrasal and clausal form: *God who is invisible* or *in his invisibility, has created the world which is visible.* Or in more succinct modification, *Invisible God has created the visible world.*[1]

Of these, the first is more strongly predicative and sequenced with its three statements. The second is subordinative, like the boy on the path. The most loaded form is the adjectival: having cut away the predicates of attribution, it assumes the attributes and by such assumption can build a multiplicity of qualified nouns upon a single verb. Classically, such richness of condensation was recognized also in verse, in the "golden line" of which Dryden reminds us in his Preface to the *Fables*. In parallel to *Dieu invisible a créé le monde visible* is the Latin *ultima$_A$ cumaei$_A$ venitiam$_V$ carminis$_N$ aetas$_N$*. Both present a proportion of two adjectives and two nouns to one verb instead of three, and represent therefore an economy by relative paucity of assertion, relative generosity of assumption. Between these extremes are the partial assertions, partial assumptions of explicitly clausal and phrasal structure, working in forms not fully sentences yet not simply words.

These three alternative structures provide the chief possible choices in sentence-making in English; and, therefore, establish the grounds for the three styles distinguishable on the basis of structural choice: the predicative, the connective-subordinative, and the adjectival. Structure supports substance. In addition to the primary relation of *who* to *what*, the material to be explicated, we have the material of our questions *where, when, how,* and *why;* questions, that is, of time and place, of manner and consequence, our normal settings of relation in context. Logic makes these same distributions in sentence structure: conjunctive *and . . . and*, with *then . . . then*, and *there . . . there* for time and place; *either . . . or*

[1] Noam Chomsky, *Current Issues in Linguistic Theory* (The Hague: Mouton & Co., 1965), p. 15.

for alternatives; *if . . . therefore* for consequence; along with the cor-respondent disjunctive *but, nor, though.* Logic and grammar thus work with content and furnish out the situation of statement, allowing single words, subsentences, or extra sentences to do the work of specification. So just as a single word or a whole paragraph may serve the function of one sentence with its subject-verb and affixes, so also a single word, sentence, or paragraph may function as affix or adjunct to a primary assertion; that is, supply material of *where, when, how, why* to a basic predication of *who-what.*

A "characteristic passage" in prose must mean, therefore, not just any section of given length, inasmuch as we should not expect or wish for such homogeneity of character throughout a text, but rather a "passage," a pro-gression which does actually move forward by a major predicate in ways, with segmentations or subordinations, representative of those habitual in the text when it is making such progress. A whole sentence or a whole long paragraph may take one main step: *I came*; where, why, or how. It may take three: *I came, I saw, I conquered*; where, when, why, how. Or it may take only part of one, a substep (I came): *The place I came to was distant and disturbed*; when, where, why, or how.

For these reasons of assumption and subordination, these powers of prose to expand and contract and shift its emphases, the criterion of length of word, sentence, or paragraph is an especially irrelevant one, much as it has been used by critics of prose style. Is a short word more economi-cal than a long one, or must three be used as equivalent? Is a sentence that spares verbs more economical than one that spares assumptions? Economy must depend on intent. At least we may say, therefore, that a characteristic passage needs to be recognized in terms of a text's whole style of progression or its general habits of little leaps, heavy landings, or long articulated strides. Shall we carry the furniture to the new house by one trip in one large truck or by many trips in our own car. Or shall we take just the small items and leave the rest to a friend? A motor can move many different sizes and weights, one way or another. A defining feature is the delivery of the goods.

Now, with the aid of additional white space around connected sections, let us look at some passages of prose, which I suggest to be characteristic of the texts from which they come, and note how their differences in sentence-structures make for a perceptible difference in effect of manner, even of traditional styles. Then, later, we can turn to the larger and more abstract proportions in structure which these passages illustrate.

5

Consider D. H. Lawrence's command of many independent verbs in a paragraph from "The Spirit of Place" in *Studies in Classic American Literature*.

> The real American day hasn't begun yet. Or at least, not yet sunrise. So far it has been the false dawn. That is, in the progressive American consciousness there has been the one dominant desire, to do away with the old thing. Do away with masters, to exalt the will of the people. The will of the people being nothing but a figment, the exalting doesn't count for much. So in the name of the will of the people get rid of masters. When you have got rid of masters, you are left with this mere phrase of the will of the people. Then you pause and bethink yourself, and try to recover your own wholeness.

The dozen verbs carry the line of thought: . . . *hasn't begun* . . . *so far it has been* . . . *that is, the desire to do away* . . . *to exalt* . . . *doesn't count* . . . *so get rid* . . . *you are left* . . . *pause and bethink*, and *try to recover*. . . . A persistent chronology supports the argument. *When* . . . *then* . . . with only one *so* to enforce the logic. The adjectives *real* . . . *false* . . . *dominant* . . . *mere* . . . *own* are thematic, too, but fewer and are in a supporting relation. Repetitions work also to support thematically, to do some of the work that subordinate connections might otherwise do; the repeated phrasal *will of the people* is thematically put down by the repeated imperative verb *get rid of*.

Characteristic as is such an active sequence in the prose of Lawrence, it is famed also as the early native English style: the active sequences of Tyndale's Biblical prose; the narrative arguments of More, Lyly, Sidney, Dryden; even to Joyce in our own day. Indeed, at least half of our best-known writers use this jaunting tone — the curt wit of predicative concept.

If we would call this a plain, a sequential style of process, then we could read in contrast the subordinating prose of Bertrand Russell's essay "Philosophy's Ulterior Motives," noting particularly the complexly related steps in its explicitly connected subordinations: *as opposed to* . . . *from* . . . *to* . . . *belief that* . . . *and that* . . . *but* . . . *such as* . . . and again *as opposed to*.

> Philosophy, as opposed to science, springs from a kind of self-assertion: a belief that our purposes have an important relation to the purposes of the universe, and that, in the long run, the course of events is bound to be, on the whole, such as we should wish. Science abandoned this kind of optimism,

but is being led   towards another: that we,   by our intelligence,
can make the world such   as to satisfy a large proportion   of our
desires: This is a practical,   as opposed   to a metaphysical, op-
timism. I hope   it will not seem   to future generations   as foolish   as that   of Dr. Pangloss.

We sense here not just colorful references but their perspective at different levels in the fabric of connection. The careful subordinations in interior thought may develop partially from the state of prose language in
Russell's time, which he accepts naturally and works with companionably,
partially from his own biases of character and tone. The *that* clauses, the
practical and metaphysical contrast, are to be found in paragraph after
paragraph, in essay after essay by Russell, and reflect in their close design
a weighing and arguing, an active and balancing mind and mode of
thought, which makes use of the various alternatives that the language
offers. In precise terms of proportions, we may say that this style balances
adjectives and verbs, phrases and clauses, and that its explicit connectives
are strong in the same way, balancing prepositions and conjunctions, with
emphasis on the subordinating relative pronoun and on prepositions like
by and *to* in phrases of motion.

We may call this style classical inasmuch as logic, subordination, and
poise are its strong characteristics; we may also call it modern because it is
used by so many of Russell's contemporaries: Churchill, Shaw, Read, and
Orwell. If we look back in time, we will see it also in the work of Bacon,
of Hobbes, of Milton, of Clarendon, of Locke, of Burke, of Alison and
Arnold; and, inasmuch as many of these have been traditionally called
both classical and modern, we may tentatively use both labels. The earlier
writers share with Russell his moderate alternatives: his sense of balance
on the one hand and on the other his strong substantial sense of nouns,
phrases, and relative clauses. For example, Bacon's essay "Of Friendship"
in its final form possesses a number of passages in style and structure
similar to Russell's.

Both the free independent verb of Lawrence and the bound subordinate
verb of Russell are modern as well as traditional, but they do not provide
the only possible choices. A third style is characterized by the infrequent
verb, heavily loaded with noun modifications, as in the highly adjectival
style of Huxley's "Uniqueness of Man" in *Man in the Modern World*.

Man's opinion   of his own position   in relation   to the rest
of the animals   has swung pendulum-wise   between too great   or
too little a conceit   of himself,   fixing   now too large a gap   be-

tween himself and the animals, now too small. The gap, of course, can be diminished or increased at either the animal or the human end. One can, like Descartes, make animals too mechanical, or, like most unsophisticated people, humanize them too much. Or one can work at the human end of the gap, and then either dehumanize one's own kind into an animal species like any other, or superhumanize it into being a little lower than the angels.

The many epithets — *too great, too little, too large, too small, animal, human, mechanical* — are crucial to the thought and overweigh the fewer verbs, themselves nearly adjectival — *has swung, can be diminished, can work, dehumanize, superhumanize.* Such proportioning is accentuated by a choice of participial modifiers like *fixing* instead of verb clauses with *which.* So, even though this paragraph deals with the kind of balance of contrasts we think of as classical, its procedure is not classical. Its choices are not subordinative; it slights clauses for phrasal *of, in, at, to, like,* and it explicitly compares, with *either, or, than,* setting up contrasting structures.

In other traits, this style of Huxley's is to be contrasted rather to Lawrence's than to Russell's. What for Huxley and Russell is one sentence, for Lawrence is two or three. Like Russell, Huxley does not progress temporally, with Lawrence's sense of immediate process, but works within the generality of a pendulum swing. The point of view of Huxley's general *one* is closer to Russell's *we* than to Lawrence's *you,* though all are talking about human nature. Other scientists and pre-scientists — Darwin, Adam Smith, Gibbon, Browne, Ascham — write in this mode of Huxley's.

Not subject merely, but attitude, purpose, and sense of verbal tradition establish these distinctions in expression. Out of varieties of choice, persistent nuclei of choice recur. The tongue twists; the hand, the *stylus* or pen, slants in ways perceivably guided by language as by spirit. We find an interplay, with its flexibility disconcerting to causal analysis, between the singularity and community of a work of literature as between the singularity and community of a person.

Happily, there is good Greek precedent for grounding personal rhetorical choice in general grammatical structure. Demetrius in Alexandria in the third century B.C. characterized styles by rhetorics of purpose within the potentialities of certain grammatical constructions. The plain style, he said, is simple, using many active verbs and keeping its subjects spare. Its purposes include lucidity, clarity, familiarity, getting its work done crisply and well; so it uses few difficult compounds, coinages, or qualifications; avoids harsh sounds or odd orders; employs helpful connective terms and clear series with firm endings; and in every way tries to be natural, following the order of events themselves with moderation and repetition as in dialogue.

The eloquent style, in contrast, changes the natural order of materials in order to effect control over them even before predication. So the style may be called, in a form of *pathos*, passive in contrast to active. As strong assumptions are made, subjects are tremendously amplified without the activity of predication, because inherent qualities rather than new relations are stressed. Sentences are lengthy, rounded, suspended, with a great deal of elaborately connected material. Words can be unusual, coined, figured; sounds can be mouth-filling, even harsh; and meanings can be implied, oblique, symbolic.

The modern student of prose may quickly praise plainness and condemn the eloquent, which he often calls high or flowery, but after consideration may remember that purposes differ and that if he wishes to move, to enhance, to persuade, some language of flowers, some structure of suspense and excitement, may be valuable, in contrast to a plain naturalness.

Demetrius cut across this contrast with another — one between styles energetic on the one hand and polished on the other: between short and harsh phrases, broken, loose, and spontaneous, as if under great stress, with a choice of terms symbolic like the eloquent, though not so elaborated, and without interconnected qualifying structures; and the polished, smoothly connected, aesthetically pleasant in reference and tone, which embellishes the familiar with charm and grace. Two centuries later, Dionysius of Halicarnassus characterized Pindar by this contrast: his harmony natural, stately, spacious, articulated by pauses rather than smoothly polished and joined by connectives; naturally off-balance, not rounded and symmetrical.

Note that this contrast is another version of the first, between an art of naturalness and an art of inventiveness: the first contrast grammatically stressing the choice between predication or qualification; the second, between implicit or explicit connection; these grammatical choices providing the structural basis for choices of reference, reason, and tone. Gradually the choices, in certain combinations, settled into three — plain, middle, and high — because, though the high could not easily descend or blend, the plain could easily be somewhat energetic, somewhat polished, even somewhat eloquent and thus effect a middle style. In grammatical terms, the predicative style could be either implicitly or explicitly connected, abrupt or smooth; while the high qualifying style, because of its greater mass and extension, could not so easily get along with the abruptness of connectives merely implied. For the high style, the terms of reference are implicative of further qualities rather than of further active relations. The gamut in choice between sparest and fullest materials of qualification is mediated by the choice along the way of sparest or fullest signals of relation. The sentence is a synthesis; a composition; an arrangement of sounds, references, and structures; put to a purpose of showing, weighing, moving, and of pleasing along with these. From the high style of Aeschylus and Demosthenes and the smooth of Isocrates to the moderate fullness of Cicero and to the loose or intense brevity of the Stoics, classic prose tradition came into English with all its variations still possible in the new language, so that More, Ascham, and Bacon all within one century could well disagree on what different styles would be appropriate even to similar subject matter. Still today all three basic styles and their variations are useful and are, indeed, still discernible by the measures of the most technical linguistic analysis, as beneath the differing surfaces of procedure may be seen the simple kernel forms for the plain style and what we now call the further levels of transformations for the high.

The work of authorship in its rhetoric involves not only the horizontal ordering, or disposition, but also the vertical ordering, or invention, of the hierarchies of emphasis: the selecting, from any set of possible transformations, what is chosen to be predicated and what to be modified in what form of modification. In such selectivities of substance and structure, we may vividly recognize the functioning of choice, which, when habitual, becomes style, closely limited by its material into certain kinds and developments, yet profoundly variable in individual identity.

Metaphysically, one may speculate a little about these styles, what attitudes they may be concerned with. Most simply, the predicative style is statement-making. It has much to say and says it sequentially, leaving context to establish relations between statements, making the most important relation the statable one between verb and noun. In other words, it creates situations. The adjunctive style, on the other hand, assumes situations and therefore is able to express them in form of additive words and phrases — *old Jacob . . .* or *Jacob, one of the oldest . . .* rather than *Jacob ages* or *Jacob is old*. This is the spatial attitude — as distinguished from the temporal — which Joseph Frank, for example, considers characteristic of the modern novel; and, inasmuch as we note the strong decline of the use of connectives, especially conjunctions, in the English essay also, we may surmise a central defining characteristic of the present-day literary prose style. I have recently read in newspapers supposedly word-of-mouth reports so suspensive, substantive, and adjectival, so lacking in the many verbs which normally, according to Fries, characterize the colloquial, that I have wondered whether even everyday speech was being affected by the attitude of assumption and was moving in the same direction as literary prose, toward "presenting" in preference to "stating." Perhaps also a central problem in writing may be put in this way: writers are far more adept at assuming, at naming and presenting, than at stating and connecting. The freer they are to do either one, the freer they may be to choose.

The balanced and adjunctive style, which Russell used, has the advantage of complexity, in making direct statements in the express terms of subordinate assumptions and thus weighing the evidence. It lacks, however, the simplicity both of the rapid-fire statement with which English began and the noncommittal naming toward which, at times, we seem to move. At any rate, we may see that stating, naming, and connecting are not only forms but functions of the language. More than parts of speech, they are parts of thought.

We may suggest as ideas important for fuller analysis of prose styles: The participating nature of art makes it simple to analyze without distortion; clear strands of agreement run through it, from form to form, from time to time, and from individual to individual. On the other hand, each form and time, even each individual work, has its own structures of relevance that need to be fairly discerned, so as not to be subordinated to others. In the language in which art works, certain patterns are given by speech and certain patterns are formalized by prose and poetry; for example, in complex discursive writing, word, phrase, and clause structures play across sentence structures in ways that build certain clear types of recognizable wholes. The artist's choices are not atomistic and infinitely various, but already shapely when he comes to them in the language. By recognizing the general proportion and continuity of these choices, we may sooner recognize what we value in the artist's specific integrity.

Proportion is a concept important for the analytical study of an art because it concerns not only the structure in the discernible parts of the material and not only the content or reference of the parts but also the relation between material and structure, the relation between *what* and *how* in *how much what?* So, for example, an architect will care not only about the character or function of the room he is designing and not only about its links to other rooms but also about its own proportions and its proportionate relations, in shape, size, and arrangement. Or a cook will care not only about the order of combination of salt and sugar in a sauce but also about the amounts of salt and sugar, the proportion of one to the other for very different effects.

11

Proportion is, so to speak, an aesthetic, a sensory interest, as this relates to interest in identity and function. It is the relation of the old *quadrivium* of geometry, music, architecture, astronomy, with its patterns in numbers, to the *trivium* of grammar, rhetoric, logic, with its patterns in letters. The figures 235 can mean a sum checkable in fact or a sum functionable for a purpose or within itself have an aesthetic relevance of shape, an ascending pattern of 235 as distinguished, for example, from a balanced one of 232. Many theories of beauty have their basis, as they did for Pythagoras and for Leonardo da Vinci, and still do today, in a consciousness of "right" proportions. So in language, for the Romans, a recommended proportion for language in verse was the two nouns and two adjectives to one verb, which they called the "golden line." Interest in the interworking of parts in structure leads also to interest in proportioning of parts.

Modern grammar, with its emphasis on functioning parts, aids in the discerning of proportions in the use of language and thus in the discerning of some of the choices in prose and poetry as arts of language. Asking such questions as whether prose is similar to poetry in its uses and whether the histories of the two run parallel in continuity and change, I have found more and more illumination in their grammars as well as in their vocabularies, in the ways that proportionings of materials reflect proportionings of structures.

Certain more commonly discussed characteristics of style I examine less systematically either because they have already been thoroughly treated or because they will be subsumed under topics here. For sentence structure, as an instance, writers have often treated sentence lengths and sentence rhythms without treating sentence parts and groups. Their findings have therefore seemed to me too atomic. True, Macaulay's sentences are half Milton's in length; but how much of the difference is punctuational? What is a sentence unit? Macaulay's lesser use of clausal connectives and thus of bound interior verb forms seems to me the more helpful clue to the difference. Again, rhythms are treated as cadences, as ends of sentences, without an overview of varying sentence structures. As for diction, the common distinction, by Quayle and others from Aristotle down, is between rare and usual terms or between Saxon, Norman, and Latin terms, with a tendency to assume norms never explicated and thus to emphasize oddity apart from patterns of usage.

There is perhaps a feeling that long Latinate words, much affixed, make for long, periodic sentences, much balanced and subordinated; while, in contrast, short, crisp sentences are pronounced in short, crisp monosyllables. But there are a number of difficulties in such a dualism. One is that the chief short, crisp monosyllables (the Englishness of which Dryden complained of) are the connectives, as distinguished from affixed forms; subordinating and phrasal structures, therefore, in all their complexity, can be as English as Latin. On the other hand, short, simple sentences may easily use multisyllables for weight. The contrasts are not one but many: content, order, subordination, generality, abstraction, figurativeness, connotation, and the complexities of reference — all supply their multiple interrelations. My purpose therefore is to follow out the main lines provided by proportion in both content and structure, and then to see how these are variable in individual combinations in individual texts.

An important objection to the literary relevance of proportion is that it is not specific, that it is expressible as an average or norm, not as descriptive of actualities of prose. The important answer is that it is both general and specific; that is, I have not yet found a text of which the general proportions are alien to central specific passages. Of course, no writer is apt to write in monotone without variation. But if a proportion shows many connectives, for example, then paragraphs illustrating just this ratio of connectives come immediately to view. The most fundamental part of the objection is that proportion is abstracted from order, from context. True, it is by such abstraction that I hope to follow out certain main lines of emphasis; but these abstractions need ultimately to be seen in order and context again, the specific adjectives with their specific nouns, the emphasis and choices in their correlative progressing.

The advantage of thinking about grammar, logic, and rhetoric together is to see their interconnections more plainly. This *trivium* of letters, as distinguished from the *quadrivium* of numbers, establishes the full relations of letter to letter, letter to reference, and letter to intent and effect, which a system of symbols makes pertinent. As representing sound and syllable, unit of meaning from morpheme to word and utterance, the letter of *logos* conveys spirit in the signs of speech. Each specialist sees the proliferations of complexity in the process, the exceptions and ambiguities that make the borderlines of distinctions; the subtle differences between one verb form and another, the habits of tautology, the artifices of rhetoric as device. But the contemplation of lettered, of literary, language in general can afford to blur these distinctions for the sake of focusing upon the whole use of the medium in a paragraph or stanza, to learn how one sentence, one word, one syllable fits with another, and how all fit the pattern of their intent. Not a geometer, musician, astronomer, or architect, I nevertheless think that proportion, the basis of the *quadrivium*, is pertinent to language as well as to structural forms. Properties of sound, syllable, grammatical unit, and rhetorical scheme in composed language are just as significant as properties of perceived design in stone or constellation.

Specifically, the pattern of proportions I present in concentrated form on pp. 16, 17 is the proportion of adjectives, nouns, verbs, and connectives used by sixty poets and sixty prose writers in English in the past five centuries. Because my earlier interest was in frequencies of reference in the major vocabulary of poetry, I paid little attention in *Eras and Modes* and the *Continuity of Poetic Language* to questions of syntactic proportion, to connectives, and to prose structures. Then, when I recognized the close relations between syntactic structures and the proportioning of parts of speech, I supposed that prose would differ in its uses especially by an emphasis on connectives. As can be seen, this idea did not turn out to be wholly true. But it led to the selective emphases of the present study: upon certain parts of speech and upon poetry and prose in parallel through the centuries.

First, to be more specific about the parts of speech: the terms commonly called terms of reference or content are nouns, adjectives, verbs. Words used chiefly for linking and connecting, prepositions and conjunctions, then are usually grouped as "grammatical terms." These two kinds of terms, referential and grammatical, constitute the language of our study. Of the other parts of speech, the pronouns, and the articles or determiners so neatly treated by Rostrevor-Hamilton, both are so closely related to the noun that they belong to a fuller study of the noun itself; their absence here limits the validity of what is indicated about the noun's functions in other forms as the absence of adverbs limits the view of the verbs.

The chief specified pattern then is the proportion, in a sequential text of one thousand lines of poetry (six to eight thousand words) and eight thousand words of prose, of adjective to noun to verb, the referential pattern; and of these to connectives, the grammatical pattern. These proportions, simply established, allow us to see the overall structure of the text — its dominant subordination or its dominant qualification, for example — more easily than a close structure-by-structure scrutiny would do. It allows us to see the trees within the forest.

Note needs to be made of inclusion in categories: in a simpleminded way, all nouns and gerunds as nouns; numerical or limiting adjectives and present and past participles as adjectives when used so, as in *sparkling broken glass*; infinitives as verbs; all connectives, prepositional and conjunctival, together as connectives. As Jespersen says, "The difference between the various functions of one and the same word, e.g., *before* in . . .

'using this before my marriage,' and 'many times before I was married,' is not important enough to cause it to be placed in different categories." [2] Of the seventy most used connectives, half, like *before*, are used as either prepositions or conjunctions, so that the tendency of the language seems to relate the two; and this relation simplifies the habit of the reader to note all connective material as of a kind, whatever the further possible subdivisions. In the distinguishing of verbs, it seems to me that the forms *I go, he goes, he is going, he has gone, he hopes to go* all share a predicative force which the assumptive form, a *going* or *gone concern*, lacks. At any rate, it has turned out that adjectival writers are the large users of participial adjectives, so that they seem to concur in my feeling of affinity in such parallelism as that of *England's green and pleasant land*.

The two pages which follow give an overview of English poetry and English prose in their pattern of structural variation. Most immediately visible is the similarity of the two patterns. On both pages, the writers cluster first at lower left, then at upper center, then at middle right, with an effect of motion through five centuries from one extreme through midpoints to another extreme and then back to midpoint. The great difference between the two is that the prose motion first leads, then follows the poetic, developing a middle style earlier than poetry, but then not moving into the adjectival heights until a century later, coming in the twentieth century to much the same agreement with which it had begun, though closer to mid level.

In closer detail, the reader may note, starting at the left, that each century-column contains the names of the ten writers publishing in that century, in order, from bottom to top, of the dominance of verb over adjective: strongest verbs at bottom, balance in the middle, least verbs at top. So in prose Tyndale's Bible, More, Sidney, and others, like the Ballads, Wyatt, and Sidney in poetry, use the active English of three verbs to every one or two adjectives; while a few experimenters, Bacon and Ascham in prose, like Spenser, Shakespeare, and Sylvester in poetry, try a stronger set of attributions. Connectives, somewhat more numerous for prose, tend to follow nouns in number; that is, to relate to the extra noun called for in phrase or clause. The average sixteenth-century proportion for prose is 2–4–3–5, for poetry 2–4–3–4, as these numbers represent reduction by the least common denominator of four hundred, of proportions such as 800–1000–1200–2000 adjectives, nouns, verbs, connectives in 6000–8000 cursive words of text.

[2] Otto Jespersen, *Essentials of English Grammar* (London: Allen & Unwin, 1933), p. 12.

TABLE 1A PROPORTIONS IN ENGLISH POETRY*

All values are given in A-N-V-C order (Adjective-Noun-Verb-Connective).

	16th century	17th century	18th century	19th century	20th century	AMERICAN 19th & 20th centuries
Adjectival	Sylvester 3-5-2-3p	Blackmore 3-5-2-4 Milton 3-4-2-4	Thomson 4-5-2-4p Blake 3-6-2-6cp Bowles 3-5-2-4 Collins 3-5-2-4 Gray 3-5-2-3 Cowper 3-4-2-4c	Keats 4-6-2-5cp Swinburne 4-6-3-6crp Tennyson 3-4-2-3	Thomas 3-6-2-4p Spender 3-5-2-4p	Whitman 3-7-2-5p Crane 3-5-2-4 Dwight 3-5-2-4
Balanced	Shakespeare 3-4-3-4cr Spenser 3-4-3-4r	Waller 3-5-3-4r	Pope 3-5-3-4 Johnson 2-5-2-3 Wordsworth 2-4-2-4	Shelley 2-5-2-4p Hopkins 2-5-2-3 Yeats 2-4-2-4c	Lawrence 3-4-3-4c Sitwell 2-6-2-5cp Nicholson 2-5-2-4p	Bryant 2-4-2-4 Emerson 2-4-2-3 Eliot 2-4-2-3 Roethke 2-4-2-2 Robinson 2-3-2-2
	Dunbar 1-3-1-3	Dryden 2-5-2-4	Crabbe 2-4-2-3		Graves 2-4-2-3	Lowell 2-5-3-3
Predicative	Sidney 2-5-3-4r Gascoigne 2-5-3-4cr Surrey 2-4-3-4r Wyatt 2-3-3-3 Coverdale 1-2-2-3 Ballads 1-3-3-3	Jonson 2-4-3-4cr Herrick 2-4-3-4c Herbert 2-4-3-3 Donne 2-3-3-6cr Marvell 2-3-3-3 Vaughan 2-3-3-3		Coleridge 2-4-3-4c Byron 2-4-3-4 Browning 2-4-3-3 Hardy 1-3-2-3	Jennings 2-4-3-4 Gunn 2-4-3-3 Muir 2-4-3-3 Auden 2-4-3-3	Dickinson 1-3-2-2
(total)	2-4-3-4	2-4-3-4	3-5-2-4	2-5-2-4	2-5-3-4	2-4-2-3

A-N-V-C Adjective-Noun-Verb-Connective
c clausal or phrasal
r relative
p phrasal

*Note that proportions for Pindar's Odes (Olymp. 1,2; Pyth. 1,8,9; Ist. 5,6,7) are 1260-2050-760-970. For other proportions in other languages, see Appendix. Eras and Modes, rev. ed. 1964.

TABLE 1B PROPORTIONS IN ENGLISH PROSE

	BRITISH					AMERICAN
	16th century	17th century	18th century	19th century	20th century	19th & 20th centuries
	A-N-V-C	A-N-V-C	A-N-V-C	A-N-V-C	A-N-V-C	A-N-V-C
Adjectival						
Ascham	3-4-2-5c					
Browne		3-5-2-4p				
Gibbon			3-6-2-5p			
Smith			3-5-2-5p			
Macaulay				3-5-2-5p		
Ruskin				3-5-2-6cpr		
Pater				3-5-2-5		
Carlyle				3-4-2-4		
Darwin				3-4-2-3p		
De Quincey				2-4-1-3p		
Huxley					3-5-2-4	
Whitman						3-5-2-5p
				_3-5-2-4_	_3-5-2-4_	_3-5-2-5_
Balanced						
Bacon	2-4-2-5cpr					
Hobbes		2-5-2-5				
Burnet		2-5-2-5				
Clarendon		2-4-2-5				
Milton		2-4-2-5cr				
Locke		2-3-2-5cr				
Alison			2-5-2-5p			
Burke			2-5-2-5p			
Godwin			2-4-2-4p			
Swift			2-4-2-4			
Arnold				2-5-2-4		
Shaw				2-5-2-4		
Russell					3-5-3-5p	
Orwell					3-4-3-4	
Churchill					2-5-2-4	
Read					2-5-2-4p	
Wain					2-5-2-4	
Twain						3-5-3-4
Eliot						3-4-3-4
Paine						2-5-2-4
Predicative						
Holinshed	2-5-3-5p					
Hooker	2-4-3-5c					
Dekker	2-4-3-5c					
Sidney	2-4-3-4					
Lyly	2-4-3-4					
More	2-4-3-4c					
Latimer	1-4-3-4c					
Tyndale	1-4-3-5cpr					
Donne		2-4-3-5				
Jonson		2-4-3-5				
Dryden		2-4-3-4				
Bunyan		1-4-3-5cpr				
Addison			2-5-3-5			
Johnson			2-5-3-4			
Shaftesbury			2-4-3-4p			
Berkeley			2-4-3-4			
Hazlitt				2-5-3-5		
Frazer				2-5-3-4p		
Connolly					2-5-3-4	
Lawrence					2-5-3-3	
Joyce					2-4-3-4	
West					2-4-3-4	
Lardner						2-6-3-4
Emerson						2-5-3-4
Baldwin						2-5-3-4
Edwards						2-4-3-5
Santayana						2-4-3-4
Hemingway						2-4-3-4
	_2-4-3-5_	_2-4-2-5_	_2-5-2-5_			

A-N-V-C Adjective-Noun-Verb-Connective   r relative
c clausal or phrasal   p phrasal

If read across the bottom of the page, the averages reflect the similarities of tendencies in the two forms: for prose, the seventeenth-, eighteenth-, and nineteenth-century decrease of verbs with increase of nouns; the nineteenth-century increase of adjectives; the twentieth-century increase of verbs, which with lessening of connectives would seem to be not clausal but independent. Nearly the same pattern for poetry: a similar portioning at first and last, and in between a later lessening of verbs, an earlier gain and then loss of adjectives, a persistently smaller number of connectives except in the present day; in America, more oddity of meagerness in poetry than in prose.

These pages are full of amazement for me both because they show in their fundamental likenesses the whole basis of the art in the language and because they show in their differences the power of literary forms and of individuals working within those forms to vary even the chief characteristics of structure in the medium through which they work.

Our prose has moved in good array from much clausal subordination to much phrasal subordination to much adjectival assumption, through three standard styles — plain, middle, and high. Our present day has made the change, noted by many commentators, toward a variant, a lessening of connectives while the referential forms are at their height: a device of juxtaposition, it would seem, in relation to strong statement and assumption. Through the temporal stages of general usage, the types are to be found, whether in general favor or not, in individual practice. For example, the simpler statement in favor now, as in the work of Lawrence, was early emphasized by Hazlitt and still earlier by Lyly and Sidney. In the midst of the early predicative stress we yet find Ascham's complex modificational bent, notable in the prose of Sir Thomas Browne, before its cumulative force in Gibbon in the eighteenth century. The balanced choice too has its range of use, early in the work of Bacon and of Milton, as well as late in Orwell; for all of whom the poise of adjective and verb, of phrase and clause, presents equivalent emphases before and after the chief time of classical strength. As a whole we may say that about half the writers favor the early clausal qualification; a fifth, the nineteenth-century phrasal qualification; and the rest, between and at present, some variety of balance, now tending toward the simple. Yet again we may note writers who move out from any of these possibly generalizable types to further extremes. Ben Jonson is such a one, who, even in literary criticism, employs such a variety of verbs that one might think he was writing the narrative of Bunyan or Joyce; while many more actual narrative writers, as in the histories, do not so predicate.

Condensation of proportions provides a still recognizable view of English prose. In its terms, the traditional three styles are visible: the early increase of noun phrases and recent decline of connectives; the accepted contrasts, between More and Ascham, for example, or between Donne and Browne or between Hazlitt and De Quincey; and the accepted comparisons between Hooker and Milton, Hobbes and Russell, Burke and Churchill, Swift and Shaw.

On the other hand, some less familiar lines of relation come into view. The likeness of Lyly's and Sidney's so-called euphuistic and "curt" juxtapositions to Dryden's, Johnson's, and the moderns'; the clear difference between Dryden's and Addison's modernity; the striking relation of Julian Huxley to Adam Smith and the technical writers as well as the dreamers.

Analysis works to support and invite intuition. Often today we hear skepticism of the analytic because we ask it to do more than it can do. It does not create, invent, imagine, lead to values; but given values, it clarifies and discerns, helping us to understand the relation between what we feel and what we know.

A generation ago, most criticism was not analytical. It was discovering and rediscovering values through aesthetic impression and, if historical, was historical in a general sense, in studies of what were called sources and analogues. Now, after a generation of close criticism of individual and autonomous texts, we may find that criticism has still further steps to take, to reach poetry as well as poems, extensions as well as intensions, participations as well as isolations. Though my first purpose in studying the language of poetry was to be able to recognize a poem of any poet by the singularity of his choices, now I have learned that singularity of choice is a part of the commonality of choice that serves a poet in the making of poetry. Both in kinds of substance and in kinds of arrangement, one work is like, as well as different from, another; they share great stores of interest and assumption, from artist to artist, throughout an era, throughout a tradition, and even throughout a literature in a specific language. It is impossible to treat the autonomy of the work without considering also its patrimony and hegemony. The intrinsic criteria and extrinsic criteria, though they are separated in such an established work as Wellek and Warren's *Theory of Literature*, extend in strands through the work from outside to inside, from inside to outside again, so that their pattern is not static but dynamic in its effect. In the metaphors of R. S. Crane and others, an object may be both an icon and a message; a construct, at once a gift, a mirror, and a lamp; a poem, a part of poetry.

Poets and prosaists work in the same language: the same sentence structures, the same references, even the same terms of value. But thus far we have learned less about prose's procedures than about meter and other intensifying poetic structures. Relatively few studies of prose style have been made, and these have been either in poetic terms of cadence or in rhetorical terms of figure or in quantitative terms of sentence length, but all with little attention to the working wholes we have come to appreciate in poetry.

In recent years, two philosophical schools, the ordinary-language philosophers and the structural linguists, have been raising new and different questions: the first covering the reaches of usage, in relation to specific lexical definition, and the second concerning the structure of basic minimal sentence units. The one so subjective *a priori*, the second so objective and universal, their divisions are yet part of one larger whole. My suggestions for analysis work in the no-man's-land that theorists have encouraged to stretch between them unexplored — the realm of art. This realm, as it gives us our best direct experience of generality in particularity can serve to close the gap between the infinite particulars of the ordinary-language theorists and the generated laws of transformation theorists, by showing the actual structures of evaluative choice and the way particulars do actually work within them. In such a realm, we need not limit our questions to utterances either as speech in ordinary-language phrases or as all the possible sentences of a language.

Rather we can start at the other end, the complex realm of values already uttered and recorded in writing, with an intricacy alien to the precise formalities of our predecessors, yet susceptible of just that degree of working and observable generality that is provided by the common agreements of artists in language when they make choices of materials and structures; that is, a generality not rigorously generated but freely observed, a particularity not infinitely variable but focused in patterns of actual choice. When we speak, we paraphrase and reparaphrase our statements, seldom echoing statements in exact repetition, but using different words and different forms each time, so that by a sort of cumulative redundancy, if not by simple clarity of situation, we may make ourselves understood. But in literature the writer is responsible for constructing both the situation and its phrasing, and must find patterns that will stand fixed to do the work for many readers in many times. There is in literature a normative function, a preserving of choices that will hold good.

That the normative function is present and that it functions for more than mere analysis is testified to by the tradition of comedy or joke on this subject of tone in grammar. Comedy enjoys pulling the chair from under that very person who most fully assumes its stability. So, much of the comedy of language plays upon the contrast between adjectival assumptions and verbal assertions, assertions and assumptions that we have been noting in styles. "Why does Uncle Sam wear red, white, and blue suspenders?" The puzzled responder is hung up on those adjectives because he assumes their importance. The more straightforward listener gets to the actual predicate and replies, "To keep his pants up." Pliny supposedly reported just such a joke: "How would you like to be shaved, sir?" asks the barber. "In silence," replies the customer, shifting the assumption of manner from passive to active. Even the ambiguity of qualification itself can be played upon; does the phrase qualify noun, verb, or predication in "Would you hit a woman with a child?" "No, I'd hit her with a brick." The shift is double: from *woman with* to *hit with*, turning upon the predicate *would you hit?*

Such jokes play upon and across the breaks of the language: the breaks between nucleus and adjunct, between assertion and assumption, between the act of sitting on a chair and the assumption that it is there to sit on. In their humor, they seem to me a trustworthy guide to art in language, both in what they suggest about the usable segments of language and in what they suggest about the bases of emphasis.

TWO

Styles in British Prose

PROSE HISTORY

The descriptive term for English prose style in its first modern form, its Renaissance form, was *sinewy*. *Sinewy* meant connected, articulated, clearly jointed, without fat or even a fine complexion. It was a style to think and move with, a difficult style to analyze because it did not stay still but rather shifted temporal or structural ground from sentence to sentence. It was the style of the Bible, through William Tyndale, its chief translator; the style of Biblical preaching by Latimer and Donne; the style of history for Holinshed and Hooker; the style of More, Lyly, Sidney, and Jonson in noble discourse; of Dekker and Bunyan in colloquial narrative; and of Dryden, Addison, Shaftesbury, Berkeley, Johnson, and Hazlitt in moral meditation. Until mid-eighteenth century, with a few purposeful exceptions, it was all of a piece, the strong prose of English deliberation, asking rather than assuming, asserting rather than qualifying, declaring rather than presenting. It shared this character not only with the Bible but also with the classical traditions of Cicero and Seneca, both of whom, despite their differences, wrote a sinewy prose.

Of fifty chief prose writers from the sixteenth century to the twentieth, nearly half chose to work in this style, so that we may call it English as well as Biblical and Classical. On the other hand, we may learn that the other half of our distinguished writers moved toward a style more qualified, or more complexioned, and we must take into account the fact that even in Tudor and Stuart prose, some moves were being made in these directions: by Bacon, Milton, Hobbes, and Locke toward the symmetries of today's reasonable prose; and by Roger Ascham and Thomas Browne toward the higher style which nineteenth-century science would embrace.

Among these names that I have grouped together, the reader may sense enough differences to raise some doubts about grouping them at all.

Of course, each stylist is singular in his complex of habits. Nevertheless, because major possibilities in grammatical construction are limited in number, choices among them cannot be singular, and therefore reveal strongly characterizing agreements.

The major choice of maximal verb statement with minimal qualification held for a large portion of the sixteenth and seventeenth centuries. The average proportion of verbs was three to every four nouns, two adjectives, and five connectives, high in proportion inasmuch as the classical norm of the "golden line" was only two verbs to four nouns, two adjectives, and four connectives. Of the average, More provided an instance, as did Holinshed, Hooker, Lyly, Sidney, Dekker, Jonson, Donne, Dryden, Addison, Johnson, and finally Hazlitt, Joyce, Lawrence, Connolly, and others — the chiefs of English prose lessening in dominance after Addison and Johnson. Theirs was a vocabulary of concept: adjectives of *good, great, true;* qualifying *God, father, man, law, life, mind, name, nature, matter, manner, reason, time, truth, way, word, work, world;* put in action by verbs of operations, chiefly of *bring, come* (and *go*), *find, hear, give* (and *take*), *know, let, make, see, seem, speak, think, write;* with connectives of choice and logic, *either-or, because, so, therefore, yet, though,* and the *after-before, over, against, through, where* of time and place.

Consider the sound and structure of this passage of Elizabethan and Stuart prose. In the Epistle of Paul to the Romans, 8–16, in its Authorized Version representing in large part the work of Tyndale — and thus to be taken as an early sixteenth-century text — we may read as follows, distinguishing the connective structures by spacing:

> First, I thank my God   through Jesus Christ   for you all   that your faith is proclaimed   throughout the whole world.

> For God is my witness   whom I serve   in my spirit   in the gospel   of his Son   how unceasingly I make mention   of you always   in my prayers   making request   if   by any means now   at length   I may be prospered   by the will   of God   to come   unto you.

> For I long to see you   that I may impart   unto you   some spiritual gift   to the end   ye may be established   that is,   that I   with you   may be comforted   in you   each   of us   by the other's faith   both yours   and mine.

> And I would not have you ignorant . . . I am debtor . . . So . . . I am ready. . . .

This parallelism of structure, *paratactic* as it is called, moves forward in sequences of small steps, then back to its starting point to begin again.

Unlike much modern parataxis, it does not avoid connectives, but rather uses them — as do Milton and a few others — in as great abundance as we can see anywhere in English prose. Especially like Milton is the use of the clause with *that, who,* and *which;* the temporal *then* or *when;* the causal *if, therefore, yet;* and the main prepositions like *by, in, of, to.* Noteworthy in the passage is the use of *for;* though all use it, we find no other writer using it so strongly except the preacher Latimer, Tyndale's close contemporary.

Paul's vocabulary is moral and evaluative, in the persons of God, Christ, and man, and the subjects of faith, spirit, and prayer. Further dominant in this text are the terms *death, flesh, grace, law, righteousness, sin;* the modifiers *dead, free, good, holy, own;* and such predicates as *believe, die, know, judge, justify, make, obey, save, work* and *write* — a list of active moral responsibility, of which most of the terms were frequently used by many other Renaissance authors.

The colloquialism of Paul's dictated message demanded plain English, the one or two thousand fundamental and common words that make up English speech.[1] The basic structure of Tyndale's translation has endured through all subsequent changes, at least a third still in his exact wording and the rest following "the general pattern of the underlying structure as Tyndale laid it down." [2] Behind him was the narrative tradition of romances by Malory and others, the religious tradition of meditation and the Gospel of St. John, and the data of exposition. The Gospel seemed to require curtness. "It is prose written in short lengths and the old punctuation of bars drawn across at the end of the rhythmical close brings this out more clearly than the modern commas. . . . It is difficult to include qualifications and niceties, afterthoughts and nuances, in fact it is difficult to render abstract thought in this old measure." [3] The old sentences are inverted and look back, as ours look forward.

From Tyndale's point of view, Sir Thomas More was a "poet" — too literary. Yet More also drew from pulpit and devotional vernacular of the fifteenth century and from the plays given at Cardinal Morton's house, and achieved examples of progression that Dr. Johnson in the Preface to his *Dictionary* called models of pure and elegant style, though Tyndale had called them "painted poetry, babbling eloquence." [4] Of English, More

[1] *Interim Report on Vocabulary Selection,* 1936.
[2] *The New Testament Octapla,* Luther Weigle, ed. (New York: Thomas Nelson & Sons, 1962), p. ix.
[3] G. D. Bone, "Tindale and the English Language," in Rev. A. L. Greenslade, *The Work of William Tyndale* (London and Glasgow: L. Blackie and Son, 1938).
[4] F. Th. Visser, *A Syntax of the English Language of St. Thomas More* (Louvain: C. Uystpruyst, 1946–56), p. liii ff.

said, "And if they would call it barren of wordes, there is not doubt but it is plenteous enough to express our mindes in any thing whereof one man hath used to speke with another." [5]

Sir Thomas More's *Apology* [6] gives us what seems a complex prose, not readily readable by a modern eye, partly because of its multiple connectives:

> So stand I not (thank God) good reader   in mine owne conceit,
> and thereby so much   in mine owne light,   but   that I can some-
> what   with egall judgment   and an even eye, behold   and con-
> sider   both my self   and mine own.

Most simply, this sentence reads: I stand not so well in my own conceit and thus in my own light that I cannot behold myself and my own. Such simplification removes inversions of subject and verb, doublets, parentheses, and odd terms, with a substitution of *not* for *but*. Even so, difficulty remains in choice of terms, especially the inextricable punning of *in* (*by* my own conceit, but *in the way* of my own light). But note that underlying both removable oddity of structure and unremovable oddity of meaning, the form of the sentence is basically recognizable — *I am not so* self-concerned *that I cannot* be self-scrutinizing.

> Nor do I follow Isopes ape   that admires her own babies,   nor
> the crow   that accounts her bird the fairest.   But   as there are
> some   who know less   than I,   yet write   about it, I perceive
> there are many   who know more,   and   if they were to write, I
> should not.
>   And therefore   since I know   that many excell me, I was never
>   so foolish   as to hope   that my own faults should be passed
> over,   but rather sought out, sifted, reproved.   But   since the
> things I write are consonant   with the Catholic faith and are con-
> futations   of doctrines   by Tyndale,   and Baron, no really destruc-
> tive faults will be found. Now   as to the minor faults . . .

Part of the awkwardness here is the awkwardness of many beginnings — a kind of argumentative self-consciousness. In contrast, note a few of the sentences of the conclusion, more balanced and interwoven:

> But first I think better to bestow some time   uppon an nother
> thing   and leaving   for a while   both defence   of mine own
> faults   and finding   of other mens'   in writing, think better to
> bestow some time   about the mending   of mine own   in living,
>   which is a thing now   for many men more necessary   than is

[5] *Works*, p. 243.
[6] Taft, ed., 1930.

> writing.   For   of new book makers   there are now mo   than
> ynough.

The repetition of "think better to bestow some time," in the positive contrast of *living* to *writing*, strengthens the structure and lets the reader feel the final decisiveness in the prose.

Another paragraph by Sir Thomas More begins as follows:

> In this counterfeit kind   of pleasure   they put them   that I spoke
> of before: which   the better gown they have on, the better men
> they think themselves: in which thing they   do twice err   for
> they be no less deceived   in that they think their gown the better
>   than they be   in that they think themselves the better.   For
> if you consider the profitable use   of the garment   why should
> wool   of a finer-spun thread   be thought better   than the wool
> of a coarse-spun thread?

In less than a hundred words we find different levels of subordination, because More's subjects are thinking, arguing, opining and are at the same time characterized in action, so that both how and what they think are conveyed in predicates. *Of* phrases and *which* clauses are followed by balanced, explanatory, and illustrative instances, themselves contrasted by *of* phrases, with a resulting proportion of more verbs than adjectives and a substitution of pronouns for nouns. Drawing on classical Latin more than the Hebraic-based Latin Bible, More uses more adjectives than Tyndale does and less connective material, with more subordination than parallelism. It was his model that would be followed, more often than Tyndale's, through the English centuries.

Close to his extreme is the prose of Hugh Latimer, a preaching, like Wyclif's and Wesley's, based on Biblical spirit and thus on Biblical syntax. His Christmas sermon of 1529 read: "Who are thou?" "I am a Christian man." "What requireth Christ of a Christian man?" When he was to be burned to death, he used the same active, short, and "low" language with its familiar grace: "Be of good comfort, master Ridley, and play the man. We shall this day light such a candle, by God's grace, in England, as I trust shall never be put out."

Thomas More has been called the founder of modern English literature.[7] The founding was difficult, and the development continued to be so in the sermons which Latimer himself thought plain. His fifth sermon begins:

> What doctrine is written   for us   in the parable   of the judge
> and the widow, I have opened it   to you, most honourable audi-

[7] M. Delacourt, *Essai sur la langue* . . . , p. 311.

ence. Something   as concerning the judge, I would wish   and pray
   that it might be a little better kept   in memory,   that   in the
   seat   of justice   no more iniquity and unrighteousness might reign.
   Better a little well kept,   than a great deal forgotten.

Here we see in the second sentence the same sort of difficulty of structure
that is to be found in Latimer's contemporaries: for example, an allusive *it*
different from our own usage. But here we see also the kind of crisp balance that makes Elizabethan prose readable to us: the "curtness" of such
a sentence in Latimer's penultimate paragraph as "If after Samuel's death
the people had asked of God a king, they had not faulted; but it is no
small fault to put an innocent out of his office."

For quite other reasons the prose of Holinshed's *Chronicle* was predicative, by the data-giving, rather than the action-giving, process. He fostered
a sense of stability and convention — the sense of "a fair and fertile country, well-wooded and well-watered, a pleasant place wherein it is good to
dwell." [8] His statements were simple and sequential, his qualifications by
time and location.

Holinshed begins with "Descriptions of Britain and England" and moves
them to the "History of England," continuing a descriptive pace:

   What manner   of people   did first inhabit this our country,
   which hath most generallie and   of longest continuance   beene
   knowne   among all nations   by the name   of Britain   as yet is
   not certainly knowne;   neither can it be decided   from whence
   the first inhabitants there of came,   by reason   of such diversitie
      in judgements   as have risen   amongst the learned   in this be-
   halfe.

Again, order and reference provide the difficulty for the modern reader.
For us, too many noun phrases are joined together by *which* and *thereof*.
Best structured are the main verbs: *is not certainly knowne; neither can
it be decided*. Holinshed's relatively few adjectives and verbs — *ancient,
diverse, sundry, call, pass* — and abundant nouns and connectives —
country, earth, history, name, according to, out of, over, under, within —
suggest a special sort of survey even when the concern is chronological. The
first book is probably most static in this fashion. Yet the static quality con-
tinues, for even at the end of the seventh book we find such phrasing as,

   But to let this piece   of curiositie   passe, this land felt   that
   they had a time   of arrival,   a time   of invading,   and a time
   of overruling the inhabitants   of this maine continent.   Whereof

[8] Christabel Fiske, *A Study of . . . Holinshed's Chronicle* (Bloomington, Illinois, 1950), p. 7.

> manifest proofes are   at this day   remaining   in sundrie places,
> sundrie ruines I meane   and wastes committed   by them.

Finally, with the good services of Hooker, Lyly, and Sidney, these difficult colloquial beginnings of English prose settled into greater skill and ease. Hear the opening of *Ecclesiastical Polity* and then the reminiscent concessions of its second paragraph:

> He   that goeth about to persuade a multitude,   that they are
> not   so well governed   as they ought to be, shall never want attentive and favorable hearers;   because they know the manifold defects   whereunto every kind   of regiment   is subject,   but the
> secret lets and difficulties,   which   in public proceedings   are
> innumerable and inevitable, they have not ordinarily the judgment
> to consider.   And   because such   as openly reprove supposed disorders   of state   are taken   for principal friends   to the common
> benefit   of all,   and   for men   that carry singular freedom   of
> mind;   under this fair and plausible colour   whatsoever they utter
> passeth   for good and current.   That which wanteth   in the
> weight   of their speech,   is supplied   by the aptness   of men's
> minds   to accept and believe it . . .
> Albeit therefore much   of that   we are to speak   in this present
> cause   may seem   to a number   perhaps tedious, perhaps obscure,
> dark,   and intricate;   (for many talk   of the truth,   which never
> sounded the depth   from whence it springeth;   and therefore
> when they are led thereunto they are soon weary,   as men drawn
>   from those beaten paths   wherewith they have been inured;)
> yet this may not   so far prevail   as to cut off   that   which the
> matter itself requireth,   howsoever the nice humour   of some   be
> therewith pleased   or no.

This, like More's, is the early standard. Sidney, Lyly, and later Dryden modified the texture by reducing its fiber of connectives in the "curt" manner; thus, Sidney's *Apologie for Poetrie* begins:

> When the right vertuous Edward Wotton   and I were   at the
> Emperor's Court together   wee gave ourselves to learne horsemanship   of John Pugliano: one   that   with great commendations
>   had the place   of an Esquire   in his stable.   And hee   according to the fertilness   of the Italian wit   did not only afoord us the
> demonstration   of his practice,   but sought to enrich our mindes
>   with the contemplation therein   which he thought most precious.

As this is characteristic of the introductory prose, so the following is characteristic of the development:

Nowe dooth the peerlesse Poet performe both: for whatsoever the Philosopher sayeth should be doone, hee giveth a perfect picture of it in someone, by whom hee presupposeth it was done, so as hee coupleth the generall notion with the particular example. A perfect picture I say, for hee yeeldeth to the powers of the minde an image of that whereof the Philosopher bestoweth but a wordish description which dooth neither strike, pierce nor possesse the sight of the soul so much as that other dooth.

This is a predicative prose, not highly connected. The verb statements are strong, the subordinations largely phrasal.

Lyly's verbs reflect a logical system of parallels and subordinates, especially, in Lyly's philosophy, disjunctive. "A logical style, to say it summarily, is one that marks out divisions of thought, that inspects things in order to classify and subdivide them either into antithetic or complementary components, which strives for clarity and syntax by opposing clause to clause, phrase to phrase, and word to word . . . and tends to develop its ideas in terms of some of the traditional topics of logic still felt as logical today: definition, cause and effect, antecedent and consequent, alternative hypotheses and the like." [9]

A verb style, as we see here and in Sidney, is not always plain and certainly not always homogeneous. As Donne's style has been described: "Donne's sentences, when he chooses, can be as terse, pithy, and colloquial as Bunyan's, or as eloquent and rhetorical as Milton's." [10] Donne mastered the long and subordinated Latinate style, yet, like Latimer, stayed by the Bible on which he preached.

As Barish and Trimpi have shown, the plain style was extended to higher subjects by the urging of Erasmus, even by interpretations of Horace and Cicero, so that not only Donne but Jonson could become "baroque" stylists, spontaneous, asymmetrical, nonlinear, with syncopation and dominance, and, as Barish says, "a reluctance to fulfil the syntax." [11] The new prose essay of the seventeenth century, following Montaigne, was of "mind in motion," [12] to which both the Ciceronian period and Elizabethan rhetoric were unsuited. Learned as he was, Burton, for example, insists that he writes "with as small deliberation as I do ordinarily speak, without all affectation of big words, fustian phrases, jingling terms, tropes,

[9] Jonas Barish, "The Prose Style of John Lyly," *Journal of English Literary History*, March, 1956.

[10] *The Sermons*, George R. Potter and E. M. Simpson, eds. (Berkeley: University of California Press, 1953), I, 91.

[11] *Op. cit.*

[12] F. P. Wilson, *Seventeenth Century Prose* (Berkeley and Los Angeles: University of California Press, 1960).

strong lines, — which many so much effect." [13] His allegiance is to Bacon's matter, not Ascham's "words"; to the fist of logic, not the palm of rhetoric; to the acts of a life, not to its panegyric.

Ben Jonson gives us a more structured proportioning, active and connected, subordinative, with relatively few adjectives, which is the classical form of the Biblical aphoristic structure. The assertive verbs rebegin the statements; the connectives introduce more verbs in the qualifying clauses. Jonson's *Explorata* begins:

> Ill Fortune never crush't that man whom good Fortune deceived not. I therefore have counselled my friends never to trust to her fairer side though she seem'd to make peace with them: But to place all things she gave them, so as she might aske them againe without their trouble: she might take them from them not pull them: to keepe always a distance betweene her, and themselves. He knows not his own strength, that hath not met Adversity.

First the balance: *ill* and *good, never crush't* and *deceived not.* But then the piling up: *I have counselled . . . never to trust . . . though she seem'd to make . . . But to place . . . she gave . . . as she might aske . . . she might take . . . not pull . . . to keep.* There is a great activity of thought, concept, and relation, much like More's and Hooker's; but Jonson maintains a kind of wiry flexibility by using infinitives and by intonations, as well as by the connectives *who, therefore, though, but, as, without, between;* connectives, that is, which seem not so much to build up the substance of phrases as to act adverbially for the verbs.

Again note the structure in the third paragraph:

> No man is so foolish, but may give an other good counsell sometimes; and no man is so wise, but may easily erre, if hee will take no others counsell, but his owne. But very few men are wise by their owne counsell; or learned by their owne teaching. For hee that was onely taught by himselfe, had a foole to his Master.

We see that the shape is *no man . . . but, no man . . . but, if . . . none but, But few, by . . . or by, for he that was . . . had a foole to.* The close interrelations are such that no terminals or periods are necessary; the units are basically subject–verb–object (or qualifier), and the structure of *so–but–for,* intensive–opposition–explanation, is basically simple. This passage does use many adjectives, especially the intensive *own,*

[13] Quoted in Wilson, *op. cit.*, p. 42.

30

but many scantier passages also proceed in this interlocked, short-clausal way. In its lack of phrasal and clausal elaboration, this style differs from the balanced and phrasal styles. The simple sentence unit provides the basic structure, and thus even connectives over longer stretches are minimal. Says Jonson, "Of the two (if either were to be wisht) I would rather have a plaine down-right wisdome, then a foolish and affected eloquence."

Main and connected subordinate verbs dominate this structure; so too for Donne, Addison, and Hazlitt. But not for the twentieth century. The twentieth century goes back rather to the Senecan curtness of Sidney, Lyly, Dryden, and much of Samuel Johnson, and is somewhat freer with adjectives but less free with clausal connectives. That Jonsonian clausal structure we just examined is to be contrasted to the Sidneyan-modern. From the perspective of the modern, Dryden's development from Sidney, Hobbes's and Milton's from Bacon, and Browne's from Ascham represent the persistent, though often theoretically obscured, lines of conscious choice and practice.

Passages of Clarendon, Burnet, and Dryden exemplify the basic and developing English predicative style: an active, ordered proportion of nouns and connectives, each twice the number of adjectives and verbs, with appreciably more verbs than adjectives.

Clarendon's *History* [14] begins elaborately and adjectivally, in Latin style:

That posterity may not be deceived,   by the prosperous wicked-
ness   of those times   of which I write,   into an opinion,   that
nothing less   than a general combination,   and universal apostacy
   in the whole nation   from their religion   and allegiance,
could,   in so short a time,   have produced such a total   and
prodigious alteration   and confusion   over the whole kingdom; . . .

But by the end of this brief introduction, the normal tone is established:

I shall not then lead any man farther back   in this journey,
for the discovery   of the entrance   into those dark ways,   than
the beginning   of this king's reign.   For I am not so sharp-sighted
   as those, who have discerned this rebellion contriving   from
(if not before)   the death   of Queen Elizabeth,   and fomented
   by several princes and great ministers   of state   in Christen-
dom,   to the time   that it brake out.   Neither do I look so far
back   as I do,   because I believe the design to have been so long
since formed;   but that,   by viewing the temper, disposition,
and habit,   at that time,   of the court   and   of the country,

[14] Oxford, 1826.

31

we may discern the minds of men prepared, of some to act, and of others to suffer, all that hath since happened; . . .[15]

Or, for narrative proper, see:

> These reflections were so terrible to him, that they robbed him of all peace of mind; insomuch as when the prince and duke came to him about the dispatch, he fell into a great passion with tears, and told them that he was undone, and that it would break his heart, if they pursued their resolution; that, upon a true and dispassionate disquisition he had made with himself, he was abundantly convinced, that, besides the almost inevitable hazards of the prince's person, with whom his life was bound up, and besides the entire loss of the affections of his people, which would unavoidably attend this rash action, he foresaw it would ruin the whole design, and irrecoverably break the match.[16]

Similarly, Gilbert Burnet's *History of the Reformation* begins with a highly descriptive style:

> England had for a whole age felt the miseries of a long and cruel war between the two houses of York and Lancaster; during which time, as the crown had lost great dominions beyond sea, so the nation was much impoverished, many noble families extinguished, much blood shed, great animosities every where raised, with all the other miseries of a lasting civil war:
> but they now saw all these happily composed when the two families did unite in King Henry the Eighth.[17]

But then Burnet settles into the steady narrative and explanatory mode:

> The king loved to raise mean persons, and upon the least distaste to throw them down: and falling into disgrace, he spared not to sacrifice them to public discontents. His court was magnificent, and his expense vast; he indulged himself in his pleasures: and the hopes of children (besides the Lady Mary) failing by the queen, he, who of all things desired issue most, kept one Elizabeth Blunt, by whom he had Henry Fitzroy, whom in the seventeenth year of his reign he created Earl of Nottingham, and the same day made him Duke of Richmond and Somerset, and intended afterwards to have put him in the succession of the crown after his other children; but his death prevented it.[18]

[15] *Ibid.*, p. 5.
[16] *Ibid.*, p. 26.
[17] Oxford, 1829, p. 1.
[18] *Ibid.*, p. 18.

Adjectival and phrasal introductions, predicative developments — these are not surprising. Yet the differences represent not only rhetorical demands but more general states of mind about prose. Consider Dryden as representative at the end of the seventeenth century.

George Williamson illustrates the contrast between styles by giving two sentences from Dryden, the first from the *Essay of Dramatic Poesie*:

> It was that memorable day,   in the first summer   of the late war,
>   when our navy engaged the Dutch; a day   wherein the two most
> mighty and best appointed fleets   which any age had ever seen,
> disputed the command   of the greater half   of the globe,   the
> commerce   of nations,   and the riches   of the universe.

The second is the opening sentence of the Preface to the *Fables*:

> 'Tis   with a Poet,   as   with a man   who designs to build,
> and is very exact,   as he supposes,   in casting up the cost before-
> hand;   but   generally speaking, he is mistaken   in his account,
> and reckons short   of the expense   he first intended.

Mr. Williamson comments: "The oratorical idiom predominates as much in the first sentence as the controversial does in the second; the difference appears not only in the diction and turn of phrase but also in the sweep and modulation of members. This appears nowhere more clearly than in the way the phrasing of the second follows the various movement of the mind; it commits itself less obviously to any continuous development. In all respects, from diction to rhythm, the first is as formal as the second is informal." [19]

The first is what we call adjectival, with its *memorable, first, late, most mighty and best appointed,* and also highly connective, with its *in, of, when, wherein, and, which, of, of, of,* and *of.* The informal is the style built upon the verb, implying other verbs in its non-verbal forms. Not the first but the second passage is characteristic of Dryden. The praise that Dr. Johnson gives to both Dryden and Addison for their modernization of English prose is praise for their emphasis on the native forms that he himself also follows — the active predicative forms.

So we may come more clearly to understand how, at the beginning of the eighteenth century, which has been considered the beginning of "modern" prose, Dryden's moderation in connectives, like Sidney's, was in the long run closer to modernity than Addison's apparently more progressive generosity.

[19] George Williamson, *The Senecan Amble* (Chicago: University of Chicago Press, 1951), p. 60.

Dryden's Dedication to *The Aeneis* begins with few connectives in proportion to verbs:

> A heroic poem, truly such, is undoubtedly the greatest work
> which the soul   of man   is capable to perform. The design   of it
>   is to form the mind   to heroic virtue   by example;   'tis con-
> vey'd   in verse   that it may delight   while it instructs. The action
>   of it   is always one, entire,   and great.

Said Hopkins in a letter to Bridges in 1835, Dryden "is the most masculine of our poets; . . . [he] puts the strongest stress on the naked thew and sinew of the English language." Yet Dryden fretted, "We are full of monosyllables, and those clogged with consonants," [20] though "after all, our language is both copious, significant, and majestical." [21] He allowed for shadow and silence, even for the obscurities of Pindar, and found in Denham's *Cooper's Hill* "the exact standard of good writing." He argued "by senses to allure the soul into the practice of that which it admires," and that imagery is the height and life of poetry. But most strongly he felt, "The argument of the work, that is to say, its principal action, the discovery and disposition of it, these are the things which distinguish copies from originals." [22] So, though he was aware of a multiplicity of conflicting values in thought and prose, he settled at heart for action.

Meanwhile, certain learned predecessors, notably Bacon, Hobbes, and Milton, devoted themselves to a moderating of native action toward a more classic balance. In Bacon's "Of Friendship," the second to the last paragraph begins:

> Heraclitus saith well   in one   of his enigmas   *Dry light is ever*
> *the best.*   And certain it is,   that the light   that a man receiveth
>   by counsel   from another   is drier   and purer   than that
> which cometh   from his own understanding   and judgment;
> which is ever infused   and drenched   in his affections   and cus-
> toms.   So   as there is   as much difference   between the counsel
> that a friend giveth,   and   that a man giveth himself,   as there
> is   between the counsel   of a friend   and   of a flatterer.   For
> there is no such flatterer   as is a man's self;   and there is no such
> remedy   against flattery   of a man's self   as the liberty   of a
> friend.   Counsel is   of two sorts;   the one concerning manners,
> the other concerning business.   For the first: the best preservative
> to keep the mind   in health   is the faithful admonition   of a
> friend.

[20] Dedication to *Troilus*.
[21] Dedication to *Aeneis*.
[22] Preface to Ovid's *Epistles*.

Note the many explicit connectives, particularly the *and*'s, *of*'s, *that*'s, and *which*'s; note the balance of adjectives and verbs, of phrases and clauses. Note, as in Russell, the comparative structure, "For there is no such flatterer as is a man's self: and there is no such remedy against flattery of a man's self as the liberty of a friend." In this very contrast we may see how phrases and clauses provide alternative choices: first Bacon writes the modifying clause, "no such remedy . . . as the liberty of a friend," the second seeming to be the simpler and more assured form of the first.

Such sentences of one essay by Bacon exemplify general facts of his practice: balanced and alternative forms; comparative methods; strongly explicit connectives, especially *and*'s, and *of*'s among phrasal connectives, and *and*'s and relatives among conjunctions; that is, a weighing mode. Or see again the connectives in the beginning of his essay "Of Truth."

> *What is truth?* said jesting Pilate,   and would not stay   for
> an answer.   Certainly there be that delight   in giddiness,   and
> count it a bondage to fix a belief; affecting free-will   in thinking,
> as well as in acting.   And   though the sects   of philosophers
> of that kind   be gone,   yet there remain certain discoursing wits
> which are   of the same veins,   though there be not so much blood
> in them   as was   in those   of the ancients.

Or, toward the end of the essay,

> To pass   from theological and philosophical truth,   to the truth
> of civil business: it will be acknowledged,   even   by those
> that practice it not,   that clear   and round   dealing is the honour
> of man's nature;   and that mixture   of falsehood   is like alloy
> in coin   of gold and silver;   which may make the metal work
> the better,   but it embaseth it. For these winding   and crooked
> courses are the goings   of the serpent;   which goeth basely   upon
> the belly,   and not   upon the feet.

Later, Hobbes, Milton, and Locke further this connective quality. See Milton's *Areopagitica*:

> I deny not   but   that it is   of greatest concernment   in the
> Church and Commonwealth,   to have a vigilant eye   how Bookes
> demeane themselves   as well as man;   and thereafter to confine,
> imprison,   and do sharpest justice   on them   as malefactors:
> For Books are not absolutely dead things,   but doe contain a po-
> tencie of life   in them   to be as active   as that soule was
> whose progeny they are; nay, they do preserve   as   in a violl   the

purest efficacie   and extraction   of that living intellect   that bred
them. . . .[23]

Lords and Commons of England, consider   what Nation it is
whereof ye are   and   whereof ye are the governours: a Nation not
slow and dull,   but   of a quick, ingenious, and piercing spirit,
acute to invent, suttle and sinewy to discours, not beneath the reach
of any point   the highest   that human capacity can soar to.
Therefore the studies   of learning   in her deepest Sciences   have
bin so ancient   and so eminent   among us,   that Writers   of
good antiquity   and ablest judgment   have bin perswaded   that
ev'n the school   of *Pythagoras*   and *Persian* wisdom took beginning   for the old Philosophy   of this Iland.[24]

The *Areopagitica* begins with a descriptive *who, which, such, as,* an
alternative *or,* a contrasting *some* and *others.* It joins *private* to *public,*
doubt and *fear* to *hope* and *confidence,* with strongly explicit connectives.

They   who   to states and governors   of the Commonwealth
direct their speech, High Court of Parliament,   or, wanting such
access   in a private condition,   write that which they foresee may
advance the public good; I suppose them,   as   at the beginning
of no mean endeavor,   not a little altered and moved inwardly   in
their minds: some   with doubt   of what will be the success,
others   with fear   of what will be the censure; some   with hope,
others   with confidence   of what they have to speak.

Or, similarly, the famous sentence of contrast:

I cannot praise a fugitive   and cloistered   virtue, unexercised
and unbreathed,   that never sallies out   and sees her adversary,
but slinks   out of the race,   where that immortal garland is to be
run for,   not without dust   and heat.

The connective *and*'s, in which Milton is as strong as Bacon; the relative
that and *where;* the verbs turned negative, then rising to the positive *where
that immortal garland is to be run for* — these are the traits of the whole
essay, of what we have called classic composition.

Within the two centuries of plentiful and serious prose writing and
printing, we see not simply two but a third mode of work based on grammatical choice as that reflects a rhetoric of concern, and on a rhetoric as
that reflects a logic. Rhetorical and rounded as Cicero seemed to Erasmus
and the Senecans, he was a very model of direct emotion when compared
to the artful structures of Isocrates. Perhaps only such an extreme as Greek

[23] Oxford, 1898, p. 5.
[24] *Ibid.,* p. 44.

rhetoric is suitable then for the endeavor of Roger Ascham to write effectively in the midst of native crudity.

Ascham wrote:

> Once I commerced with a man which reasoned the English tongue to be enriched and increased thereby, saying, "Who will not praise the feast where a man shall drink at a dinner both wine, ale and beer?" "Truly," quoth I, "they be all good, everyone taken by himself alone, but if you put malmsey and sack, red wine and white, ale and beer, and all in one pot, you shall make a drink neither easy to be known, nor yet wholesome for the body."

See then *The Schoolmaster*'s beginning:

> After the child hath learned perfectly the eight parts of speech, let him then learn the right joining together of substantives with adjectives, the noun with the verb, the relative with the antecedent. And in learning farther his syntax by mine advice, he shall not use the common order in common schools for making of Latin, whereby the child commonly learneth: first, an evil choice of words (and right choice of words, saith Caesar, is the foundation of eloquence) than a wrong placing of words; and lastly, an ill framing of the sentence, with a perverse judgment both of words and sentences. These faults, taking root in youth, be never or hardly plucked away in age.[25]

The vintage which enriches this paragraph is that of evaluative adjectives, *common, evil, wrong,* and so on; the participial *taking root;* and the serial phrases. With values of sound in musical phrasing, with ellipsis of verbs, and with statement weighted by Latin and Saxon language, more Greek than usual, more Isocratean than Ciceronian, Cantabridgean with a stress on need for examples and instances, with Lever's compounds of *witchcraft* for reason, *saywhat* for definition, and the method of doublet translation, Ascham had provided an emphasis, if not from Isocrates, at least from Cicero's other hand, his smooth Greek hand. "Like most of his contemporaries, moreover, he did not clearly differentiate poetics from grammar and rhetoric, so that, in approaching literary works, he is interested primarily in their formal and rhetorical aspects: diction, phrasing, metrics, and, above all, style and decorum." [26] In mid-sixteenth century,

[25] New York, 1902, p. 11.
[26] Lawrence V. Ryan, *Roger Ascham* (Stanford: Stanford University Press, 1963), p. 271.

this style of his letters was described by a friend at Louvain: ". . . [t]he utmost sweetness without slackness, brevity with vitality, on the other hand, copiousness without luxuriance; well turned also and artistic, but without that unremittent corruscation for which the age of Pliny labored, eloquent without effeminate devices, their diction polished and pure, but without that scrupulous anxiety, through which the Ciceronians of our age wear themselves away, as though they had loaded themselves with fetters . . ." [27]

Ascham was more than Ciceronian, freer, sweeter, and more eloquent than Cicero, closer to Greek tradition; and these traits lead us to expect what we find: a more qualitative and adjectival style in Ascham, as in his inheritor Sir Thomas Browne. Praised as elegant by Hoskyns, Sidney, and others, Ascham was called "Master Isocrates" by Harvey for his parallel structures in paramoion, isocolon, and parism. He was distinguished for his art as was Sidney for his wit.[28] But Ascham belongs more, I think, in the descriptive epideictic tradition of historians like Thucydides and Tacitus, of Gibbon and Macaulay, with their ongoing participles of process and generalization.

Browne too was praised for his art, as by Henry Wotton: "The African idea of St. Augustine's Age, full of sweet Rapture, and of researched Conceipts, nothing borrowed, nothing vulgar; and yet all flowing from you (I know not how) with a certaine equal facility." [29]

Without Ascham's especial humanism, Browne nevertheless shared his meditative interest in forms and operations, in a kind of science of life that called for descriptive observation and then a flight into speculative, associative, non-logical high style. On the flyleaf of *Vulgar Errors*, by no means the flightiest of Browne's works, Coleridge wrote, "He is a quiet and sublime Enthusiast, with a strong tinge of the Fantast. . . ." The vital thing for Browne was phenomenon, and as Dewey Ziegler comments in his *In Divided and Distinguished Worlds*, the consequence is Browne's detachment from readers and his fellow men.

For Browne the adjective tests the fabric, as in the first and last paragraphs of *Hydriotaphia:*

> In the deep discovery of the subterranean world, a shallow
> part would satisfy some inquirers; who, if two or three yards were
> open about the surface, would not care to rake the bowels of

[27] *Ibid.*, p. 140.
[28] *Ibid.*, pp. 280–284.
[29] Quoted in F. Huntley, *Sir Thomas Browne* (Ann Arbor: University of Michigan Press, 1962), p. 118.

Potosi, and regions towards the centre. Nature hath furnished
one part of the earth, and man another. The treasures of
time lie high, in urns, coins, and monuments, scarce below
the roots of some vegetables. Time hath endless rarities, and
shows of all varieties; which reveals old things in heaven,
makes new discoveries in earth, and even earth itself a discovery. That great antiquity, America, lay buried for a thousand
years; and a large part of the earth is still in the urn unto
us. . . .

To subsist in lasting monuments, is to live in their produc-
tions, to exist in their names and predicament of chimeras,
was large satisfaction unto old expectations, and made one part
of their Elysium. But all this is nothing in the metaphysics
of true belief. To live indeed, is to be again ourselves, which
being not only a hope but an evidence in noble believers, 't is
all one to lie in St. Innocent's churchyard, as in the sands of
Egypt, ready to be any thing, in the ecstasy of being ever,
and as content with six feet as the "moles" of Adrianus.

Deep, shallow, high, endless, in the urn unto us — this is not a weighing
but a presenting, a relishing, of qualities.

Erasmus and the humanist philosophers had asserted against rhetoric the
virtues of philosophical prose: "more genuine, more concise, more forceful,
. . . more masculine," a sententious density rather than a chiming ca-
dency. It was a native prose, colloquial, aggregative, with loose time-and-
space joints. As Krapp said, "The style which lay at the base of Tyndale's
translation was the easy, polysyndetic, and naïve style of simple narrative"
(p. 239) — by which the King James Bible was still characterized, in its
general acceptance of Tyndale's text, a century later. Such style prevailed
well into the eighteenth century — the Senecan, as contrasted to the Ciceronian that Erasmus opposed. The Ciceronian was rhetorical, periodic,
copious, cumulative, deriving its energy from its fullness and suspense, its
rhythm, and climax of vividness, its symphonic complexity.

There were classical precedents for both these styles and for the third,
with its highly formalized set of parallelisms. The Sophist, Gorgias, led to
Isocrates, the Asiatics, and Ascham; as the Ciceronians to Milton; and the
Attic Stoics from Thucydides to Sallust, Tacitus, Lucan, Seneca, to many
Elizabethans and moderns. But then the questions begin. Different critics,
contemporary and present, put different authors in different categories. Are
More and Lyly Isocratean because of their parallelisms, parison and
paramion, or Stoic because of their brevities? Are Ascham's formalisms
from Cicero or Isocrates and do they tend to Lyly's Euphuism? The "natu-

ral," progressive order of thought, with free and loose connectives, may give us verbs; so may curt parallels as substitutes for connectives.

We see that various distinctions need to be made. Following the Renaissance interest of Erasmus, we should first of all distinguish Seneca from Cicero, philosophy from rhetoric, the natural from the artificial; or, from another position, the curt or loose from the elevated and consciously constructed. Professors Croll and Williamson have given great help with these distinctions, though Professor Trimpi suggests that the Latin structures of Cicero and Seneca are so different from the English that they cannot provide parallel contrasts. If we explore this proposal a little further, we may see that Cicero and Seneca, when treating similar subject matter, as in their essays on old age, differ mainly in connective structures. Cicero, in talking gently about death, uses many more verbs than adjectives, and a strong number of connectives to subordinate them: *atque, autem, cum, enim, qui, ut* — in all of which he far exceeds Seneca. Seneca, on the other hand, in *De Brevitate Vitae* and *De Consolatione*, while also using more verbs than adjectives, uses fewer connectives than does Cicero, the only ones used more frequently being *dum, inter, quando, ubi*, terms of place and time, of phrase and clause, rather than of logical relation or relative reference. This is the same difference as between Bacon and Jonson, between strong relative and logical subordinates like Bacon's *of, to, that, which, and, for, or, because, if, so, therefore,* and strong temporal and spatial modifications like Jonson's *about, against, with, so, than, yet.*

In general vocabulary, too, Seneca is, as one would expect of a plain stylist, more fond of emotional terms, such as *alienus, humanus, otiosus, ultimus, bonum, cupiditas, dolor, fortuna, malum, memoria, spes, tempus, cogito, opto, puto, scio, voco*; and number terms like *alius, primus, totus*; in addition to terms like *miser, omnis*, and *multus* used also by Cicero; and abstractions like *vita* and *res* in which Seneca exceeded Cicero. More of Cicero's vocabulary is of sensory substance: *beatus, aetas, ager, annus, fructus, locus, natura, opus, senex, studium, voluptas, ego, audio, fero, venio, video*. Again we see that there is a basic distinction between the "plain" Senecan expressive style and the more structured and substantial Ciceronian, and this contrast helps illuminate the difference between Jonson's or Dryden's English style and Bacon's or Addison's more classical version. The main difference between the Latin pair and the English is the scantiness of adjectives in both the English; and it was perhaps this sense of meagerness that moved Ascham and Browne to try a still "higher," more adjectival style. At any rate, note the two effects in the following passages. Cicero's is from *De Senectute*, V, 13.

Nec tamen omnes possunt esse Scipiones aut Maximi, ut urbium expugnationes, ut pedestris navalisve pugnas, ut bella a se gesta, ut triumphos recordentur. Est etiam quiete et pure atque eleganter actae aetatis placida ac lenis senectus, qualem accepimus Platonis, qui uno et octogesimo anno scribens est mortuus, qualem Isocratis, qui eum librum, qui Penathenaicus inscribitur, quarto nonagesimo anno scripsisse dicit vixitque quinquennium postea; cuius magister Leontinus Gorgias centum et septem complevit annos, neque umquam in suo studio atque opere cessavit.

Seneca's is from *De Consolatione,* XXIII, 3–4.

Quicquid ad summum pervenit, ab exitu prope est. Eripit se sufertque ex oculis perfecta vitus, nec ultimum tempus expectant quae in primo maturuerunt. Ignis quo clarior fulsit, citius extinguitur; vivacior est, qui cum lenta ac difficili materia commissus fumoque demersus ex sordido lucet; eadem enim detinet causa, quae maligne alit. Sic ingenia quo inlustriora, breviora sunt; nam ubi incremento locus non est, vicinus occasus est.

Such brisk temporal progression as Seneca's has suited perhaps half our stylists in English. The others have sought to move less quickly and to carry more as they went, either in the suspensive modificatory manner or in the complex balances of the Ciceronian. Inasmuch as the Elizabethans themselves recognized and described these distinctions (though, as one would expect, most often in terms of figures) and inasmuch as even today we are able to discover their emphasis in our own stylists, we may learn to trust traits of style that support each other — the orders and proportions of words and structures.

The sinewy prose of the Renaissance has persisted and serves a purpose even today. Its predicative units are least amply filled out with substantives and modifications beyond the basic unit of predication, with the least spelling out of assumptions of quality and location. It capitalizes upon the flexible Saxon monosyllabic and connective traits of native English, capitalizing also upon the structural ordering and minimal qualifications of Biblical language; yet, it makes moderate use of the abstracting and subordinating forces of Latin. It is a durable mode for thinkers as well as narrators, for Lawrence's essays as well as Molly Bloom's monologues, for following the process of thought.

Even in early Elizabethan England, however, there was a restive sense of other possibilities. Though the plain style dominated, many arguments and many examples by such expert practitioners as Ascham and Browne, Bacon and Milton were set against it. Despite the common tendency, then as now, to think in terms of two opposing styles, plain and some other, these four authors provide not one other pole but two, two different sets of variation from the plain.

As one may surmise, one clear opposition to the plain style is the elaborate. In terms of grammar, this sort adds qualifications by way of adjectives, appositives, and connected phrases and clauses. It proliferates, it leafs out from its branches, as the Elizabethan metaphor would have it. But though we have noted the parallel between the plain style and Senecan prose and should expect a contrast in the parallel between the elaborate style and the Ciceronian, the contrasts are not so simple. Cicero himself thought of himself as plain, clear, perspicacious, Attic, in contrast to the elaborate Asian style of Isocrates and the Sophists.

Despite the French fashion of a diligent negligence in the curt *style coupé* and despite the support of Hebraic Biblical structures, more and more was to be heard in the seventeenth century, as from Cowley, against too spidery fine a spinning or against "The dry chips of short-lung'd Seneca." There was more stress on balance. A eulogist of Glanvil countered the older view of Erasmus by saying:

> You have remov'd the old Antipathy
> Twixt Rhetorick and Philosophy.

Waller, in his *Instructions* of 1659, recommended propriety of choice: "A short period loseth as much of smoothness as a long and round one of acuteness. One is more harsh, and the other blunt." [30]

Along with the endeavors of the Royal Society to simplify, to achieve sense with every word, went the efforts of the many rhetoric books of mid-century to moderate and mollify toward propriety and decorum. So in 1698 John Hughes could praise Sprat for a quality of style with which Dryden and many others would agree — sweet, fluent, with a soft cadence of periods "like the current of a pleasant stream" — a compromise.

Different philosophies of reality lay behind contrast and compromise: The "Ciceronian" Ascham had said, "Ye know not what hurt ye do to learning that care not for words but for matter," thus emphasizing the means of expression, the *how*, or rhetoric. The "Senecan" early Bacon noted, in contrast, that it is vanity when men begin "to hunt more after words than matter." He was for wit and weight, as was Jonson. Similarly Hobbes praised the curt Thucydides: "For he is so full of matter that the number of his sentences doth almost reach to the number of his words; and in his words he is so apt and close that it is hard to say whether his words do more illustrate his sentences, or his sentences, his words." Similarly

---

[30] Quoted in Williamson, *op. cit.*, p. 275.

Cowley praised "the Pindaric way" of the prophets in that "they pass from one thing to another with almost invisible connexions, and are full of words and expressions of the highest and boldest flights of Poetry." He explained that while "we," the Hobbesians, expressed all that is meant, as in syllogisms, "they," the older prophets, left half out, as in enthymemes. Thus Cowley proposed a new basis, sparing of connectives, neither fully explicit nor cryptic, but implicative. Both Hobbes and Dryden supported this basis of contrast.

Hobbes stressed a new, though partly Ciceronian, basis for the old distinction between Reason and Passion: the one is an elegant and clear view of things and concepts; the other is a "commotion of the passions of the mind, such as are *hope, fear, anger, pity*; and derives from a metaphorical use of words fitted to the passions. That forms a speech from true principles; this forms opinions already received, what nature soever they are of. The art of that is logic, of this rhetoric; the end of that is truth, of this victory."

Can we perceive more explicitly what were the results in style? Demetrius gives us a clue: "As verse is articulated by measures, so prose style is articulated by members." [31] Members we may take to mean independent forms: subject-predicate, modifiers, and the segments linked by explicit prepositions or conjunctions. The singly-predicated sentence, the epigram, formalizes words, as the complex sentence formalizes more complex members; or either may proceed informally, in loosely additive steps. For the three kinds, then, one traditional tripartite division was based on degree of ease: terse style, dry, Attic, Sallust; clear style, Rhodian, Isocrates; grand style, fluent, long periods, symmetrical, non-masculine, Seneca, in loose form. But the famed divisions of Erasmus in the Renaissance were more moral on the basis of attitude: Senecan, or Lipsian, terse, stoic, philosophical, natural; Ciceronian, elaborate, periodic, rhetorical, artificial; Isocratean, possibly then, even more artificial in symmetry.

Consider what we know about English: terse style, native, predicative; moderate style, fuller, more consciously classical, Ciceronian, balancing verb and adjective, clause and phrase; grand or high style, adjectival and phrasal, less active, more receptive and artificial. We see not only a scale of degrees but three contrasting centers with differing clusters of attributes.

The conscious and explicit contrasts of English critics may then help us further; not only do they note Attic-Rhodian-Asian, low-middle-high, Senecan-Ciceronian-Isocratean; but, with emphasis on their own work: English-Roman-Greek, wit-argument-rhetoric, nature-art-artifice, plain-regu-

[31] *On Style*, I.

43

lar-ornate, sinew-flesh-raiment, conversation-oratory-meditation; terse-asymmetry–symmetry–loose-asymmetry; sobriety-eloquence-ornateness; clarity-glitter-darkness, or vice versa; roots-fruits-leaves; water-beer-wine; intellect-reason-feeling; and so on. The scales are more consistent than the values, which shift from one end to the other; *artificial*, for example, being sometimes a good word, sometimes a bad.

For many decades in the sixteenth century, learned writers felt that the sinews of English, its monosyllables, its connectives, its Saxon terms had been barbarous and inadequate for decent expression or translation. As Jones has shown, from Caxton's "rude and symple englysshe" to Gascoyne's praise of its monosyllables and apt epithets is a slow, but patient, way.[32] The literary virtue of "epithets" increases as the language grows more classical.

A chief metaphor was that of raiment. Rough cloth was to velvet as sinews to flesh. Thomas Wilson in translating the Greek eloquence of Demosthenes wrote, "But all cannot weare Velvet, or feede with the best, and therefore such are contented for necessities sake to weare our Countrie cloth, and to take themselves to harde fare than can have no better." [33] Artifice could be a good and learned power — "The Latine Tongue being so copious and plentifull, so darke and doubtfull, so necessarie and fruitfull, . . . "[34] This was another popular figure — the contrast of leafy darkness and fruitful spareness, here obscured by their combination. Leaf made for shadow, as Chapman liked it in Ovid's *Banquet of Sense*, and epithet for leaf. Yet some stressed the need to stay bare, rather than to "glyster with vague eloquence of words." [35] Vries' *De Ratio Dicendi* too had warned against the shade of Asian foliation, the lack of productive sunshine.[36] The baser the language of English translation, said Thomas Bean, "the higher doth it excel other, not with windiness and vague bablying, but with soliditie and grave doctrine." [37] *Glister* seems to be the word of the poet of real language for his more rhetorical opponents. It was Wordsworth's term, in the form of *glitter*, for the "gaudiness and inane phraseology" of the eloquent poetry of the sublime.

Many writers though opposed to glister were not for bareness either, but for that well-rounded form they called classical, which did indeed call upon devices of classical language. Thomson contrasts the simple clarity of

[32] Richard Foster Jones, *The Triumph of the English Language* (Palo Alto: Stanford University Press, 1953), pp. 59–60.
[33] Quoted in Jones, *op. cit.*, p. 19.
[34] A. Fleming, quoted in Jones, *op. cit.*, p. 24.
[35] Vries, quoted in Jones, *op. cit.*, p. 31.
[36] Williamson, *op. cit.*, p. 54.
[37] Quoted in Jones, *op. cit.*, p. 31.

44

Herodotus with the imagination of Thucydides.[38] The argument for *art* was a persistent one. Early, Demetrius had identified the Greek periodic sentence of Demosthenes as building clauses or phrases within the sentence. Thus, for example, "Mainly also for the sake of Chabrias' son, I have agreed to speak, to the best of my ability, on their behalf." This is a verb-saving structure, in contrast to the looser and plainer: "I shall speak on their behalf, gentlemen. The son of Chabrias is a friend of mine." Like the "dithyrambic compound," on the order of "the fiery-lanced host of stars," the periodic sentences reduce the particles of action. Consider too that for many in the Renaissance *enargeia* was the vividness of imitated nouns, of concreteness.[39] Is reality things or nouns? Or is it, for poetry, as Sidney said, between the two? As logic and dialectic and wit dealt with sentences and contradictions, rhetoric worked with vivid examples in arguments using authorities, definitions, properties, and oppositions. "Art" then was especially concerned with the sensory particular, not with verb or logical connective. The logical topics were devices for finding how various kinds of predication could be attributed to a subject, usually by differences of Genus, Integer, Quantity, Mode, Time, Place, in Whole, Part, Cause, Effect, Corruption, Use, Concomitants. Even for Locke, genus and species had this status of topics, conveniences for disjuncting and classifying in language. But we note that these were the verbalists. The pro-art writers were more concerned with the qualities of instance.

Bacon, as one who tended to compromise, advised subordinating "conceits intellectual to images sensible, which strike the memory more." [40] So Milton was to agree in his view of poetry as "more simple, sensuous, and passionate" than rhetoric.

> Pure phrase, fit Epithets, a sober care
> Of Metaphors, descriptions clear yet rare,
> Similitudes contrasted smooth yet round,
> Not next to learning, but with Nature crown'd.
> . . . Strong figures drawn from deep invention's springs,
> Consisting less in words, and more in things.

This was English poetry for John Beaumont in 1629. Again in 1692 Walsh was writing that modern writers were less "surprising and glittering," more "tender, passionate, or natural."

[38] J. A. K. Thomson, *Classical Influences on English Prose* (New York: Collier, 1962).

[39] See, for example, Patrizi and Beon, in Baxter Hathaway, *The Age of Criticism* (Ithaca: Cornell University Press, 1962). And compare Raymond Howes, ed., *Historical Studies of Rhetoric and Rhetoricians* (Ithaca: Cornell University Press, 1961).

[40] George Williamson, *The Proper Wit of Poetry* (Chicago: University of Chicago Press, 1951), p. 13.

Even in matters of fact, the modes of styles were not always easily separable, and are not now. Feuillerat and Whipple disagreed, for example, in whether the Isocratean style was euphuistic. Clearly Latimer was plain — "more genuine, more coarse, more forceful . . . more masculine" — in the native and colloquial tradition of Tyndale's translation of the Bible. But is the free flow and parallelism of Ascham more like Isocrates or more like Cicero? As Williamson says, "Structurally, of course, style is conceived primarily with the relation of members, although the character of the members, such as form and length, is also important." [41] He raises the question of Dionysius: Is the middle style achieved by fusing or eliminating extremes? Then he helps answer these questions by showing first that Cicero's sentences are complex; Isocrates', coordinate, rhythmic, phrasal, more repetitive than conjunctive. We begin to see the contrast between Cicero's style and Isocrates', between a balance and an extreme. Besides, we have Harvey's confirmation that Ascham followed Isocrates. Also, "Seneca, when he spoke of style, always preferred things to words for weight, as Bacon did, and as Hobbes would do." [42] So it was not mere fusion but a philosophy of value of subordinating evidence that led to balanced style in the seventeenth century. As Trimpi says, "The persistence of stylistic qualities reflects a persistence of attitudes toward experience." [43]

At the end of the seventeenth century we therefore recognize at least three clear persistences: Dryden's strengthening of predicative style, to be confirmed later by Johnson, Hazlitt, and others; the moderate and subordinating Ciceronians like Bacon and Milton, suited to the deliberateness of the new psychological exploration; and, finally, the high style of science in its subjective mode.

MODERN PROSE

At the end of the seventeenth century, as at the end of the sixteenth, writers tried and tested and consciously contrasted the chief possibilities of prose style; and the original predicative forms remained dominant. Indeed, they were reasserted by Dryden and Addison with conscious approbation: Addison's connective clausal patterns; Dryden's less connected, more progressively juxtaposed; both still "native" in their combinations of Biblical and classical colloquialism. At the same time, the cases for contrasting styles were fully argued in rhetorical terms: high and middle as well as low, oratorical and epideictic as well as conversational, copious and well-

[41] *Ibid.*, p. 38.
[42] *Ibid.*, p. 150.
[43] Wesley Trimpi, *Ben Jonson's Poems, a Study of the Plain Style* (Palo Alto: Stanford University Press, 1962), p. viii.

complexioned as well as sinewy, artistic as well as natural, natural as well as conceptual; finally, in a new terminology, passionate and aesthetic as well as rational. The Royal Society had its say, yet words and concepts still dominated objects in prose as in poetry.

In the eighteenth century, objects began to gather strength. First nouns, then adjectives, increased at the expense of verbs. The efforts of Bacon became in sequence the efforts of Hobbes and Locke, then satirically of Swift, then soberly and naturally of Burke, Alison, and others, to present and to name. The grammatical result was the noun phrase, and then, with additional qualification, the increased use of adjectives. Purposes of exemplification and illustration, of "imaging," became amplified by purposes of more detailed description of properties. The result was, for Gibbon and Adam Smith, a new beginning of what Ascham and Browne had started: the high style as presentative and epical in new ways, in the surveys of new materials of knowledge.

The middle style predominates in twentieth-century England and America. But along with it, and along with such rich scientific prose as Huxley's, we need to remember the continuing vigor of predication. Jan Lennering begins his study of Addison's prose style by saying it is the forerunner of Johnson's style. "It can hardly be contested that Johnson represents the culmination of the neo-classical ideals of style." [44] And Johnson himself called Addison's "the model of the middle style [45] — without glowing words or pointed sentences; Blair also names him the safest model for imitation." [46] Addison challenged the current loose style of Montaigne, the Gothic turns and conceits, and recommended the more planned periods of Cicero, the shortened and parallel classical structures. He thought about effects, aiming for clarity, economy, and organization. He used much symmetry, parallelism of predicate elements, relating few different words and phrasal structures.[47] He can indeed sound quite balanced, as in *Spectator* 1:

> I was born to a small Hereditary Estate, which (according
> to the tradition of the village where it lies) was bounded by
> the same Hedges and Ditches in *William* the Conqueror's Time
> that it is at present, and has been delivered down from Father
> to Son whole and entire, without the Loss or Acquisition
> of a single Field or Meadow, during the Space of six hundred

[44] *Studies in the Prose Style of Joseph Addison* (Uppsala, 1951), p. 10.
[45] *Works*, I, 367.
[46] Hugh Blair, *Lectures on Rhetoric and Belles Lettres*, 1762 *et seqq.* (London, 1813), II, 37.
[47] Zilpha Chandler, *An Analysis of the Stylistic Technique of Addison, Johnson, Hazlitt, and Pater* (University of Iowa Humanistic Studies), Vol. IV, No. 3 (1928).

Years. There (runs) a Story   in the Family,   that   when my
Mother was gone   with Child   of me   about three Months,
she dreamt   that she was brought   to Bed   of a Judge . . .

But like his admirer Johnson, Addison was in general more "English,"
more predicative than balanced, more active than he aimed to be.
Samuel Johnson's "On Biography," reads:

All joy or sorrow   for the happiness of calamities   of others   is
produced   by an act   of the imagination,   that realizes the event,
   however fictitious,   or approximates it,   however remote,   by
placing us,   for a time,   in the condition   of him   whose fortune
we contemplate;   so   that we feel,   while the deception lasts,
whatever motions would be excited   by the same good   or evil
happening   to ourselves.

Johnson's verbs and connectives *is produced . . . that realizes . . . or*
approximates . . . by placing . . . of him whose . . . so that . . . which
. . . whatever also, in their own elegant, deliberate way, build a content of action. We speak of the poise, the architecture, of Dryden and
Johnson, but also we should stress their forward momentum, the unfolding
of action from action and verb from verb, in purposeful direction.

If the biographer writes   from personal knowledge,   and makes
haste to gratify the publick curiosity, there is danger   lest his interest, his fear, his gratitude,   or his tenderness, overpower his
fidelity,   and tempt him to conceal,   if not to invent.

This is Johnson, a few paragraphs further on. The *if* provides one vivid
situation, the consequences another moving from it. Not only the clear
connectives but the order of consequence is vital. As Ben Jonson had said,
order is at the heart of plainness in prose style.

W. K. Wimsatt warns us that Johnson's power is that of momentum,
not the monumentality of Burke and Gibbon.[48] The forty-fourth paragraph of the *Life of Pope* provides an example of Johnson's active style in
brief:

As the end   of method   is perspicuity, that series is sufficiently
regular that avoids obscurity;   and   where there is no obscurity it
will not be difficult to discover method.

Or, from the third paragraph:

Pope was   from his birth   of a constitution tender   and deli-
cate;   but is said to have shown remarkable gentleness   and sweet-

[48] *The Prose Style of Samuel Johnson* (New Haven: Yale University Press, 1941),
p. 99.

ness of disposition. The weakness of his body continued through his life, but the mildness of his mind perhaps ended with his childhood.

Or, for a paragraph less possibly involved with temporal sequence, the beginning of the Preface to *Shakespeare*:

> That praises are without reason lavished on the dead, and that the honours due only to excellence are paid to antiquity, is a complaint likely to be always continued by those who, being able to add nothing to truth, hope for eminence from the heresies of paradox; or those, who, being forced by disappointment upon expedients, are willing to hope from posterity what the present age refuses, and flatter themselves that the regard which is yet denied by envy, will be at last bestowed by time.

Other examples are the first paragraph of the *Idler, #72; Rambler,* 155, paragraph five; *Rambler,* 154, last paragraph; *Rambler,* 144, an active portrait of moderation; and the last paragraphs of the Preface to the *Dictionary.* In all these, representatively, as in the *Lives,* the sense of forward purpose, off-balance, is carried by the predication, making Johnson, grammatically and effectively, a far more restless writer than Gibbon, with whom he is so often linked.

William Hazlitt is famous for his essay in defense of the familiar style and for all the active, familiarly characterizing essays he wrote to illustrate this style. He used the old Elizabethan term *sinewy* for his own style, and added, "The continuity of impression is the only thing on which I pride myself." [49] As Baker says, he was incapable of detachment, would not stoop to elegance, opposed Locke, those he called Sophists, and writers of cadence and hieroglyph: [50] "Personifications, capital letters, seas of sunbeams, visions of glory, shining inscriptions, the figures of a transparency, Britannia with her shield, or Hope leaning on an anchor, make up their stock in trade. . . . Images stand out in their minds isolated and important merely in themselves, without any groundwork of feeling. . . ." [51] He wrote of isolation as Wordsworth did with reference to Ossian; and he praised, instead, familiarity, as in his essay on Familiar Style:

> It is not easy to write a familiar style. Many people mistake a familiar for a vulgar style, and suppose that to write without affectation is to write at random. On the contrary, there is

[49] Quoted in Herschel C. Baker, *William Hazlitt* (Cambridge, Mass.: Harvard University Press, 1962), p. 472.
[50] *Ibid.,* p. 470.
[51] William Hazlitt, quoted in Baker, *op. cit.,* p. 228.

nothing that requires more precision, and, if I may so say, purity of expression, than the style I am speaking of.

Note the effect of separate statements, each simple and direct, filled with the actions of *to write, mistake, suppose, requires, say, speak of,* and the characteristic connective *than,* which throws the comparison off-balance by moving toward a superlative.

How different another Romantic concept; Coleridge's "On Method" praises a learned man's order: "The evidently habitual arrangement of his words, grounded on the habit of foreseeing, in each integral part, or (more plainly) in every sentence, the whole that he then intends to communicate. However irregular and desultory his talk, there is method in the fragments. . . . Listen, on the other hand, to an ignorant man, though perhaps shrewd and able in his particular calling whether he be describing or relating. . . . The necessity of taking breath, the efforts of recollection, and the abrupt rectification of its failures, produce all his pauses; and with exception of the 'and then,' the 'and there,' and the still less significant 'and so,' they constitute likewise all his connections."

Such a description is a reminder of the earliest English "native" style, as characterized by Matthews: "The statements, short and of even length, set end to end or limited by a few conjunctions — with only an occasional clausal subordination lending its formal aid to the logic of the matter itself." [52]

At the same time, we see the learned and sophisticated interest in the native simplicities, as earlier by Sidney and Jonson, so later by Lawrence and Joyce. Indeed, the line of interest is direct, as Joyce tells us: Jonson was one of his most read writers. [53]

Cyril Connolly shows the same consciousness of tradition. In his predicative style, he says:

> An expert should be able to tell a carpet   by one skein   of it; a
> vintage   by rinsing a glassful   round his mouth. Applied   to
> prose, there is one advantage   to this method — a passage taken
> from its context is isolated   from the rest of a book,   and cannot
> depend   on the good will   which the author has cleverly estab-
> lished   with his reader. [54]

Thus he isolates the Mandarin, in Valéry's term; the style of rest, in Con-

[52] William Matthews, ed., *Later Medieval English Prose* (London, 1962).

[53] J. B. Bainsborough, "Joyce and Jonson," *Review of English Literature,* I (October, 1960), 45–51.

[54] "The Next Ten Years," *Enemies of Promise* (Garden City, N.Y.: Doubleday & Co., 1960), p. 13.

nolly's: the grand or baroque to be distinguished from the puritan because it wishes to convey more than it means or feels: "The Mandarin style at its best yields the richest and most complex expression of the English language. It is the diction of Donne, Browne, Addison, Johnson, Gibbon, De Quincey, Landor, Carlyle, and Ruskin, as opposed to that of Bunyan, Dryden, Locke, Defoe, Cooper, Cobbett, Hazlitt, Southey, and Newman." [55]

What skein is here? Ours, though not quite ours. Most of Connolly's Mandarins are what we call phrasal or adjectival, but not Donne, Addison, Johnson. And certainly the opposite sort is Bunyan, Dryden, Hazlitt, with Locke somewhat less. Connolly's skein is more complex than ours — a sampling of the qualities in a passage — but it is interesting that it so closely parallels the distinction between adjectival and predicative, varying for a few because it ignores the force of the verbs, which Connolly in his own structure does not ignore.

But though a modern theorist like Connolly may wish to employ the plain style even to convey a redefinition of the Mandarin, neither the old Renaissance colloquial nor the new nineteenth-century elaborate seems the force in prose or poetry today. While noun phrases and qualifiers have remained strong, verbs have returned, to effect a reasoning complexity of style, as for those early moderns, Bacon, Hobbes, Locke, Alison, and as recently for Shaw, Churchill, Russell, Orwell, Wain, and many Americans, like Baldwin. While we may well think of the middle style as a balance between predicative and adjectival, sharing a moderate portion of the characteristics of each, we should see that it has, also, characteristics of its own. What Bacon and Milton established, in their efforts to involve the English vernacular of process in a more complex, classical deliberation, Hobbes, Locke, Swift, and the reasoning writers continued: a cognizant style. Hear it in Locke, "Of the Beginning of Political Societies":

> He must show a strange inclination to deny evident matter of fact,
>   when it agrees not   with his hypothesis,   who will not allow
> that the beginning   of Rome and Venice were   by the uniting
> together   of several men, free and independent one   of another
> amongst whom there was no natural superiority   or subjection.

Adjectives equal verbs, or nearly, and nouns and connectives are about twice as many; clauses do the work upon the basis of thought and relation: *deny, agree, allow, amongst whom there was.* The thought is bodied forth in examples and from more than one point of view.

[55] *Ibid.,* p. 23.

So we see also the work of Swift, which, for its perspicuity and energy, received approval by later rhetoricians.

> Man is said to be a Sociable Animal, and, as an Instance of it, we may observe, that we take all Occasions and Pretences of forming ourselves into those little Nocturnal Assemblies, which are commonly known by the name of *Clubs*. When a Sett of Men find themselves agree in any Particular, tho' never so trivial, they establish themselves into a kind of Fraternity, and meet once or twice a Week, upon the Account of such a Fantastick Resemblance.

Hugh Blair agreed with Dr. Johnson, with Bishop Lowth, and with Priestley that this style was "easy, vigorous, plain," and rested upon sense, with few Latinate terms, few synonyms or figures, little "pomp or glare of expression." [56] Blair even praised exactly that trait of adverbial connectives which distinguishes most of the writers in this style: the use of adverbs of direction, as, for example, *towards* instead of *for*. He perceptively groups Swift with Locke as plain in contrast to Dryden and Addison as elegant, showing that for him elegance, as distinguished again from floridity, involved a certain figurativeness beyond Swift's.

Blair's rhetorical successor, Whately, was also helpful in defining clarity, setting it between the curt and the prolix as moderate because of its use of repetitions. Concreteness, not generality or abstraction, was also part of it; and Whately said that here was a real crux of choice — against the high generality of epithet as against abstract concept.

It is easy to perceive how an aesthetician like Alison would continue and enhance presentative correctness and how Arnold would argue for it. As both Lionel Trilling and E. K. Brown remind us, Arnold, like other classicists — T. S. Eliot, for example — had a strong sense of detachment in the midst of action, art as the isolation of the practical. Therefore, argument and the stating of positions were important, as in Arnold's "Literature and Science": "The necessary style of the life of such a world Plato regards with disdain; handicraft and trade and the working professions he regards with disdain; but what becomes of the life of an industrial modern community if you take handicraft and trade and the working professions out of it?" Here is the thinking about thinking which is made clear, as Whately suggests, by repetition, so as to be neither loose nor curt.

Likewise Bertrand Russell in "Philosophy and Politics": "Hobbes, though less skeptical than Hume, was equally persuaded that government is not of divine origin and was equally led, by the road of disbelief, to

---

[56] Blair, *op. cit.*, XXIV, pp. 67, 90.

advocacy of extreme conservatism." The subject-noun *Hobbes* carries its clause *though* in relation to its adjective *skeptical*.

Winston Churchill's prose in 1947 proceeds with a similar enthusiastic moderation:

> No one pretends   that democracy is perfect   or all-wise. Indeed it
> has been said   that democracy is the worst form   of government
>   except all those other forms   that have been tried   from time
> to time.

The verbs and adjectives work equally to give significance to the nouns, in forms explicitly connected and subordinated. Even more emphatically, in 1944:

> At the bottom   of all the tributes paid   to democracy is the little
> man, walking   into the little booth,   with a little pencil making a
> little cross   on a little bit   of paper — no amount   of rhetoric
> or voluminous discussion can finally diminish the overwhelming im-
> portance   of that point.

The *little, little,* and *little* adjectives, *walking* and *making,* culminate in the final adjective *overwhelming.* Even in his most characteristic balanced form, Churchill may stress the epithet, as in 1945:

> The inherent vice   of Capitalism is the unequal sharing   of bless-
> ings; the inherent value   of Socialism is the equal sharing   of
> miseries.

Here is the classic matching of adjective to noun in both subject and predicate as these are joined by the single verb; in addition, phrase parallels phrase.

Of his own style, Churchill wrote: "I affected a combination of the styles of Macaulay and Gibbon, the staccato antithesis of the former and the rolling sentences and genitival endings of the latter; and I stuck in a bit of my own from time to time." But also, "Broadly speaking, the short words are best and the old words are best of all." The elaborateness of the first combination is balanced by the simplicity of the second.

In the presence of a prose style so moderate as our own, it is tempting to ask whether this moderation is merely a kind of running down into entropy, a loss of the energy for extremes. As in poetry, however, we see that this moderate style persistently recurs between extremes and seems to provide a true alternative choice. When we ask what Arnold, Shaw, Russell, Churchill, Read, Orwell, Wain have in common, or what they could share with their great moderating predecessors Bacon, Milton, Hobbes,

Locke, Swift, Burke, Godwin, and others, it is necessary to remember that a multitude of variations exist for any likeness; and that a likeness here is significant in contrast to two other different modes.

We have already certain general qualities to go on. There has been a discrimination of a middle or balanced style, and it has been called classical. It is supposed to be poised, well-wrought, smoothly connected. Looking back, we may remember how Bacon, in revising his essays, worked for just these qualities; how Milton built upon them; and how Swift borrowed them for satire, to capitalize upon their effect of normalcy. Nevertheless, they do not merely temper actions by qualities and connectives at a mid position along a gamut of usage. They provide discernible traits of their own: essentially, a substantive structure that is yet active through its strong use of the relative clause. These writers are, so to speak, the realists. Like Bacon, they are for the weight of matter: for the external honey of the bee, not the internal spinnings of the spider; like the eighteenth century, they are for *growth*; that is, for organic forms in development, for an inner harmony rather than an outer embellishment; like Burke they are for the embodiment of general truths in concrete images; [57] like Godwin they are for an inner reason, expressed by clarity in style.

Like Swift, Shaw endeavors to make his Prefaces as reasonable-sounding as possible, and as substantial, considering all the paradoxes he plans to spring. Orwell too works in the surface normalcy of absurdity, a directly imaged, vividly presented world of fact. Read and Russell have the aesthetic of observation and of instance; Churchill, too, especially the sense of instance.

All stress represented image. Shaw said that drama was "truth to natural history." He said that his own language was the language of Swift, not of nineteenth-century journalism, and that while the Englishman is wholly at the mercy of his imagination, having no sense of reality to check it, the Irishman with "a far subtler and more fastidious imagination, has one eye always on things as they are." [58]

Henry Treece quotes Herbert Read as saying, "I had discovered myself and my style — that is to say, I had made an equation between emotion and image, between feeling and expression." [59] And Michael Roberts says of this style, "The voice is never raised, there is no overstatement, no

[57] James Boulton, *The Language of Politics in the Age of Wilkes and Burke* (London: Routledge and K. Paul, 1963).

[58] Woodbridge, *Shaw*, pp. 65, 106.

[59] *Herbert Read* (London: Faber and Faber, 1944), p. 10.

collapse into a false rhetoric, and there is a curious austerity in the imagery, an absence of harsh contours and strong lights. . . ." [60]

Orwell was sensitive both to sight and to the language conveying it. He abandoned his early liking for floridity and turned to Swift and Shaw, to "an aura of plausibility." He warned against dead metaphors and abstractions like *inevitable* and *phenomenon, romantic* and *human,* or verbal operators like *picking out* instead of *choosing.* "Of course the greatest wastage is in the verbs and adjectives." [61] He referred to four modes of writing English: two of them bad, the debased scant, or flowery; two of them good, the clarity of Bunyan or Addison, plus the tradition of rich imagery.

Fact, sight, object, image, noun — these, rather than syntax and structure, provide the focus of description of style for the modern critic; these provide the solidity, the observational accuracy, that we call classical. A structure does follow, as we have seen: substantival, with phrasal and clausal modification of the substantives.

Far more concerned with assumption are the adjectival prosaists, who developed from Ascham to Browne to, a century later, Adam Smith and Gibbon. See the early brief paragraph in *The Wealth of Nations:*

> This great increase in the quantity of work, which, in
> consequence of the division of labour, the same number of
> people are capable of performing, is owing to three different
> circumstances; first, to the increase of dexterity in every par-
> ticular workman; secondly, to the saving of the time which
> is commonly lost in passing from one species of work to an-
> other; and lastly, to the invention of a great number of ma-
> chines which facilitate and abridge labour, and enable one
> man to do the work of many.

The proportioning here is twelve adjectives to seven verbs. The abundance of adjectives is not decorative but analytical, part for part and item for item. Such a sentence as the following, a few paragraphs later, is representative:

> It is the great multiplication of the productions of all the differ-
> ent arts, in consequence of the division of labour, which oc-
> casions, in a well-governed society, that universal opulence
> which extends itself to the lowest ranks of the people.

[60] *Ibid.,* p. 13.
[61] Quoted in J. W. H. Atkins, *George Orwell, A Literary Study* (London: J. Calder, 1954), p. 321.

There is a sense of qualitative savour in the technical quantities, a sense, one may say, of natural and generous distribution.

In Gibbon, there is an even stronger structural sense; the famous poise of his first paragraph suspends itself between modified phrase and modified phrase.

> In the second century of the Christian era, the Empire of Rome comprehended the fairest part of the earth, and the most civilized portion of mankind. The frontiers of that extensive monarchy were guarded by ancient renown and disciplined valour. The gentle but powerful influence of laws and manners had gradually cemented the union of the provinces.
> Their peaceful inhabitants enjoyed and abused the advantages of wealth and luxury. The image of a free constitution was preserved with decent reverence: the Roman senate appeared to possess the sovereign authority and developed on the emperors all the executive powers of government. During a happy period of more than fourscore years, the public administration was conducted by the virtue and abilities of Nerva, Trajan, Hadrian, and the two Antonines. It is the design of this, and of the two succeeding chapters, to describe the prosperous condition of their empire; and afterwards, from the death of Marcus Antoninus, to deduce the most important circumstances of its decline and fall; a revolution which will ever be remembered, and is still felt by the nations of the earth.

In the second century of the Christian era . . . by the nations of the earth — this is the frame; and the content, *the fairest, the most civilized . . . ancient renown and disciplined valour . . . peaceful inhabitants, free constitution . . . decent reverence . . . important circumstances,* introduced by prepositions *in, of, by,* and Gibbon's favorite, *during,* each verb set between and protected by its braces of nouns, adjectives, and phrases.

Peter Quennell has commented "Than the *Decline and Fall*, there is probably no book of equal size and scope more thoroughly imbued with the characteristic quality of a single man's intelligence. It is not that the historian makes arbitrary or unjustified incursions into the pages of his history; he has no reason to intrude himself, for, in fact, he is always there — not as a figure rising impertinently between the reader and his subject, but as an influence that colours every scene, moderates the verbal rhythm of each successive period and links episode to episode in the same harmonious pattern. Naturally, such a feat of literary assimilation could only be achieved at the price, here and there, of a certain loss of sharpness.

Detachment as complete as Gibbon's is not without its dangers. It is at a distance that we hear the tramp of iron-shod Russian legions. . . ." [62]

In contrast: "Johnson's style was grand, and Gibbon's elegant; the stateliness of the former was sometimes pedantick, and the polish of the latter was occasionally finical. Johnson march'd to kettledrums and trumpets; Gibbon moved to flutes and hautboys; Johnson hew'd passages through the Alps, while Gibbon levell'd walks through parks and gardens." [63]

C. V. Wedgwood quotes Horace Walpole as saying, "Lo, there is just appeared a truly classic work . . . the style is as smooth as a Flemish picture, and the muscles are concealed and only for natural uses, not exaggerated like Michaelangelo's to show the painter's skill in anatomy." [64] Walpole's figure fits the contrast as we have seen it. The classic high style is smooth, the sinews of language fleshed out in substance in the manner the nineteenth century thought Greek.

Among his contemporaries, De Quincey was most conscious of this new sense of prose: "Simple narratives and a pathos resting upon artless circumstances, elementary feelings, — homely and household affections, — these are most suitably managed in the old indigenous Saxon vocabulary." But a "passion which rises into grandeur, which is complex, elaborate, and interveined with high meditative feelings, would languish or absolutely halt without aid from the Latin moiety of our language." [65] As a consequence, he dislikes the stiffness of "natural" writers like Addison, Lamb, Hazlitt. "Hazlitt was not eloquent, because he was discontinuous." [66]

Procter says that De Quincey's analysis is at its best when applied to a contrast between Johnson's plain and Burke's more classical modes. Burke he saw as elastic, in motion, letting truth grow; Johnson as "an intellect retrogressive, retrospective, and throwing itself back on its own steps," demanding subjects teaming with elements of known contradictory opinion.[67] Ruskin too proclaimed that he could not waste time arguing. Dialectic was not the goal of nineteenth-century subjectivism. Rather, the music of cadence, or, as in a dream, in Saintsbury's fine phrasing, "the greatest possible *variety* with the least possible *disturbance*." [68]

[62] *The Profane Virtues* (New York: Viking Press, 1945), p. 98.
[63] *Ibid.*, p. 101.
[64] *Edward Gibbon* (London: Longmans and Green, 1955), p. 16.
[65] *The English Language*, reprinted in *Collected Writings*, XIV, 157.
[66] De Quincey, *Collected Writings*, V, 231–236.
[67] Sigmund Procter, *Thomas De Quincey's Theory of Literature* (Ann Arbor: University of Michigan Press, 1943), p. 222.
[68] George Saintsbury, *A History of English Prose Rhythms* (London: The Macmillan Co., 1912), p. 311.

De Quincey's *Confessions of an English Opium-Eater* has often been called "poetical" in times when adjectives and artfulness have been thought poetic:

> I have often been asked   how it was,   and   through what series of steps,   that I became an opium-eater.   Was it gradually, tentatively, mistrustingly,   as one goes   down a shelving beach   into a deepening sea,   and   with a knowledge   from the first   of the dangers lying   on that path;   half-courting those dangers,   in fact,   whilst seeming to defy them?   Or was it,   secondly,   in pure ignorance   of such dangers,   under the misleadings of mercenary fraud?   since oftentimes lozenges,   for the relief   of pulmonary affections,   found their efficacy   upon the opium   which they contain,   upon this,   and this only,   though clamorously disavowing   so suspicious an alliance. . . .[69]

The adjectives, we may see, are strongly participial, so that a leaning, suspended effect is achieved, with high pattern — "down a shelving beach into a deepening sea . . . half-courting those dangers, in fact, whilst seeming to defy them." Then the intensive *pure* and the earnestly technical *pulmonary*, for a full setting of the complex, wistful, yet authoritative tone.

How well Carlyle joins this tone with the earlier busy, practical one of Adam Smith. *Past and Present* begins:

> The condition   of England,   on   which many pamphlets are now   in the course   of publication,   and many thoughts unpublished are going on   in every reflective head,   is justly regarded as one   of the most ominous,   and withal one   of the strangest, ever seen   in this world.   England is full   of wealth,   of multifarious produce,   supply   for human want   in every kind;   yet England is dying   of inanition.[70]

And again, with its reference to Browne's *Hydriotophia*:

> O,   what a waste is there;   of noble   and thrice-noble   national virtues;   peasant Stoicisms, Heroisms;   valiant manful habits, soul of a Nation's worth, —   which all the metal   of Potosi   cannot purchase back;   to which the metal   of Potosi,   and all you can buy   with *it*,   is dross and dust! [71]

From external mode to internal sympathy, "the changes of many-coloured existence," the poet as a seer of inner truth, this step Carlyle took with

[69] Everyman ed., p. 13.
[70] Everyman's ed., p. 1.
[71] *Ibid.*, p. 13.

vigor, not musicality. "My style is like no other man's." [72] Not for "Art," but for *intelligence of fact* — "the *fact*, deep as Hades, high as Heaven, and written *so*, as to the visual face of it, on our poor Earth!" [73] If this made for "heterogeneous, lumbering, interminable sentences," for qualifications, compounding, and plethoric fullness, so much the better for sincerity. Grace Calder has shown that for Carlyle, revision meant the building of words and phrases, the expanding by subordinated modification.

More aesthetic in their morality were the artists of the era. Take, for example, Ruskin:

> To be precise, I believe   that   among the agents   or instruments
> of human evaluation,   art is extremely important. I believe
> that the aesthetic faculty has been the means   of man   first ac-
> quiring,   and then refining, consciousness. Form, the progressive
> organization   of elements   otherwise chaotic, is given   in percep-
> tion . . . The realization   of formal values is the aesthetic ac-
> tivity.[74]

As John Rosenberg says, "Not diffuseness, but an almost licentious amassing of detail characterizes the purple patches of *Modern Painters*." [75] At another point, Rosenberg says that Ruskin introduces into modern English "the rich resources of Donne and Browne, the majestic sonorities of the King James Bible." [76] Hilda Hagstolz quotes Ruskin, predictably, as saying, "I never waste a moment of life in dispute or discussion." [77]

Equally aesthetically, Pater's *Renaissance* begins:

> The history   of the Renaissance   ends   in France,   and car-
> ries us away   from Italy   to the beautiful cities   of the country
> of the Loire.   But it was   in France   also,   in a very important
> sense,   that the Renaissance had begun;   and French writers,
> who are fond   of connecting the creations   of Italian genius   with
> a French origin,   who tell us   how Saint Francis of Assisi took not
> his name only,   but all those notions   of chivalry and romantic
> love   which so deeply penetrated his thoughts,   from a French
> source.   How Boccaccio borrowed   the outlines   of his stories

[72] *Journal*, 1833.
[73] Letter to Sterling, January, 1842. Compare Grace Calder, *The Writing of Past and Present* (New Haven: Yale University Press, 1949), pp. 120–121.
[74] Quoted in Solomon Fishman, *The Interpretation of Art* (University of California Press, 1963), p. 159.
[75] *The Darkening Glass* (New York: Columbia University Press, 1961), p. 4.
[76] *Ibid.*, p. 171.
[77] *Educational Theories of John Ruskin* (Nebraska, 1942), p. 60.

from the old French *fabliaux,* and how Dante himself expressly connects the origin of the art of miniature-painting with the city of Paris, have often dwelt on this notion of a Renaissance in the end of the twelfth and the beginning of the thirteenth century, a Renaissance within the limits of the middle age itself — a brilliant, but in part abortive effort to do for human life and the human mind what was afterwards done in the fifteenth.[78]

And proceeds:

And so from the rooms of this shadowy house by the Seine side we see that spirit going abroad, with its qualities already well defined, its intimacy, its languid sweetness, its rebellion, its care for physical beauty, its worship of the body, which penetrated the early literature of Italy, and finds an echo even in Dante.[79]

The prose of the scientists carries some of this qualitative force. Note Darwin's Introduction to the *Origin of Species:*

When on board H.M.S. 'Beagle,' as naturalist, I was much struck with certain facts in the distribution of the organic beings inhabiting South America, and in the geological relations of the present to the past inhabitants of that continent. These facts, as will be seen in the latter chapters of this volume, seemed to throw some light on the origin of species — that mystery of mysteries, as it has been called by one of our greatest philosophers. On my return home, it occurred to me, in 1837, that something might perhaps be made out on this question by patiently accumulating and reflecting on all sorts of facts which could possibly have any bearing on it.[80]

Eleven of our fifty writers or about a fifth of them, and half the number of classic writers, follow this mode. Ascham in the sixteenth century, Browne in the seventeenth, Adam Smith and Gibbon in the eighteenth, a large group in the nineteenth from De Quincey to Pater, and Julian Huxley in the twentieth are examples. This style followed the seventeenth and eighteenth century classic style in time, but has not kept pace with it in the twentieth century.

Yet its characteristic vocabulary is intensely modern. Classical writers

[78] London, 1935, p. 1.
[79] *Ibid.,* p. 5.
[80] London, 1920, p. 1.

emphasize terms of generality for man, society, and values: nouns like *business, government, liberty, association, culture;* and adjectives like Locke's *certain, evident, necessary,* Burke's *political,* Alison's *beautiful, capable, material,* and Arnold's *harmonious, moral, religious.* The phrasal writers, on the other hand, include among their main terms sensable ones like *body, form, structure, element;* with qualities like Browne's *large,* Smith's *simple,* Carlyle's *deep.* Theirs is, in other words, a vocabulary of more direct sense, and at the same time, their structure is more static and receptive. Note the dominant introductory phrase, the passive verb, and the verbs turned to nouns, in Huxley's concluding sentences:

> In the perspective of biology, our business in the world is seen to be the imposition of the best and most enduring of our human standards upon ourselves and our planet. The enjoyment of beauty and interest, the achievement of goodness and efficiency, the enhancement of life and its variety — these are the harvest which our human uniqueness should be called upon to yield.

The message of enjoyment and enhancement is supported by the form of its statement in the verbs made nouns and passives. Grammarians and poets of our day tend to praise one style or another, just as the Renaissance moralists did. L. A. Sherman approves the lightness, the economy, achieved by the reduction of verbs in favor of phrases and adjectives. But Otto Jesperson applauds what he calls nexus, "the dog runs," in preference to what he calls junction, "the running dog." "There is more life, more dramatic movement in nexus than in junction, which is like a picture." [81] He supports Hugh Blair's earlier contrast between the energy of Dryden's verbs and metaphors, and the plainer sense-imagery of Locke's epithets and of Swift's lack of metaphors.[82] R. A. Sayce most vividly makes the contrast between Pascal's motion and Montaigne's material, as he grounds literary tone in grammatical construction. Most critics simplify the contrast into dualism, but Gertrude Stein manages even to take account of the third force, the particle: "Words have to do everything in poetry and prose and some writers write more in articles and prepositions and some say you should write in nouns, and of course one has to think of everything." [83]

So, in the twentieth century, one tries to do.

[81] Jesperson, *op. cit.*, pp. 17, 67.
[82] Blair, *Lectures on Rhetoric* (Boston, 1850).
[83] *Lectures in America* (New York: Random House, 1935), p. 209.

⊷⊂ THREE ⊃⊱

Styles in American Prose

We seem to have come a traceable way in prose, though not to a pre-dictable future; a way that has led from one sort of strong predication through many substantival ramifications to a new sort of strong predication supported by qualities rather than by connections — another level deeper, or higher, as we may choose to see it.

To test this view of a progression in styles, we may look more briefly at a parallel series, separated spatially by an ocean and temperamentally by a revolution, but joined in common language. We speak of an American prose style — that active, rationalistic structure that seems to be character-istic of our best known prose writers and related closely to its English sources in the Renaissance. Its form is patent in its famous early preacher, Jonathan Edwards. His first of twenty sermons is dated September, 1740, and proceeds after the statement of text, doctrine, and some comment on the first proposition, as follows:

> Noah's undertaking was   of great difficulty,   as it exposed
> him   to the continual reproaches   of all his neighbors,   for that
> whole hundred and twenty years. None   of them   believed
> that he told them   of a flood,   which was about to drown the
> world.   For a man to undertake such a vast piece   of work,
> under a notion   that it should be the means   of saving him,
> when the world should be destroyed, it made him the continual
> laughing-stock   of the world.   When he was about to hire work-
> men, doubtless all laughed   at him,   and we may suppose,   that
>   though the workmen consented to work   for wages,   yet they
> laughed   at the folly   of him   who employed them.   When the
> ark was begun, we may suppose   that every one that passed by

and saw such a huge hulk stand there, laughed   at it,   calling it *Noah's folly.*[1]

Here we have the familiar Renaissance structure, strong in verbs and connectives. We see the simple subject-predicate combination loaded with following phrases within following clauses. The peroration is vividly active, much like Emerson's, but characteristically more negative:

> You have been once more warned to-day,   while the door   of the ark   yet stands open. You have,   as it were,   once again heard the knocks   of the hammer   and axe   in the building   of the ark,   to put you   in mind   that a flood is approaching. Take heed therefore   that you   do not still stop your ears, treat these warnings   with a regardless heart,   and still neglect the great work   which you have to do, lest the flood   of wrath suddenly come   upon you,   sweep you away,   and there be no remedy.[2]

Sir Thomas More or John Donne could claim these moving progressions.

Paine's *Common Sense* reflects a familiarly eighteenth-century tradition closer to classical. It begins:

> Some writers have so confounded society   with government, as to leave little   or no distinction   between them;   whereas they are   not only different,   but have different origins. Society is produced   by our wants   and government   by our wickedness;   the former promotes our happiness *positively*   by uniting our affections,   the latter *negatively*   by restraining our vices. The one encourages intercourse, the other   creates   distinctions. The first is a patron, the last a punisher.[3]

Along with his vigor, Paine has taken on more nouns, fewer verbs; though still he keeps more verbs than Burke. His balanced structure, here strongly used, is doing the work of the connectives, as in "The first is a patron, the last a punisher."

The next section is ended by the balanced peroration:

> In England   a king hath little more to do   than to make war and give away places;   which,   in plain terms,   is to empoverish the nation and set it together   by the ears.   A pretty business indeed   for a man   to be allowed eight hundred thousand sterling

[1] *Works* (New York, 1830), VI, 7.
[2] *Ibid.*, p. 22.
[3] *Complete Writings*, ed. Philip Foner (New York, 1945), I, 4–23.

a year for,   and worshipped   into the bargain!   Of more worth
is one honest man   to society;   and   in the sight   of God,
than all the crowned ruffians   that ever lived.[4]

The balance is set in the modified nouns: *honest man, crowned ruffians.*
The American speaks substantially as the Englishman.

Mid-nineteenth-century America provides us, in the work of Emerson,
Twain, and Whitman, with the same range of variation we have seen in
England: Emerson colloquial as Hazlitt; Twain balanced, in some ways an
earlier Shaw; Whitman even beyond Gibbon, beyond Macaulay, in a
copious combination of adjectives, nouns, connectives — all but verbs.
Note how predicative, crisp, unconnective Emerson sounds in the first
short paragraph in *Self-Reliance*:

Trust thyself: every heart vibrates   to that iron string.   Accept
the place the divine Providence has found   for you;   the society
of your contemporaries,   the connexion   of events.   Great men
have always done so,   and confided themselves childlike   to the
genius   of their age,   betraying their perception   that the Eternal
was stirring   at their heart,   working   through their hands, pre-
dominating   in all their being.   And we are now men,   and must
accept   in the highest mind the same transcendent destiny;
and not pinched   in a corner,   not cowards fleeing   before a
revolution,   but redeemers   and benefactors,   pious aspirants to
be noble clay plastic   under the Almighty effort,   let us advance
and advance   on Chaos   and the Dark.[5]

In contrast, the beginning of Whitman's *Democratic Vistas*, with its
three adjectives for every verb:

As the greatest lessons   of Nature   through the universe are perhaps the lessons   of variety   and freedom,   the same present the
greatest lessons also   in New World politics   and progress.   If
a man were ask'd,   for instance,   the distinctive points contrasting modern European,   and American   political   and other   life
with the old Asiatic cultus,   as lingering-bequeath'd yet   in
China   and Turkey,   he might find the amount   of them   in
John Stuart Mill's profound essay   on Liberty   in the future,
where he demands two main constituents,   or sub-strata,   for a
truly grand nationality — 1st, a large variety   of character — and
2d, full play   for human nature to expand itself   in numberless
and even conflicting directions — (seems to be   for general hu-
manity   much like the influences   that make up,   in their limit-

4 *Ibid.*, p. 16.
5 Everyman's ed., 1938, p. 31.

64

less field, that perennial health-action of the air we call the weather — an infinite number of currents and forces, and contributions, and temperatures, and cross purposes, whose ceaseless play of counterpart upon counterpart brings constant restoration and vitality.) With this thought — and not for itself alone, but all it necessitates, and draws after it — let me begin my speculations.[6]

After a few paragraphs:

And now, in the full conception of these facts and points, and all that they infer, pro and con — with yet unshaken faith in the elements of the American masses, the composites, of both sexes, and even consider'd as individuals — and ever recognizing in them the broadest bases of the best literary and esthetic appreciation — I proceed with my speculations, Vistas.[7]

And:

There is, in sanest hours, a consciousness, a thought that rises, independent, lifted out from all else, calm, like the stars, shining eternal. This is the thought of identity — yours for you, whoever you are, as mine for me.[8]

Compare the fresh objectivity of a third sort of stylist, Mark Twain, in *Life on the Mississippi*:

Imagine the benefits of so admirable a system in a piece of river twelve or thirteen hundred miles long, whose channel was shifting every day! The pilot who had formerly been obliged to put up with seeing a shoal place once or possibly twice a month, had a hundred sharp eyes to watch it for him now, and bushels of intelligent brains to tell him how to run it. His information about it was seldom twenty-four hours old. If the reports in the last box chanced to leave any misgivings on his mind concerning a treacherous crossing, he had his remedy; he blew his steam whistle in a peculiar way as soon as he saw a boat approaching; the signal was answered in a peculiar way if that boat's pilots were association men; and then the two steamers ranged alongside and all uncertainties were swept away by fresh information furnished to the inquirer by word of mouth and in minute detail.[9]

[6] New York: Pellegrini & Cudshy, 1948, p. 208.
[7] *Ibid.*, p. 216.
[8] *Ibid.*, p. 232.
[9] Bantam ed., 1945, p. 121.

Here are nearly equal adjectives and verbs, and we see that the structure reflects the content: each subject and predicate modified as the sentences go, each sentence direct and complete in its statement, working toward the clear, repeated predications of the last of the paragraph. This is simplicity of structure rather than complexity; it is not interwoven. But though it is simple, it is not bare.

See again a paragraph from "Racing Days":

> In the old times, whenever two fast boats started out on a race, with a big crowd of people looking on, it was inspiring to hear the crews sing, especially if the time were nightfall, and the forecastle lit up with the red glare of the torchbaskets. Racing was royal fun. The public always had an idea that racing was dangerous; whereas the opposite was the case — that is, after the laws were passed which restricted each boat to just so many pounds of steam to the square inch. No engineer was ever sleepy or careless when his heart was in a race. He was constantly on the alert, trying gauge-cocks and watching things. The dangerous place was on slow, plodding boats, where the engineers drowsed around and allowed chips to get into the "doctor" and shut off the water-supply from the boilers.[10]

Here is a pattern similar to the first. We see that Twain likes to give us the "color" of the situation — *In the old times* — *if the time was nightfall . . . when his heart was in a race* — and the final pile of modification — *where* they drowsed and allowed chips *to get into* and *shut off*. At the same time, the material is not convoluted like Baldwin's, but flatly put: *Racing was royal fun . . . the opposite was the case . . . no engineer was ever sleepy or careless*. These are Twain's basic tones: the one of downright assertion, the other of enthusiastic qualification by description. They provide, too, when in unexpected combinations, the basis for his humor: "By and by, all the useless, helpless pilots, and a dozen first-class ones, were in the association, and nine-tenths of the best pilots out of it and laughing at it."

Since Twain, discursive American prose has been close to his, close to balance in active progression. Santayana, Eliot, and Baldwin provide examples, in contrast to the stronger colloquial verbs and weaker connectives of a Hemingway or a Lardner. A paragraph from Baldwin's *Notes of a Native Son*, written with — a critic notes — "bitter clarity and uncommon grace" reads (and from now on I shall leave it to the reader to do his own mental spacing):

[10] *Ibid.*, p. 128.

The American student colony in Paris is a social phenomenon so amorphous as to at once demand and defy the generality. One is far from being in the position of finding not enough to say — one finds far too much, and everything one finds is contradictory. What one wants to know at bottom, is what *they* came to find: to which question there are — at least — as many answers as there are faces at the café tables.

The symmetry in repetition is noteworthy and is characteristic of the writing as a whole. Compare, for example, the last, and more elaborate, sentences of the essay:

It is, indeed, this past which has thrust upon us our present, so troubling role. It is the past lived on the American continent, as against that other past, irrecoverable now on the shores of Europe, which must sustain us in the present. The truth about that past is not that it is too brief, or too superficial, but only that we, having turned our faces so resolutely away from it, have never demanded from it what it has to give. It is this demand which the American student in Paris is forced, at length, to make, for he has otherwise no identity, no reason for being here, nothing to sustain him here. From the vantage point of Europe he discovers his own country. And this is a discovery which not only brings to an end the alienation of the American from himself, but which also makes clear to him, for the first time, the extent of his involvement in the life of Europe.

The repeated relative clauses and participles underpin the thought: . . . this *past* which . . . *the past lived* . . . that *other past* . . . which, *not that* . . . but *only that, having turned* . . . having *never demanded* . . . this *demand which, a discovery which.* Such deliberating prose provides our American counterweight to the colloquial tradition of Emerson, which flourishes now in Hemingway, as in Joyce and Lawrence.

Speaking of stylistic choice, a friend once said of Emerson's: "His noun had to wait for its verb or its adjective until he was ready." These are two of the choices; the third, a connective, was certainly less Emerson's, and he worried about the omission. Because of his lively consciousness of questions of style — in prose as in poetry — and because of his importance in the plain or colloquial British and American traditions, it may be profitable to consider his work more fully in its relations of theory to practice. What are the special traits and traditions of this essayist of ours that set him apart from any other we may know — from Cicero and Seneca on old age, from Montaigne on life and friendship, from the Elizabethan essayists whom he read with such pleasure as a boy, from the sermons he heard, from the eighteenth- and nineteenth-century philosophic and journalistic prose that he read in the English reviews, from Carlyle, whom he admired so directly, from his own American contemporaries, from the wisdom-literature of China, Persia, India, and from his own Bible?

If we read the beginning of his perhaps most famous essay, "Self-Reliance" (which, in the 1840's, followed "History" in introducing his increasingly popular series of "Essays"), we may catch his mode of expression. After presenting three quotations on the theme "Man is his own star," Emerson begins:

> I read the other day some verses written by an eminent painter, which were original, and not conventional. The soul always hears an admonition in such lines, let the subject be what it may. The sentiment they instill is of more value than any thought they may contain. To believe your own thought, to believe that what is true for you in your private heart, is true for all men, — that is genius. Speak your latent conviction, and it shall be the universal sense; for the inmost in due time becomes the outmost, and our first thought is rendered back to us by the trumpets of the Last Judgment. Familiar as the voice of the mind is to each, the highest merit we ascribe to Moses, Plato, and Milton is that they set at naught books and traditions, and spoke not what men, but what *they* thought. A man should learn to detect and watch that gleam of light which flashes across his mind from within, more than the lustre of the firmament of bards and sages.

The tone of this beginning is particular and personal: *I read . . . your own*; general and confident: *the soul always hears*; evocative: *the trumpets of the Last Judgment*; wide-reaching: *Moses, Plato, and Milton*; recommendatory: *speak . . . learn*; figurative: *that gleam of light . . . more than the lustre of the firmament.*

In this combination of qualities, Emerson's style is more focused and condensed than Cicero's, say, or Seneca's, or Montaigne's; it sets its generalities in specific actions and analogies. It is not what we traditionally call a classic style, either in Latin or in English, because it does not progress as a full and logical unfolding of thought, but rather moves as if by flashes of illumination. This is not to say that it is illogical; merely that it does not give the effect of explicit stress on logical connections. Nor does it stress the literal qualifications and descriptions with which classical prose is concerned. So both adjectives and connectives are relatively subordinated to direct active verbs in the passage. The prose is carried not so much by the contrast, *original and not conventional*, though this is a basic contrast; nor by the adjectives *eminent, true, private, latent, universal, first, last, familiar, highest*; and not so much by the connectives *by, which, in, than, that, for* and so on; as it is by the verbs *I read, the soul hears, they instil, may contain, to believe, what is true, that is genius, speak, it shall be, what they thought, should learn to detect and watch, light which flashes*.

In abstract terms, this is to say that characteristically Emerson, in this paragraph, throughout this essay, and again twenty years later in "Illusions," writes a very active, predicative style, one in which the structure is basically simple statement, to which both modification and connective addition are only minimally necessary, and the sentences relatively short, the central statements relatively unqualified.

Closest to Emerson are the sermon-makers, like the pre-Elizabethan Latimer or Tyndale's Epistle of Paul to the Romans, who write in the "low" style that Walton found noteworthy in the *Complete Angler*; or narrative writers like the Bunyan of *Pilgrim's Progress* or the Joyce of Molly Bloom's soliloquy. But these are styles we do not probably think of as Emersonian. Yet even less so are the classic arguers in the tradition of Hooker, Bacon, and Locke, or the soaring describers he often loved, like Sir Thomas Browne, his own contemporaries, like Carlyle, or what he himself called a "mock-turtle nutriment as in Macaulay." [11]

But in the tradition there is one writer with whom he is so closely allied that we cannot help but recognize what was, as a youth, his own favorite reading: Ben Jonson, in his prose *Discoveries*, as in his poetry. Jonson was as singular in his own time as Emerson in his; their sense of the English language as best used in active, concise statements, often making connections by implication, was a sense shared in its extreme by few others, and thus especially lively both in its singularity and in its function as a bond between them. Even their use of specific connectives — the proportion of relative clauses to causal clauses and locational phrases — is striking. Not Plutarch, not Montaigne, nor Bacon, but specifically the aphoristic Jonson of *Timber* is Emerson's direct model. Jonson sounds like this, in "Claritas Patria," from *Timber*:

> Greatness of name, in the Father, oft-times helpes not forth, but ore whelmes the Sonne; they stand too neere one another. The shadow kils the growth; so much, that we see the Grand-child come more, and oftener, to be the heire of the *first*, then doth the *second*; He dies betweene; the Possession is the *thirds*.

[11] *A Correspondence with John Sterling* (Boston: Houghton Mifflin Co., 1897), p. 62.

In contrast is Montaigne's flow of easy subordinates, at least in modern translation, in "To the Reader":

> This book was written in good faith, reader. It warns you from the outset that in it I have set myself no goal but a domestic and private one. I have had no thought of serving either you or my own glory. My powers are inadequate for such a purpose. I have dedicated it to the private convenience of my relatives and friends, so that when they have lost me (as soon they must), they may recover here some features of my habits and temperament, and by this means keep the knowledge they have had of me more complete and alive.[12]

Many a discussion of Emerson's style has expressed regret at his effect of abrupt discontinuity and illogicality; and he himself, as he wrestled with his writing, scolded about the sentences that seemed sometimes to repel rather than to attract each other. But the absence of strong explicit connectives does not mean the absence of strong implied connections. See in *Self-Reliance* how Emerson's thought, like Jonson's, specifically moves. He has read some original verses; he generalizes from such originality in such a way that it leads one to trust his own thought as true for all — "inmost" becomes "outmost." As we value great men for what they thought, so we should attend, even more than to what they thought, to what we think. The argument moves between particular and general, and from key word to key word, as *original* leads to *private* to *genius* to *inmost* to *what they thought* to *his mind from within,* using always two sets of contrasts, the *conventional* as too limiting, the *universal* and *outward* as rightly expanding, allowing us to ally our right with that of Moses and Milton.

Such thought is logical, even syllogistic. The general: All men are mortal; the particular: Socrates is a man; the conclusion: Therefore Socrates is mortal. You and I participate in this truth. But the *and*'s and *therefore*'s have been omitted or have been used with relative infrequency. In other words, the logical relation of all to one is present, but not the explicit links in the steps of relation. Further, Emerson might begin with what we would call an untenable premise: All men are immortal. He would feel this intuitively — "the blazing of evidence of immortality," [13] the "gleam of light which flashes across his mind from within" — and so he would base upon it his logical argument for anyone and for us. And further, he would treat key words like *man* in a special way, including in them all their degrees of evaluative reference from lowest to highest; so

[12] *Essays of Montaigne,* trans. Donald Frame (Garden City, N.Y.: Doubleday, 1960).
[13] Bliss Perry, *Emerson Today* (Princeton: Princeton University Press, 1931), p. 56, 70.

that "man" would mean man in his limitless degree of spirit, as well as in his limiting degree of body, thus supporting by definition, implicit or explicit, the relation between *man* and *immortal* that the syllogism makes. It is as if Emerson were essentially satisfied to say: All men are men (with all men's limitations and potentialities); a man acts like a man. The connective *therefore*'s and adjectival *mortal*'s are minimal; the subject-predicate *Men are, a man is,* central.

In the early sermons, according to Kenneth Cameron's *Index-Concordance*, key terms are *God, Jesus, man, memory, mind, Nature, self, soul, truth.* These suggest three centers: religious, psychological, scientific. Then in *Nature,* key terms are *action, beauty, God, man, mind, nature, poet, soul, spirit, thought, truth, world.* The changes make clear Emerson's motion away from religion in the shape of person toward religion in the sense of creation of beauty, whereby *action, thought,* and *world* are taken up into the forms and purposes of *spirit,* and thus made beautiful by their harmony.

Index-terms tend to be nouns, but if we look more closely at the recurrent language of specific prose texts, early and late, we will see how strong and traditional are Emerson's verbs, especially those of *feeling, knowing, thinking;* how evaluative and discriminating his adjectives, as for example in "Self-Reliance," *divine, good, great, new, own, other, same, strong, such, true,* and in the later "Fate" and "Illusions" the *fine, find,* and *hold.* The nouns of these essays also parallel the concordance sums: the early *action, being, character, fact, friend, truth, virtue;* the later *circumstance, element, form, fate;* and the shared *God, law, life, man, mind, nature, nothing, power, thought, time, world.* The shift in emphasis from early *action* and *character* to later *circumstance* and *fate* is represented in the structure of the prose, as of the poetry also: an unusually high proportion of verbs and low proportion of connectives in the early work and "Self-Reliance," establishing later a proportion of about ten verbs and ten adjectives to twenty nouns, achieving the precarious and shifting balance between action and circumstance that he argues for.

Poetry and prose for Emerson are not far apart. In syntax, in vocabulary, in idea, their likenesses are greater than their differences. The main differences are the larger proportion of sensory terms in the poetry, and the framing by meter and rhyme. His first poems appeared not in the volume called *Poems* but as epigraphs for essays. He saw poems as epigraphs, like Biblical verses, texts for sermons or essays. Therefore his poetic allegiances were divided, on the one hand to the succinctness of a Jonson, as in prose, yet on the other to the materials and moods of his own day, which were freer, more rational, more exploratory. Inasmuch as he is one of the distinguished prose writers who was also a distinguished poet, a closer look at his poetry may be helpful before we go on (in Chapter Four) to further consideration of the relation between the two forms in language.

Emerson's poetic vocabulary was strongly that of the liberal eighteenth century, from Sylvester through Thomson, Gray, and Blake. This, in its sensory quality, was often called feminine: the vocabulary of *fair, sweet, air, nature, land, morning, sea, sky, sun,* and the concepts of *good, wise, youth, fate, freedom, form, kind, home, beauty, thought, time,* of *bringing, falling, hearing, seeing, knowing;* with equal proportions of *and, of, in* of directional connectives, and of relative and logical connectives — that is, a sensorily active and receptive vocabulary like that of the English-eighteenth and American-nineteenth centuries, its especial impact in its direct joining of man and nature.

To this outreaching vocabulary he did at least consider suiting a freer form. Like Carlyle, he wearied of the "specimens" of English verse he had read. Carlyle had written him in the 1830's: "My view is that now at least we have lived to see all manner of Rhetorics and Poetics and Sermonics . . . as good as broken and abolished . . . and so one leaves the paste-board coulisses, and three unities, and Blair's lectures quite behind: and feels only that there is *nothing sacred* then, but the *speech of man* to believing men: — which will one day anew environ itself with fit modes, with solemnities that are not mummeries." [14] Emerson's own *Journals* of this time (1839) expressed his interest not only in Pope's couplets and Scott's quatrains but in freer measures like those characteristic of Words-worth's ode on immortality — "Not tinkling rhyme, but grand Pindaric strokes, as firm as the tread of a horse . . ." suggesting not a restraint "but the wildest freedom." Later, he wrote to R. W. Grimm on his *Life of Michelangelo,* "I hate circular sentences or echoing sentences, where the last half cunningly repeats the first half, — but you [Grimm] step from stone to stone, and advance ever." [15] And he expressed to Grimm his corollary lack of taste for drama: "Certainly it requires great health and wealth of power to ventriloquize (shall I say?) through so many bodies. . . ." [16] Rather, "The maker of a sentence . . . launches out into the infinite and builds a road into Chaos and old Night, and is followed by those who hear him with something of wild creative delight. [17] And in 1839: "Who can blame men for seeking excitement? They are polar and would you have them sleep in a dull eternity of equilibrium? Religion, love,

[14] *Correspondence* with Carlyle, I, 22.
[15] *Correspondence* with Grimm, p. 42.
[16] *Ibid.,* p. 52.
[17] *Heart of Journals,* 1834, p. 89.

ambition, money, war, brandy, — some fierce antagonism must break the round of perfect circulation or no spark, no joy, no event can be." [18]

He is aware, too, of freedom in natural forms. In 1841: "I told Henry Thoreau that his freedom is in the form, but he does not disclose new matter. . . . But now of poetry I would say, that when I go out into the fields in a still sultry day, in a still sultry humor, I do perceive that the finest rhythms and cadences of poetry are yet unfound, and that in that purer state which glimmers before us, rhythms of a faery and dream-like music shall enchant us, compared with which the finest measures of English poetry are psalm-tunes. I think now that the very finest and sweetest closes and falls are not in our metres, but in the measures of eloquence, which have greater variety and richness than verse. . . ." [19] Such freedom he aimed for in his prose and poetry of the sea, and such sense of freedom enabled him in 1855 to hail Whitman's new scope and form.

Yet there is a stronger controlling force for him: his note-taking interest in pithy statements. As far back as 1820 we see his mood: "Have been of late reading patches of Barrow and Ben Jonson; and what the object — not curiosity? No — nor expectation of edification intellectual or moral — but merely because they are authors where vigorous phrases and quaint, peculiar words and expressions may be sought and found, the better to rattle out the battle of my thoughts." [20] And in 1840, his philosophical reasons for condensation, "Yet does the world reproduce itself in miniature in every event that transpires so that all the laws of nature may be read in the smallest fact." [21]

Then in 1842, the recognition of the power of concentration within scope and range: "This feeling I have respecting Homer and Greek, that in this great, empty continent of ours, stretching enormous almost from pole to pole, with thousands of long rivers and thousands of ranges of mountains, the rare scholar, who, under a farmhouse roof, reads Homer and the tragedies, adorns the land. He begins to fill it with wit, to counterbalance the enormous disproportion of the unquickened earth." [22]

While his chief substance then comes from the protestant naturalism of Sylvester and the eighteenth century, in *air, sea, sky, land, cloud, star,* and its American specifications in *beautiful, river, music, morning, snow, rose,* like Whitman's *grass,* the counter, wry, limiting, and constructing tradition was his aphoristic one, the *good* and *wise thought, nature, fate, form, time,*

[18] *Ibid.,* p. 147.
[19] *Ibid.,* p. 165.
[20] *Ibid.,* p. 5.
[21] *Ibid.,* p. 149.
[22] *Ibid.,* p. 187.

of the Elizabethans. When later in life Emerson published *Parnassus,* his collection of the poems he had liked best, the most space went to Shakespeare, the next to Jonson and Herrick, Wordsworth and Tennyson. While nineteenth-century poets gave him his guide to beauty of reference, the seventeenth century, in poetry as in prose, gave him his form. From the Jonson he called "master of song," he quoted lines that remind of his own.

> Come on, come on, and when you go
> So interweave the curious knot
> As even the Observer scarce may know
> Which lines are pleasure, and which not: . . .
> Admire the wisdom of your feet:
> For dancing is an exercise.
> Not only shows the mover's wit,
> But maketh the beholder wise
> As he hath power to rise to it.

So Emerson's cryptic and summary comment on more extended thought gave to thought the close form of meter and rhyme, with which he was so concerned as a part of the structure of the universe — its recurrent tide in season and in man. For him this form was not "organic" in the sense that we sometimes use the term, as Coleridge used the term — in the individual and spontaneous unfoldment of self as a flower. This Emerson called romantic and capricious. Rather, for him "organic" meant structural, necessary, recurrent in a context of use, in material and formal cause; that is, as he said, *classic.*[23]

A close look at the form of his poetry in relation to his prose tells us much of the form of the world for him. Its lines, its regular or varied stresses, its coupled or varied rhymes are part of the body, the law, of nature. With and against them the poet's free spirit works. Similarly, names are part of the categorizing force of nature. With and against them, through metaphor, the seeing of likeness in difference and difference in likeness, the seeing poet's vision of image and symbol, of individual entity, works. Similarly, sentences and generalizations are part of the laws of nature, and with and against them the vital instance works. In structure, in reference, in sound, his poetry gives us, even more closely than his prose, the presence of all in one, the interplay of likeness and difference in every entity of art.

Among Emerson's best-liked poems — "Each and All," "Uriel," "Good-Bye," "Woodnotes," "Merlin," "Concord Hymn," "Boston Hymn," "Brahma," "Days," "Terminus" — as among his variety of longer descrip-

[23] James Cabot, A *Memoir of Ralph Waldo Emerson* (Boston, 1887), II, 766.

tions and shorter fragments, condensations and variations appear in all sorts of degrees, from the strictness of "Concord Hymn," to the obliquities of "Merlin." Even some of his choppiest addenda are likable; "Limits," for example, or "The Bohemian Hymn," or "Water" from "Fragments," or "Nature and Life," or

> Roomy Eternity
> Casts her schemes rarely,
> And an aeon allows
> For each quality and part
> Of the multitudinous
> And many-chambered heart.

Or from "The Poet,"

> That book is good
> Which puts one in a working mood.
>   Unless to thought is added will,
>   Apollo is an imbecile.
> What parts, what gems, what colors shine, —
> Ah, but I miss the grand design.

This was Emerson's steadiest complaint about his style: he dealt in parts and fragments and could not achieve the whole, which he himself bespoke. Yet his very worry about this achievement, as about his friendship and love, is indicative of its importance to him, its religious center for him. We must not take at face value his fears of coldheartedness, of infinitely repellent particles; these were the recalcitrances of substance in which his spirit worked. "It is very unhappy, but too late to be helped, the discovery we have made that we exist. That discovery is called the Fall of Man." Yet, "We are sure, that although we know not how, necessity does comport with liberty," and, "a part of Fate is the freedom of man." These are the principles of his life; they are guides, too, to the form of his art. In the speculative turns of "Merlin," as in the steady pace of "Brahma" and "Days," is the strength of freedom joined with measure.

The essay "The Poet" makes specific application of these beliefs. Ideally, the poet is the sayer, the teller of news, utterer of the necessary and causal. "For the Universe has three children, born at one time, which reappear under different names in every system of thought, whether they be called cause, operation and effect; or, more poetically, Jove, Pluto, Neptune; or, theologically, the Father, the Spirit, and the Son; but which we will call here the Knower, the Doer and the Sayer. These stand respectively for the love of truth, for the love of good, and for the love of beauty. These three are equal. Each is that which he is, essentially, so that he cannot be surmounted or analyzed, and each of these three has the power of the others latent in him and his own, patent."

The poet, by saying, makes new relations, heals dislocations and detachments, shows defects as exuberance, as in Vulcan's lameness, Cupid's blindness. "Every new relation is a new word." The world is thus "put under the mind for verb and noun" without an explicit connective. It is important to realize what this sense of saying means to Emerson's own poetry. It means that as a poet he is not an imagist, not a symbolist, but specifically a figurist. That is, he accepts image and symbol as vital, from the natural world; and then his contribution as poet is to show them in new relation. "He knows why the plain or meadow of space was strown with these flowers we call suns and moons and stars. . . ." There is a metaphoric way of speaking. He names now by appearances, now by essences, delighting in the intellect's sense of boundaries, and then in the ascension of things to higher kinds; that is, in both being and becoming, the inebriation of thought-meaning moving to fact; even in algebra and definitions, the freedom of trope. Emerson blames mystics, as he would blame modern ritualistic symbolizers, for too many fixities. "The history of hierarchies seems to show that all religious error consisted in making the symbol too stark and solid. . . . Let us have a little algebra" — a little relation and proportion! "I look in vain for the poet whom I describe." "We do not with sufficient plainness or sufficient profoundness address ourselves to life, nor dare we chaunt our own times and social circumstances."

Is Emerson a philosopher? Yes, if we agree with Dewey: "Philosophic study means the habit of always seeing an alternative, of not taking the normal for granted, of making conventionalities fluid again, of imagining foreign states of mind." [24] In this way he prepares for James, for Dewey, for Charles Peirce, the great American pragmatists. In this way too he prepares more metaphysically for Nietzsche's Dionysus. But Emerson was not systematic and did not write the connected, subordinating style of Hobbes or Russell. René Wellek, on Emerson's philosophy, Andrew Schiller on his "gnomic structure," Kathryn McEwen on his rhymes, Frank Thompson on his theories of poetry, Blair and Faust on his method, Adkins on his Bardic tradition, Yohannon on his Persian translations, Percy Brown on his aesthetics, Hopkins and Whicher on his sense of form, and Carpenter on his use of oriental materials — all suggest variations on the theme of his fragmentary illuminations. So did his elder critics like Carlyle, Arnold, Santayana.

[24] John Dewey, "The Philosophy of William James," *Southern Review*, I (1932), p. 4.

So did he. When in 1870 he began his final series, "On the excellence of Intellect, its identity with nature, its formations in Instinct and Inspiration, and relation to the existing religion and civility of the present," [25] he warned his hearers that this series would consist of "anecdotes of the intellect, a sort of Farmer's Almanac of mental moods," and even defended this method, as we have noted before, in his metaphor of the dotted line. He had reasons for not filling in the lines, for not always writing a smoothly qualified prose, poetry, or philosophy. "I think that philosophy is still rude and elementary. It will one day be taught by poets. The poet is in the natural attitude; he is believing; the philosopher, after some struggle, having only reasons for believing." "I confess to a little distrust of that completeness of system which metaphysicians are apt to affect. 'Tis the gnat grasping the world."

But in his sense of metaphysics as useful, for daily use, he had a great deal of work to do in the world. To feed the hunger of the young for ideas; to think what simple pattern of being could include man's sense of joy in being as well as his fear and falsification of it; to draw the world as newly understood by scientific thought into the world of common intuition; to combine his feeling that "the beauty of the world is a perpetual invitation to the study of the world" [26] with his explanation of such combination, as to his brother Edward in 1834, that visionary reason and toiling understanding work together "by mutual reaction of thought and life, to make thought solid and life wise." [27]

A man who has been called monist, dualist, pantheist, transcendentalist, puritan, optimist, pragmatist, mystic, may well feel dubious about the validity of labels, of adjectives. His style shows us how all of these fit him and how they work together, and over and over he tells us that it is degree he believes in; in degree, the one and the many may work together; God, man, nature may work together; all varieties of difference, from dissimilar to contrasting, will share degrees of likeness. His common term *polarity* referred not to modern positive and negative poles, and not to modern, negative correlations or annihilations, but to differences or contrasts that are unified by a common direction, a north star, a magnetic field, a spirit in the laws and limits of body, a drawing of body along in the directions of spirit — a golden mean with a lodestar. Rhyme, meter, aphorism, sermon structure gave stoical feet rather than Aeolian wings to his Aeolian natural world, and made it go at a workday pace, the early prose most radical in multiple verbs, the early poetry in minimal connectives, but all

[25] *Complete Writings,* ed. Thomas Wise (New York, 1929).
[26] First lecture, "The Uses of Natural History."
[27] *Works,* I, 181.

ready enough to state, and then to state again. By thought the transcendentalist could move from negative to positive, from literal to figurative, "a little beyond." He could write a smooth pentameter, a rough tetrameter, a smooth and soaring sermon, a rough and ready aphorism, using essentially the same sentence structures and vocabularies. It was not that sometimes he had a meter-making argument but that sometimes his argument was meter-making, coming to him in association with the old poetry he loved rather than in the work on a lecture. His relation, in prose as in poetry, was to a great, simple tradition; to Jonathan Edwards, for example, in American colloquialism. He did not take on the eighteenth- or nineteenth-century structures but rather adapted their vocabularies to older structures. He therefore prevails as an artist of *sentence*, in prose as in poetry. American prose, so far as we have sampled it, supports Emerson in this power. What was native for England persists in being native for America — predication dominant over attribution. Without seeing so full a range in American prose, we can yet see that the moderns exactly parallel the British moderns. Whitman caught epithetical echoes from overseas, Twain enlarged British classicism by more energy in adjectives and verbs at once; that is, by a high style carried along in action. Emerson (as can be seen in the Prose Table in Chapter One) shared with writers as different as Santayana and Hemingway, as Lardner and Baldwin, the propensity for straight statement-making, for aphoristic assertion, most characteristic of English prose both British and American, both Renaissance and modern.

◀◀ FOUR ▶▶

Styles in Prose and Poetry

So much has been said about the difference between prose and poetry that any suggestion of likeness can seem at once obvious and absurd. There is a clear difference in sound; there are many proposed differences in spirit, in ontology; then what about the common resources in the common language? Do we have a poetic structure, a poetic diction? Do we have poetic eras, prosaic eras? Is one of the forms a source for the other? It has been my belief that prose has provided a general source for poetry; that poetry has focused and concentrated, by means of its form, the value-terms and the patterns of statement in prose. But now I find that the directions of influence are multiple, not so simple.

The similarities in proportion can best be seen by the parallel lists of texts — for each of five centuries — that we looked at in Chapter One. The first simple comparison, between the Renaissance poets and the Renaissance prosaists, shows equal proportions of adjectives, nouns, and verbs, but distinctly more connectives for prose. Reasonably enough; there is more potentiality for subordination in prose, especially the cursive sequences in the works of Tyndale, Holinshed, Dekker, and Bacon.

In the seventeenth century there is no great difference for poetry, but a decline of prose verbs, a range from the predicates of Jonson and others in both prose and poetry to the adjectives of Browne, Waller, Milton; from the scarcity of connectives in many poets to the great abundance in Donne's poetry, Hobbes's and Milton's prose.

In the eighteenth century we find a substantial and adjectival height for poetry, a balance for prose; in the nineteenth, an adjectival increase for prose, a balance for poetry; in the twentieth century, a predicative increase for both and a continued decrease in connectives for prose, which makes it the more similar to poetry. The sequence is from prose decline of verbs, to increase of nouns and then of adjectives, to decrease of connectives and increase of verbs again — three steps of choice — verb, connective, adjective, now back to verb.

What then is the direction of effect? From poetry to prose in connective sparseness and adjectival richness; from later prose substance to poetic. So it is true, what we have heard: the *copie* of prose, the *flowers* of poetry, the *sentence* of both.

The briefer sums of American prose and poetry, covering more time, present the same relations. The Atlantic and the Revolution made no drastic alterations in literary structures. The chief notable change is what the very recent poets, perhaps under the guidance of Emerson and Dickinson, do to diminish connectives, intensifying the tendency that we see in the British also. Lowell and Roethke, Auden and Gunn support this diminishment, this curtness of poetry, more strongly than do any writers in prose.

Similarities of proportion are borne out by similarities of reference. Not only are the quantities of word-forms similar, but also their qualities, their specific contents. In the following tables we see the major terms of poetry in the first column, of prose in the second, in order of first appearance in major usage. The major words of poetry — major for at least two poets of the fifty — appear here in order of adjectives–nouns–verbs for each author for whom they were first major, with connectives in a separate table following. The terms *dear, fair, golden, good,* for example, begin as major with the Ballads and continue in major use through each of the five centuries — from nine poets for *dear* to twenty-four, or nearly half, for *good*. Note that all of these decline in use, while *old* and other following adjectives of the Ballads increase. With Dunbar and Coverdale, other new terms come into major use. The lists are longer for the earlier poets because there is greater opportunity for the later poets to follow or reject the choices of their predecessors. In all, for poetry in the five centuries, there are about 260 major terms — 60 adjectives, 60 verbs, 140 nouns — stressed by two or more poets, out of the 500 terms stressed by only one poet. Most of these, more than 200, appear in Thorndike's list of the thousand most-used words in the language.

The prose lists, beginning with the Bible, are characteristically larger, amounting to 70 adjectives, 70 verbs, and 240 nouns, or 380 major terms in the five centuries. There are about 100 more major terms than for poetry, and these 100 terms are largely subject-matter nouns, of which most are not on Thorndike's list: words like *scripture, justice, learning, perfection, courtesy, science, resolution, convention, structure, process,* for example. Also absent from Thorndike's list are many terms shared by the two forms, and thus perceivably valued and literary, though not now common: *holy, faith, grace, sin, noble, glory, youth, creature, wit, memory,* and terms of emotion like *grief, pride, hate.*

Reading down the columns of words, we see how many terms are shared by Dunbar and Coverdale with More, and by Elizabethan poets and prose writers as a whole. Lyly and Spenser both introduce *black* and *little* in abundance; Lyly and Sidney, *friend*; Sidney stresses *virtue* in both poetry and prose. Not until Locke do we find in prose the long list of terms unshared by poetry, and it is this sort of abstract noun that prose thereafter repeats in more abundance than poetry does. In the final century we see older influences coming into play in both directions, as in poetry's *hope* and *body*, which we found in Tyndale's Bible.

At the end of the table — the additions made by Coleridge and Hazlitt and following — we see again a crowding in of new terms in prose and an abstraction of concept persisting in prose as it has not done in poetry. The most recent terms in common — *last, view, want* — are supported in each form by many others of their kind: the poet's person, a *boy*; the prosaist's, a *critic* — both concerned with need and direction.

Words shared by the two forms within about a century are indicated by dashes. Arrows indicate that they may later affect or be affected. Unmarked words are those not shared. We see that half of poetry's main terms are shared by prose; and that poetry, in the early centuries, gives many: *bed, hand, leave, strong, night, fall, fire, thought, sea, wind, bad, foot, human;* later receives from prose, *soul, divine, work, glory, way, head, sense, please, country, age, truth, hope, pleasure, fancy, body, dream, house, creature, woman, self, ground, hold;* in other words, gives nature and thought to prose, and takes on its eighteenth-century psychology of sense.

The unshared adjectives and verbs in the prose have the quality, as the extra nouns do, of concept and polysyllabism — prose's *common, ancient, excellent, general, impossible, modern, beautiful,* in contrast to poetry's *green, bright, strange, sad, wild, cold;* though there are such exceptions as poetry's *pleasant* and *human* shared with prose. The great increase of adjectives in the eighteenth and nineteenth centuries involved their power to generalize certain values, as in poetry's *various, silent, distant;* prose's *simple, modern, capable, early, ideal.* So in the verbs also, the contrast between poetry's *weep, turn, watch,* and prose's *suppose, affect, develop.*

The half of the terms that is shared by the two forms consists of the most basic language: from early *good, great, long, new, old, true* to later

POETRY

Author	Word	16th	17th	18th	19th	20th	Total in 50	American Total in 10
Ballads c. 1470	dear	5	-	1	2	1	9	-
	-fair	7	4	5	3	1	20	2
	golden	1	1	3	4	1	10	-
	-good	9	8	1	3	3	24	4
	green	3	-	2	1	3	9	2
	-old	3	4	2	4	7	20	6
	red	2	-	1	-	1	4	-
	silver	1	-	1	2	-	4	-
	-young	1	-	1	1	3	6	-
	<bed	1	-	-	1	2	4	-
	-child	1	-	2	2	5	10	3
	-day	9	8	10	10	9	46	9
	-father	2	-	1	2	2	7	2
	<hand	2	3	6	5	7	23	7
	-heart	8	6	8	9	9	40	7
	home	1	-	-	1	1	3	-
	-king	2	2	3	3	-	10	-
	lady	4	-	-	-	-	4	-
	-life	7	6	6	7	6	32	8
	-lord	5	2	1	2	-	10	-
	-love(n)	9	7	7	10	6	38	-
	-man	8	9	9	8	10	44	9
	mother	1	-	-	4	1	6	-
	-son	2	1	2	-	-	5	-
	-time	6	4	4	7	7	28	7
	-word	4	-	-	3	4	11	3
	-come	7	6	7	9	8	37	8
	-die	3	3	2	4	3	15	3
	-go	8	6	4	8	7	33	6
	<leave	1	-	3	1	2	7	-
	lie	3	3	2	8	6	22	2
	-look	3	1	2	7	5	17	5
	-make	10	10	6	8	10	44	6
	-see	10	10	9	8	8	45	10
	sing	3	4	2	4	1	14	3
	-speak	3	-	1	1	1	6	-
	-take	8	7	2	3	4	23	2
Dunbar 1470	bright	3	2	3	6	1	15	3
	clear	1	-	-	1	1	3	-
	full	2	1	-	2	-	5	-
	fresh	1	-	-	1	-	2	-
	-noble	1	1	-	-	-	2	-
	sweet	7	4	5	7	1	24	4
	tender	1	-	1	-	-	2	-
	white	1	-	1	5	2	9	4
	beast	1	-	-	-	1	2	-
	<beauty	5	-	2	2	1	10	-
	bird	1	-	2	3	2	7	-
	-death	4	4	2	3	7	20	5
	field	1	-	1	1	1	4	-
	flower	1	1	3	4	2	11	-
	-god	4	7	4	5	2	22	7
	leaf	1	-	1	1	1	4	-
	light	2	4	-	5	5	16	6
	-nature	5	4	5	1	-	15	2
	queen	1	-	1	-	-	2	-
	rose	1	1	-	1	1	4	2
	sky	1	1	2	3	5	12	4
	rise	2	3	6	2	1	14	2
	-think	6	4	3	3	2	18	2
Coverdale 1488	eternal	2	-	1	-	-	3	-
	-great	8	7	4	4	6	29	3
	-holy	1	2	-	1	-	4	-
	<strong	1	1	-	-	-	2	-
	worthy	2	-	-	-	-	2	-
	-Christ	1	-	-	1	-	2	-
	-faith	2	1	-	-	-	3	-
	flesh	1	-	-	1	1	3	-
	-grace	2	2	-	2	-	6	-
	-heaven	4	7	6	5	2	24	5
	hour	1	1	3	4	1	10	2
	-law	1	2	-	-	-	3	-
	-mind	5	2	3	3	3	16	-
	-name	1	4	1	-	-	6	-
	<night	5	2	4	8	7	26	8
	pain	3	-	3	1	-	7	-
	-power	2	3	5	1	-	11	-
	-sin	1	-	-	-	1	2	-

PROSE

Author	Word	16th	17th	18th	19th	20th	Total in 50	American Total in 10
Bible tr. by Tyndale b. 1475	-good	10	7	5	6	6	34	8
	-holy	2	-	-	-	-	2	-
	-own	7	7	4	6	1	25	4
	all(n)	2	2	-	2	1	9	4
	another(n)	1	-	-	1	-	2	-
	<body	4	2	3	1	-	10	-
	branch	1	-	1	1	-	3	-
	brother	2	-	1	-	-	3	1
	-child	2	3	-	2	1	8	2
	-Christ	2	1	-	-	-	3	1
	-day	4	3	2	3	1	13	5
	the dead	1	1	-	-	-	2	-
	-death	1	2	-	1	-	4	3
	evil(n)	1	1	1	1	-	4	1
	-faith	3	-	-	-	1	4	1
	-father	4	2	1	1	1	9	-
	<glory	1	1	-	-	-	2	-
	-god	8	3	-	4	2	17	2
	the good	2	2	1	-	-	5	-
	-grace	1	1	-	-	-	2	-
	-heart	2	1	1	2	-	6	2
	<hope	1	-	-	1	-	2	-
	Jesus	1	1	-	-	-	2	-
	judgment	3	1	-	1	-	5	-
	-law	3	3	1	3	-	10	2
	-life	4	5	2	3	4	18	7
	-lord	1	3	-	1	-	5	-
	-love(n)	3	1	-	1	2	6	2
	-man	10	9	8	9	8	44	9
	-mind	5	4	3	5	1	18	3
	one(n)	3	2	1	3	3	12	6
	<people	3	1	2	4	5	15	5
	-power	1	2	5	2	1	11	4
	servant	1	-	-	1	-	2	-
	-sin	2	2	-	-	-	4	-
	-son	3	2	-	-	-	5	-
	-spirit	2	-	1	2	-	5	-
	-thing	9	7	1	5	4	26	6
	-time	7	9	5	8	6	35	9
	<truth	2	4	2	3	1	12	3
	-word	7	6	1	3	2	19	2
	<work(n)	5	3	2	2	2	14	3
	-world	6	4	4	3	4	21	6
	become	1	-	2	5	7	15	2
	believe	3	1	-	3	1	8	3
	-call	3	3	2	4	2	14	3
	-come	7	7	2	5	3	24	6
	-die	1	1	-	-	-	2	-
	-give	8	7	5	5	5	30	5
	judge	1	-	-	1	-	2	-
	-know	8	8	5	4	3	28	7
	<let	7	1	-	-	1	9	1
	-live	1	1	-	1	-	4	4
	-make	9	9	8	9	7	42	10
	obey	1	-	-	-	1	2	-
	raise	1	1	-	-	-	2	-
	receive	3	2	1	1	-	7	-
	-see	8	5	4	7	3	27	7
	work	1	-	-	-	1	2	-
	write	4	3	1	-	2	10	1
	false	1	1	-	1	-	3	-
More 1478	-great	9	8	8	7	10	42	7
	-long	1	1	1	2	2	7	2
	-new	1	2	2	1	4	10	6
	such	9	9	7	7	6	38	8
	-true	3	2	1	4	1	11	3
	whole	3	2	4	2	2	13	1
	-wise	2	-	-	-	-	2	-
	answer(n)	1	-	-	-	1	2	-
	book	2	5	1	-	1	9	1
	church	1	1	-	1	-	3	1
	deed	2	-	-	-	-	2	-
	fault	4	-	-	1	-	5	-
	matter	6	2	2	1	1	12	1
	<part	4	6	5	4	1	20	4
	-place	4	4	-	1	4	9	2
	point	2	-	1	-	-	3	-
	reader	1	2	1	-	1	5	-
	-reason	5	6	2	2	-	15	-

POETRY

Author	Word	16th	17th	18th	19th	20th	Total in 50	American Total in 10
Coverdale (cont.)	-spirit	2	1	2	4	-	9	-
	-thing	6	5	1	6	3	21	-
	-world	4	7	4	6	9	30	8
	bear	1	1	1	3	-	6	-
	break	1	-	-	1	1	3	2
	-bring	3	5	1	2	-	11	-
	-call	1	1	1	2	-	5	2
	<fall	1	2	4	5	7	19	5
	-give	7	9	5	5	4	30	-
	-keep	2	1	-	1	1	5	-
	-live	3	3	2	2	1	11	-
	-love(v)	4	3	5	4	1	17	2
	pray	2	-	1	1	-	3	-
	sin(v)	1	2	-	-	-	3	-
	-show	4	3	-	1	-	8	-
	-stand	1	1	5	5	2	14	2
Wyatt 1503	blind	2	-	-	-	-	2	-
	dead	1	2	-	-	5	8	4
	-true	4	3	-	-	-	7	-
	-cause	2	-	-	-	-	2	-
	desire	3	-	-	-	-	3	-
	<fire	3	2	1	3	-	9	2
	-fortune	2	-	-	-	-	2	-
	-place	2	1	-	1	3	7	4
	-reason	1	1	-	-	-	2	-
	tear	1	3	1	2	-	7	-
	woe	2	-	3	1	-	6	-
	-find	6	7	6	5	5	29	2
	-hear	2	3	6	5	2	18	6
	-know	5	10	7	7	7	36	9
	-seek	3	1	-	-	-	4	-
Surrey 1517	pleasant	2	-	-	-	-	2	-
	breast	2	1	1	1	1	6	-
	-eye	6	8	9	7	9	39	9
	face	1	2	-	2	3	8	4
	flame	1	-	-	-	1	2	-
	sun	3	6	7	7	7	29	6
	<thought	4	2	5	5	3	19	3
	winter	1	-	1	-	-	2	-
	-year	1	2	4	4	1	12	5
	-serve	2	-	-	-	-	2	-
	-teach	1	-	1	-	-	2	-

PROSE

Author	Word	16th	17th	18th	19th	20th	Total in 50	American Total in 10
More (cont.)	scripture	1	1	-	-	-	2	1
	sermon	1	-	1	2	1	8	2
	<soul	1	1	-	1	1	4	-
	writing	1	2	-	-	1	3	-
	-find	5	9	7	5	5	31	3
	-hear	3	2	2	1	-	8	-
	-look	3	1	-	3	3	10	1
	perceive	1	1	1	-	-	3	-
	prove	2	1	-	-	-	3	-
	put	3	-	-	-	2	5	-
	read	1	2	1	-	1	5	-
	-show	3	1	2	1	1	8	-
	-take	8	8	4	4	5	29	5
	-teach	3	-	-	-	-	3	-
	use(v)	3	-	-	1	-	4	2
Latimer 1485	sure	2	-	-	-	-	2	-
	-king	2	2	2	3	-	9	1
	justice	1	-	-	1	-	2	-
	office	1	-	-	-	1	2	-
	<way	4	5	1	2	3	15	5
	allow	1	-	1	-	-	2	-
	answer	1	1	-	2	-	4	-
	ask	2	1	-	-	1	4	-
	-so	5	4	-	4	3	16	5
	-speak	4	2	-	2	-	8	2
	-think	4	8	5	3	5	25	3
	<walk	2	-	-	-	-	2	-
	wish	2	-	-	1	-	3	-
Ascham 1515	learned	2	-	-	-	-	2	-
	common	1	-	2	3	1	7	1
	-fair	3	-	-	1	-	4	-
	hard	2	-	-	-	-	2	-
	-noble	1	1	-	2	-	4	-
	-old	1	3	1	3	4	12	3
	right	1	-	-	1	-	2	-
	same	2	7	9	5	5	28	5
	-young	2	-	1	-	3	6	-
	<end	4	1	-	1	1	7	2
	England	1	1	1	3	-	6	1
	gentleman	3	1	2	-	-	6	-
	Latin	1	-	1	-	-	2	-
	learning	3	2	-	-	-	5	-
	manner	4	2	4	1	-	11	-
	master	2	-	-	-	-	2	-
	<memory	1	1	-	-	-	2	-
	-nature	5	5	2	5	1	18	4
	note	1	-	1	-	-	2	-
	order	2	2	-	-	-	4	1
	<pleasure	3	1	-	2	1	6	-
	rule	1	-	-	1	-	2	-
	sentence	1	-	-	-	1	2	-
	teaching	2	-	-	-	-	2	-
	use(n)	1	2	2	-	-	5	-
	will	3	1	3	2	-	9	-
	-wit	3	1	1	-	-	5	-
	-youth	2	-	-	-	-	2	-
	breed	1	-	-	1	-	2	-
	-bring	3	2	-	-	1	6	-
	choose	1	-	-	-	1	2	-
	-keep	2	1	1	2	1	7	1
	-love(v)	2	1	-	-	-	3	1
Holinshed 1530	-serve	2	-	-	-	-	2	-
	ancient	1	1	2	1	-	5	-
	British	1	-	-	-	2	3	-
	divers	1	1	1	-	-	3	-
	Britain	1	1	-	1	1	4	1
	<country	1	1	4	1	1	8	1
	-earth	2	1	-	-	-	3	1
	history	2	-	-	1	1	4	2
	kind(n)	2	3	1	1	3	10	-
	-name	4	3	1	-	-	8	1
	-water	1	-	-	1	-	4	2
	wife	1	1	-	1	1	4	-
	get	1	2	-	-	1	4	2
	<pass	1	1	-	2	-	5	1

POETRY

Author	Word	Authors in Century 16th	17th	18th	19th	20th	Total in 50	American Total in 10
Gascoigne 1542	foul	2	-	-	-	-	2	-
	-high	3	5	1	1	-	10	-
	strange	1	-	1	1	1	4	-
	delight	1	-	1	-	-	2	-
	gold(n)	1	-	1	-	-	2	-
	-prince	1	1	-	-	-	2	-
	-youth	2	1	4	-	-	7	-
	behold	2	-	3	1	-	6	-
	-seem	3	2	2	2	6	15	2
	-tell	2	3	-	3	1	9	-
Spenser 1552	-black	1	-	1	3	3	8	-
	-gentle	1	1	2	-	-	4	-
	-little	1	1	3	3	5	13	2
	-new	1	3	2	-	3	8	-
	proud	2	2	1	-	-	5	2
	sad	1	1	5	3	-	10	-
Sidney 1554	gold	1	-	-	-	2	3	-
	happy	2	2	4	1	-	9	-
	-long	1	2	-	2	3	8	3
	-own	1	-	1	1	1	4	-
	poor	1	2	3	1	-	7	-
	-wise	1	1	-	-	-	2	-
	-friend	1	2	5	1	1	10	-
	muse	1	2	2	-	-	5	-
	praise	1	1	-	-	-	2	-
	sight	1	-	1	-	-	2	-
	shepherd	1	1	-	-	-	3	-
	>soul	2	7	4	6	1	20	3
	-virtue	1	1	3	-	-	5	-
	-wit	1	1	-	-	-	2	-
	learn	1	-	-	-	1	2	-
	run	1	-	-	1	1	3	-
Sylvester 1563	>divine	1	1	2	1	-	5	-
	mighty	1	1	-	-	-	2	-
	pure	1	1	1	-	-	3	-
	air	1	1	7	5	5	19	3
	-art	1	2	2	-	-	5	-
	-earth	1	3	3	7	4	18	4
	-nothing	1	-	-	-	2	3	-
	<sea	1	1	-	4	4	18	6
	-water	1	-	1	4	1	7	5
	>work(n)	1	-	-	-	1	2	-
Jonson 1573	fly	-	2	4	1	-	7	-
	grow	-	4	-	2	3	9	2
	-meet	-	2	1	-	-	3	-

PROSE

Author	Word	Authors in Century 16th	17th	18th	19th	20th	Total in 50	American Total in 10
Hooker 1554	being(a)	3	4	3	-	-	10	1
	<divine	2	-	-	-	-	2	2
	-high	2	2	-	2	1	7	1
	present(a)	1	2	-	-	1	4	2
	angel	1	-	-	1	-	2	-
	-art	2	1	1	2	2	8	1
	-cause	3	1	2	-	-	6	1
	creature	1	2	-	-	-	3	-
	degree	1	1	-	2	1	5	-
	-heaven	1	1	-	-	-	2	1
	knowledge	3	1	1	-	1	6	-
	means	2	-	1	-	-	3	1
	-nothing	2	4	6	2	2	16	5
	other(n)						4	-
	perfection	1	-	-	1	1	3	-
	sort	2	-	2	-	-	4	-
	consider	1	1	1	-	-	3	1
	observe	2	2	1	-	-	5	-
	get	3	1	-	-	-	4	-
	-seem	3	3	2	4	3	15	1
Lyly 1554	-black	1	-	-	1	-	2	1
	like	2	1	1	3	-	7	-
	-little	1	2	2	3	2	10	-
	<small	1	-	1	-	-	2	1
	>beauty	1	1	1	2	1	6	-
	conceit	3	-	-	-	-	3	-
	-friend	1	1	-	-	-	2	1
	>hand	3	1	-	1	2	7	1
	quality	1	-	2	-	-	3	1
	<woman	1	-	-	2	1	4	2
	cause(v)	1	1	-	-	-	2	-
	follow	2	1	1	-	-	4	-
Sidney 1554	excellent	2	-	-	-	-	2	-
	example	2	-	-	1	-	3	-
	force	1	-	-	1	-	2	1
	philosopher	2	-	-	-	1	3	-
	picture	1	-	-	1	1	3	-
	poet	1	1	2	-	1	5	1
	poetry	1	1	1	2	1	6	1
	question	1	-	-	1	1	3	1
	science	1	-	-	-	1	2	2
	verse	1	-	1	-	-	2	-
	-virtue	1	1	-	-	-	2	-
	wisdom	1	3	-	-	-	4	-
	-stand	2	1	-	2	1	6	2
	-tell	1	2	2	-	1	6	2
Bacon 1561	another	1	2	1	1	1	6	-
	both	1	2	-	-	-	3	-
	second	1	-	-	-	1	2	-
	according	1	1	-	-	-	2	-
	<age	1	3	-	2	1	7	-
	business	1	-	1	-	1	3	3
	-eye	1	1	-	4	1	7	1
	-fortune	1	-	-	1	-	2	-
	government	1	1	3	-	2	7	1
	philosophy	1	-	1	-	1	3	2
	<sense	1	2	1	1	-	5	1
	state	1	1	2	1	1	7	3
Dekker 1569	hair	1	-	-	-	1	2	-
	<head	1	1	-	1	1	4	1
	some(n)	1	-	1	1	-	3	1
	>year	1	3	2	4	3	13	3
	person	-	5	3	1	-	9	2
Jonson 1573	reach(v)	-	1	-	-	2	3	-

POETRY

Author	Word	16th	17th	18th	19th	20th	Total of 50	American Total in 10
Donne 1576	<bad	-	2	-	-	-	2	-
Herrick 1591	small	-	1	-	-	2	3	-
	>part	-	2	-	-	-	2	-
Herbert 1593	blood	-	2	-	2	1	5	2
	dust	-	1	-	1	-	2	-
	fear	-	1	1	-	-	2	-
	>glory	-	1	-	1	-	2	-
	joy	-	1	4	2	-	7	-
	sorrow	-	1	1	1	-	3	-
	stone	-	1	-	1	2	4	2
	>way	-	1	3	2	1	7	2
	-drop	-	1	-	-	1	2	-
	<feel	-	1	3	2	4	10	-
Waller 1606	care	-	1	1	-	-	2	-
	fate	-	2	5	-	1	8	-
Milton 1608	dark	-	2	2	1	3	8	3
	ear	-	1	1	1	-	3	-
	star	-	3	4	1	-	8	3
	<wind	-	1	3	6	4	14	5
Marvell 1621	foot	-	1	2	3	3	9	2
	garden	-	1	-	1	-	2	-
	grass	-	1	-	-	2	3	2
	>head	-	2	3	2	8	15	2
Vaughan 1622	cloud	-	1	2	3	1	7	-
	wing	-	1	-	2	1	4	-
	sleep	-	1	1	1	-	3	2
	weep	-	1	3	2	-	6	-
Dryden 1631	people	-	1	-	-	1	2	-
	>please	-	1	1	-	-	2	-

PROSE

Author	Word	16th	17th	18th	19th	20th	Total of 50	American Total in 10
Donne 1576	affection	-	2	-	-	-	2	-
	>bed	-	1	-	-	1	2	-
	<house	4	4	2	1	-	7	1
	begin	-	3	1	2	2	8	1
	express	-	1	-	-	1	2	-
	-seek	-	2	-	-	-	2	1
Hobbes 1588	past(a)	-	1	-	1	1	3	-
	account	-	2	-	-	-	2	-
	action	-	1	1	1	1	4	1
	consequence	-	1	-	-	2	3	-
	<dream	-	2	-	-	-	2	-
	<fancy	-	1	1	1	-	3	-
	image	-	1	1	1	-	3	1
	imagination	-	1	-	1	-	2	-
	motion	-	1	1	-	-	2	-
	object	-	2	2	2	2	8	-
	sign	-	1	1	-	-	2	-
	sound	-	1	1	-	-	2	-
	speech	-	1	-	-	1	2	-
	>thought	-	3	2	3	2	10	1
	train	-	1	-	-	1	2	-
	understanding	-	2	-	-	-	2	-
	conceive	-	1	1	-	-	2	1
	produce	-	1	2	1	1	5	1
	signify	-	1	1	-	-	2	-
	understand	-	3	1	2	1	7	-
Browne 1605	large	-	1	-	2	2	5	-
	Roman	-	1	1	1	-	3	-
	corn	-	1	1	-	-	2	-
	custom	-	1	-	1	-	2	-
	>fire	-	2	-	1	-	3	1
	<ground	-	1	-	2	-	3	-
	nation	-	1	1	2	-	4	2
	<peace	-	3	-	-	1	4	-
	practice	-	1	1	-	-	2	-
	the Romans	-	1	1	-	-	2	-
	Rome	-	2	1	-	-	3	-
	substance	-	1	1	-	-	2	-
	<hold	-	1	-	-	1	2	-
	>leave	-	1	-	-	2	3	-
Milton 1608	author	-	2	3	-	2	7	-
	city	-	2	-	-	-	2	-
Clarendon 1609	court	-	1	-	1	-	2	-
	crown	-	2	1	1	-	4	-
	duke	-	2	-	-	-	2	-
	kingdom	-	1	1	-	-	2	-
	majesty	-	1	1	-	-	2	-
	occasion	-	1	2	-	-	3	-
	parliament	-	2	-	-	-	2	-
	>prince	-	2	1	1	-	4	-
	Spain	-	2	-	-	-	2	-
Bunyan 1628	>fall	-	2	1	1	1	5	-
	-meet	-	1	-	-	1	2	-
Dryden 1631	character	-	1	2	3	-	6	2
	language	-	1	-	3	-	5	-
	number	-	1	2	2	-	5	1
	opinion	-	2	2	2	-	6	-
	poem	-	1	1	-	-	2	1
	verse	-	1	1	-	-	2	-
Locke 1632	certain	-	1	3	4	1	9	1
	evident	-	2	-	-	-	2	-
	general	-	1	-	-	1	2	1
	impossible	-	1	-	1	-	2	-
	innate	-	1	1	-	-	2	-
	necessary	-	1	-	2	1	4	1
	universal	-	1	-	1	-	2	-
	faculty	-	1	-	1	-	2	-
	idea	-	1	3	3	2	9	2
	impression	-	1	1	-	-	2	-
	mankind	-	1	1	-	-	2	1
	principle	-	1	3	1	-	5	-
	term	-	1	-	1	-	2	-
	suppose	-	1	-	1	1	3	1

POETRY

Author	Word	16th	17th	18th	19th	20th	Total in 50	American Total in 10
Blackmore 1655	human	-	1	1	-	-	2	-
	<superior	-	1	-	-	1	2	-
	vain	-	1	2	-	-	3	-
	various	-	1	1	-	-	2	-
	wild	-	1	6	4	1	12	-
	land	-	1	3	1	2	7	-
	>sense	-	1	1	-	-	2	-
Pope 1688	soft	-	-	5	2	-	7	2
	maid	-	-	2	-	-	2	-
	nymph	-	-	2	-	-	2	-
Thomson 1700	deep	-	-	2	4	1	7	-
	gay	-	-	2	-	-	2	-
	wide	-	-	2	1	-	3	-
	>country	-	-	2	-	-	2	-
	hill	-	-	2	-	1	3	3
	mountain	-	-	4	-	-	4	-
	-scene	-	-	6	-	-	6	-
	snow	-	-	1	-	2	3	2
Johnson 1709	>age	-	-	2	-	-	2	-
	voice	-	-	2	1	1	5	-
Collins 1721	silent	-	-	3	1	-	4	-
	>truth	-	-	1	-	1	2	2
	lead	-	-	1	-	1	2	-
Cooper 1731	distant	-	-	2	-	-	2	-
Crabbe 1754	>hope	-	-	2	2	-	4	-
	>pleasure	-	-	1	1	-	2	-
	-view	-	-	2	-	-	2	-
Blake 1757	pale	-	-	2	2	1	5	-
	bosom	-	-	2	-	-	2	-
	morning	-	-	1	1	-	2	-
	worm	-	-	1	-	1	2	-
	>pass	-	-	2	1	1	4	2
	turn	-	-	2	2	2	6	2
	>walk	-	-	1	-	1	2	2
Bowles 1762	cold	-	-	2	1	2	5	-
	>fancy	-	-	1	1	-	2	-
	pity	-	-	1	-	1	2	-
	tide	-	-	1	-	1	2	-
	wave	-	-	1	1	-	2	-
	wood	-	-	3	-	-	3	-
Wordsworth 1770	tree	-	-	1	2	3	6	2
Coleridge 1772	>body	-	-	-	2	3	5	-
	mist	-	-	-	1	1	2	-
	moon	-	-	-	5	4	9	-
	rock	-	-	-	1	2	3	-
Byron 1788	blue	-	-	-	3	-	3	2

PROSE

Author	Word	16th	17th	18th	19th	20th	Total in 50	American Total in 10
Burnet 1643	French	-	1	-	1	1	3	-
	emperor	-	1	1	-	-	2	-
	France	-	1	1	-	-	4	1
	liberty	-	1	1	-	1	5	-
	war	-	1	2	-	2	5	2
	appear	-	1	2	-	-	3	1
Shaftesbury 1667	far	-	-	2	-	-	2	-
Addison 1672	club	-	-	2	-	-	2	1
	>night	-	-	1	-	1	2	1
	-scene	-	-	2	-	-	2	-
Berkeley 1685	different	-	-	2	1	-	3	2
	external	-	-	2	-	-	2	-
	real	-	-	1	1	-	2	-
	being(n)	-	-	2	-	-	2	3
	color	-	-	2	-	-	2	-
	existence	-	-	1	1	-	2	-
	sensation	-	-	2	-	-	2	-
Johnson 1709	English(a)	-	-	1	1	1	3	-
	line	-	-	2	-	-	2	-
	>feel	-	-	2	1	2	5	3
Smith 1723	particular	-	-	2	-	-	2	-
	simple	-	-	2	1	1	4	-
	produce(n)	-	-	2	-	-		
	river	-	-	1	-	-	2	1
	>sea	-	-	1	-	-	2	-
	society	-	-	2	1	2	5	3
	carry	-	-	1	1	-	2	-
Burke 1729	political	-	-	2	-	4	6	-
	circumstance	-	-	1	1	-	2	-
	constitution	-	-	2	1	-	3	1
	election	-	-	1	-	1	2	-
	policy	-	-	1	-	1	2	-
	revolution	-	-	1	1	-	2	-
Gibbon 1737	military	-	-	1	-	1	2	-
	modern	-	-	1	1	4	6	-
	empire	-	-	1	-	1	2	-
	province	-	-	1	1	-	2	-
	soldier	-	-	1	1	-	2	-
	strength	-	-	2	-	-	2	-
Godwin 1756	>human	-	-	1	3	4	8	-
	institution	-	-	1	1	-	2	-
	species	-	-	1	1	1	3	-
Alison 1757	beautiful	-	-	1	2	1	4	-
	capable	-	-	1	1	-	2	-
	material(a)	-	-	1	1	-	2	1
	>strong	-	-	1	2	-	3	1
	animal(a)	-	-	1	1	1	3	1
	association	-	-	2	-	1	3	1
	case	-	-	1	3	1	5	1
	difference	-	-	1	1	1	3	-
	effect	-	-	1	1	1	3	-
	expression	-	-	1	2	1	4	-
	form	-	-	1	2	4	7	4
	instance	-	-	1	1	-	2	-
	taste	-	-	1	1	-	2	-
	>wind	-	-	1	1	-	2	-
	affect	-	-	1	1	-	2	-
	>consider	-	-	1	1	-	2	1
Hazlitt 1778	-last	-	-	-	1	1	2	-
	feeling	-	-	-	1	1	2	-
	moment	-	-	-	1	1	2	2
	opinion	-	-	-	2	1	3	-
	subject	-	-	-	4	1	5	1
De Quincey 1785	fact	-	-	-	3	1	4	1

POETRY

Author	Word	Authors in Century					Total in 50	American Total in 10
		16th	17th	18th	19th	20th		
Keats 1795	>dream	-	-	-	4	4	8	2
Browning 1812	>house	-	-	-	1	4	5	3
Swinburne 1837	-last	-	-	-	1	2	3	-
	darkness	-	-	-	1	1	2	-
	shadow	-	-	-	1	3	4	-
	sleep(n)	-	-	-	1	1	2	-
	summer	-	-	-	1	1	2	-
	watch	-	-	-	1	2	3	-
Hardy 1840	creature	-	-	-	1	1	2	-
	shape	-	-	-	1	1	2	-
	>woman	-	-	-	2	1	3	2
Hopkins 1844	>peace	-	-	-	1	1	2	-
Lawrence 1885	-want	-	-	-	-	2	2	-
Muir 1887	ground	-	-	-	-	2	2	-
	sand	-	-	-	-	2	2	-
	wall	-	-	-	-	2	2	-
Auden 1887	nothing	-	-	1	-	3	4	-
Nicholson 1914	street	-	-	-	-	2	2	-
Thomas 1914	boy	-	-	-	-	2	2	-
	hold	-	-	-	-	2	2	-
	260							

PROSE

Author	Word	Authors in Century					Total in 50	American Total in 10
		16th	17th	18th	19th	20th		
Carlyle 1795	success	-	-	-	1	1	2	-
Macaulay 1800	century	-	-	-	1	1	2	-
	Europe	-	-	-	1	1	2	1
	length	-	-	-	2	-	2	-
	race	-	-	-	3	-	3	3
Darwin 1809	condition	-	-	-	2	-	2	-
	period	-	-	-	1	2	3	-
	structure	-	-	-	1	1	2	-
	-view	-	-	-	2	-	2	1
Ruskin 1819	artist	-	-	-	1	3	4	-
	perception	-	-	-	1	1	2	-
Arnold 1822	moral	-	-	-	1	1	2	2
	ideal	-	-	-	1	2	3	-
	religion	-	-	-	2	1	3	2
Pater 1839	early	-	-	-	1	1	2	-
	element	-	-	-	1	1	2	-
	story	-	-	-	1	1	2	1
Frazer 1854	throw	-	-	-	2	-	2	-
Churchill 1871	German	-	-	-	2	-	2	-
	process	-	-	-	-	3	3	-
Russell 1872	reality	-	-	-	-	2	2	1
	accept	-	-	-	-	2	2	2
	develop	-	-	-	-	2	2	-
Joyce 1882	>bad	-	-	-	-	2	2	-
	hate(v)	-	-	-	-	2	2	-
	like(v)	-	-	-	-	3	3	-
	-want(v)	-	-	-	-	2	2	-
Huxley 1887	social	-	-	-	-	2	2	2
Connolly 1903	literary	-	-	-	-	2	2	-
	article	-	-	-	-	2	2	-
	critic	-	-	-	-	2	2	-
	390							

Symbols:

-     shared within a century
>   preceded
<   followed

black, little, small; from *day, death, faith, father, god, heart, hope* to later *night, scene, sea, wind, view;* from *call, come, die, give, know, live, make, see, seem* to later *fall, meet, feel, want, hold.*

The first century of adjectives for prose includes **good, holy, own,** *false,* **great, long, new,** *such,* **true,** *whole,* **wise,** *sure, learned, common,* **fair,** *hard,* **noble,** *same, right,* **old, young,** *ancient, British, divers, being* **divine, high, black,** *like,* **little, small,** *excellent, another, both, second, according.* (The fifteen terms shared with poetry are in boldface italic.)

For poetry, the adjectives include the Ballads' *dear,* **fair,** *golden,* **good,** *green,* **old,** *red, silver,* **young;** Dunbar's *bright, clear,* **noble, sweet,** *tender, white;* Coverdale's *eternal,* **great, holy, strong,** *worthy;* Wyatt's *blind, dead,* **true;** Surrey's *pleasant;* Gascoigne's *foul,* **high,** *strange;* Spenser's **black,** *gentle,* **little, new,** *proud, sad;* Sidney's *gold, happy,* **long, own,** *poor,* **wise;** and Sylvester's **divine,** *mighty, pure.*

From then until the present, poetry's newly added adjectives were Donne's **bad;** Milton's **dark;** Blackmore's **human,** *superior, vain, various, wild;* Pope's *soft;* Thomson's *deep, gay, wide;* Collins' *silent;* Cowper's *distant;* Blake's *pale;* Bowles' *cold;* Byron's *blue;* Swinburne's **last, small.** Of these, *bad* and *human* were taken up by prose, too, as were earlier *strong, small,* and *last* from prose; and twenty of the terms, or one-third, were shared.

Prose adjectives were Browne's **large,** *Roman;* Locke's *certain, evident, general, impossible;* Hobbes's **past,** *innate, necessary, universal;* Berkeley's *different, external, real;* Smith's *particular, simple;* Gibbon's *military, modern;* Godwin's **human;** Alison's *beautiful, capable,* **material, strong;** Hazlitt's **last,** *moral, ideal, early, bad, social, literary.*

Of the first century's nouns, sixty were shared. Thereafter, of prose's hundred and poetry's seventy, twenty-four were shared, or one-fourth to one-third.

The first century of poetry's verbs presented the main ones: poetry's **come, die, go, leave, lie, look, make, see,** *sing,* **speak,** *rise,* **take, think,** *bear, break,* **bring, call,** *fall,* **give, keep, live, love,** *pray, sin,* **show, stand, find, hear, know, seek, serve, teach,** *behold,* **seem, tell,** *learn, run.* Twenty-five are shared.

The first century of prose verbs presented Tyndale's seventeen: *become, believe,* **call, come, die,** *give, judge, know, let,* **live, make,** *obey, raise, receive,* **see,** *work, write;* More's eleven: **find, hear,** *look, perceive, put, prove, read,* **show, take, teach,** *use;* plus Latimer's *allow, answer, ask,* **go, speak, think, walk,** *wish;* Ascham's **bring,** *choose,* **keep, love, serve;** plus others' *get,* **pass,** *consider, observe, set* **seem,** *cause, follow,* **stand, tell.**

Later prose added: Jonson's *reach*; Donne's *begin, express,* **seek**; Hobbes' *conceive, produce, signify, understand*; Browne's **hold, leave**; Bunyan's **fall, meet**; Locke's *suppose*; Burnet's *appear*; Johnson's **feel**; Smith's **carry**; Alison's *affect*; Frazer's *throw*; Russell's *accept, develop*; Joyce's *hate, like,* **want.**

And later poetry added: Jonson's *fly, grow,* **meet**; then Herbert's *sit, drop,* **feel**; Vaughan's *sheep, weep*; Dryden's *please*; Collins' *lead*; Blake's **pass, turn, walk**; Swinburne's *watch*; Lawrence's **want**; Thomson's **hold.**

American terms, representing major use by at least two writers of ten rather than of fifty, show even more concentration in emphasis and much agreement with England.

In both content and proportion, in both countries, the basic likenesses persist and interplay over five centuries. Most of the differences lie in substantive, conceptual subject matter and in connective disjunction. The likenesses show the basic concerns in value: the adjectives *great* and *good*; the nouns *man, time, thing, world*; the verbs *come, find, give, know, make, see, take*. The poets — the fifty as well as two hundred — use these terms more intensively, that is, more share them; the prosaists use them more extensively, agree on, but vary them with polysyllabic synonyms. Except for Dryden and Milton, who stress adjectives in poetry, most writers who are distinguished for both prose and poetry maintain their similar style in the two; Sidney, Johnson, Emerson, Whitman, Eliot, Lawrence, for example.

For connectives, chronology of major appearance is less relevant than for reference terms because most were major in the language from the start, as Table 3 shows. Agreements are so common that they are not marked. Rather, unshared terms are marked with an "O." In the first century, from the Ballads to Wyatt and from Tyndale's Bible to Dekker, most of the terms appear dominant for all writers, and for the Americans as well. At times contrasts are provided by emphasis: for poetry, more use of *over, through, until, how, so, yet, like*; less of *if, either, neither, since, nor, than, around, beneath, among, therefore, because*.

Only a few terms increase: *into, upon, around*, for poetry; *under, around, thus*, for prose. That is, of the many eighteenth-century connectives for many phrases, these are the few that do persist in number.

Blocks of influence are not evident; there are three, a century apart in each direction: *until, thus*, and *around* from poetry; *whether, above, between* from prose. More noteworthy is that in the four centuries since Herbert and Browne, the major additions in the two forms have been similar ones of directional relation — *around, above, between, up, off* —

POETRY

Author	Word	16th	17th	18th	19th	20th	Total in 50	American Total in 10
Ballads	at	10	10	10	10	9	49	10
	by	10	10	10	10	10	50	10
	from	10	10	10	10	10	50	10
	in	10	10	10	10	10	50	10
	of	10	10	10	10	10	50	10
	on	10	10	10	10	10	50	10
	over	1	1	9	6	6	23	8
	through	5	7	10	9	8	39	5
	to	10	10	10	10	10	50	10
	upon	6	4	5	7	6	28	6
	with	10	10	10	10	10	50	9
	that	10	10	10	10	10	50	10
	and	10	10	10	10	10	50	10
	as	10	10	10	10	10	50	10
	but	10	10	10	10	10	50	10
	for	10	10	10	10	10	50	10
	if	8	9	8	10	6	41	7
	nor	10	8	10	9	6	43	8
	or	10	10	10	10	10	50	10
	than	7	6	5	7	4	29	6
	<until	5	5	8	7	6	31	4
	when	10	10	9	10	10	49	9
Dunbar	among	2	1	1	1	1	6	1
	within	3	1	-	1	1	6	1
	who	9	10	10	8	10	47	10
	where	9	10	10	9	10	48	10
	which	8	10	8	7	6	39	3
Coverdale	how	5	9	4	2	5	25	3
	so	8	6	1	3	4	22	2
	therefore	2	1	-	-	-	3	-
	yet	7	8	9	6	9	39	4
Wyatt	into	2	4	3	5	10	24	6
	under	1	1	-	1	2	5	3
	unto	5	5	-	-	-	10	1
	without	5	-	1	1	2	3	3
	after	1	-	-	2	3	6	4
	since	6	2	-	3	1	12	-
	though	3	8	7	5	5	28	4
Surrey	against	3	3	-	-	3	9	2
	what	5	10	9	9	6	39	8
Gascoigne	like	4	10	8	10	10	42	9
	out	2	-	-	3	3	8	2
	because	2	2	-	-	1	5	1
	while	3	7	10	7	3	30	4
Spenser	about	1	1	-	1	1	4	1
	before	2	2	1	3	2	10	6
	then	2	3	-	-	1	6	5
Sylvester	>whether	1	1	-	-	-	2	-
Herbert	now	-	1	1	-	-	2	-
	<thus	-	3	-	-	-	3	-
Milton	°ere	-	2	-	1	-	3	-
Thomson	<around	-	-	3	2	3	8	1
	°beneath	-	-	2	3	4	9	2
Gray	amidst	-	-	3	-	-	3	-
Blake	°toward	-	-	1	-	-	1	1
Wordsworth	°why	-	-	1	-	-	1	1
Swinburne	>between	-	-	-	1	3	4	1
Hopkins	off	-	-	-	1	-	1	1
Muir	>above	-	-	-	-	3	3	2
	°across	-	-	-	-	1	1	1
Nicholson	°beyond	-	-	-	-	2	2	2
Jennings	up	-	-	-	-	1	1	1

PROSE

Author	Word	16th	17th	18th	19th	20th	Total in 50	American Total in 10
Bible	after	5	5	1	3	4	18	3
	against	3	4	2	2	-	11	3
	among(-st)	4	4	2	3	-	13	1
	and	10	10	10	10	10	50	10
	as	10	10	10	10	10	50	10
	at	10	10	10	10	10	49	10
	because	8	6	2	5	6	27	5
	but	10	10	10	10	10	50	10
	by	10	10	10	10	10	49	10
	for	10	10	10	10	10	50	10
	from	10	10	10	10	10	49	10
	how	6	5	1	6	1	19	4
	if	9	10	8	9	9	45	10
	in	10	10	9	10	9	48	10
	into	9	10	6	6	8	39	7
	°neither	6	-	2	-	-	8	1
	nor	6	7	4	3	1	21	3
	now	1	-	-	-	-	1	-
	of	10	10	10	10	10	50	10
	on	4	9	10	10	9	42	10
	or	10	9	10	10	10	49	10
	over	2	1	-	1	1	5	3
	so	9	8	-	1	1	19	3
	that	10	10	10	9	9	48	10
	then	2	1	-	2	1	6	-
	therefore	2	3	1	2	-	8	2
	through	4	-	1	4	-	9	4
	to	10	10	9	10	9	48	10
	under	2	-	3	3	1	9	10
	unto	7	2	-	-	-	9	2
	upon	7	8	7	4	1	27	3
	what	5	10	6	8	9	38	10
	when	10	10	6	8	9	43	9
	which	10	10	10	10	9	49	10
	who	9	9	8	9	8	43	10
	with	10	10	10	10	9	49	10
	without	9	7	5	2	1	24	3
	yet	10	9	1	4	1	25	3
More	before	7	8	1	1	-	17	3
	than	9	10	9	7	8	43	10
	though	9	9	4	3	2	27	4
	<whether	4	2	-	1	-	3	1
	where	3	3	-	-	-	6	4
Ascham	°either	5	1	1	-	-	7	1
Holinshed	out	1	3	-	-	-	4	2
	since	2	3	-	-	1	6	1
	within	1	-	-	-	-	1	1
Hooker	<above	1	1	-	-	-	2	-
Lyly	<between	1	1	-	-	-	2	2
	like	2	1	-	1	-	3	5
Dekker	about	1	1	1	-	-	3	4
	>until	1	3	-	-	-	4	1
Browne	while	-	2	1	-	-	3	3
Milton	°unless	-	1	-	-	-	1	-
Clarendon	°however	-	1	3	-	1	5	2
Gibbon	°during	-	-	1	1	-	2	-
Alison	amid(-st)	-	-	1	-	-	1	-
Pater	up	-	-	-	1	-	1	1
Frazer	>around	-	-	-	1	1	2	-
	>thus	-	-	-	1	2	3	-
Joyce	off	-	-	-	-	1	1	-

Symbols:

°	not shared
>	preceded by about a century or more
<	followed

TABLE 4A SUMMARY OF MAJOR CONNECTIVES IN BRITISH POETRY*

	Ballads	Dunbar	Coverdale	Wyatt	Surrey	Gascoigne	Spenser	Sidney	Sylvester	Shakespeare	Jonson	Donne	Herrick	Herbert	Waller	Milton	Marvell	Vaughan	Dryden	Blackmore	Pope	Thomson	Johnson	Gray	Collins	Cowper	Crabbe	Blake	Bowles	Wordsworth	Coleridge	Byron	Shelley	Keats	Tennyson	Browning	Swinburne	Hardy	Hopkins	Yeats	Lawrence	Muir	Sitwell	Graves	Auden	Spender	Nicholson	Thomas	Jennings	Gunn	Total Poets
Prep.																																																			
about							1						1																						1										1						4
above																																										1				1	1				3
across																																										1									1
against					1				2	1				1					1	1																								1		1	1				9
amid(-st)																								2			1		2																						3
among(-st)		1	1												1								1											1										1							6
around																						1					1	1					1		1						1	1					1				8
at	3	1	1	2	2	4	4	2	2	1	3	4	1	1	3	2	3	2	2	2	3	3	4	1	2	4	2	1	3	4	3	3	3	3	2	5	2	3	4	3	3	3	2	5	3	3	2	2		4	49
beneath																						1	1								1		1		1							1				1	1		1		9
between																																					1										1		1	1	4
beyond																																															1		1		2
by	3	1	4	4	5	5	3	4	3	5	3	8	5	3	3	2	2	2	7	5	2	4	4	2	6	5	5	3	2	4	3	3	3	4	2	2	4	3	3	3	1	2	2	3	3	3	2	4	3	4	50
during																																																			
from	2	1	5	3	4	2	2	1	3	4	2	4	2	2	6	3	2	3	4	5	5	6	5	4	5	4	4	6	7	5	5	4	9	7	4	2	8	4	2	4	2	4	7	5	2	5	5	6	4	4	50
in	6	9	12	13	17	14	13	12	16	15	10	12	6	8	9	11	11	9	11	11	15	12	9	10	11	11	10	19	9	10	11	13	10	16	10	9	12	11	13	10	12	16	17	12	9	13	14	22	11	19	50
into				1					1			1		1	1	1						2				2		4			1		2	1		1				2	2	1	1	1	2	3	2	1	2	1	24
like						1	2	2		2	2	1	1	7	3	1	2	2	1	1	1		1		3		1	2	2	2	3	3	8	3	1	1	3	1	2	1	5	6	9	1	5	4	5	4	1	1	41
of	7	15	8	11	15	19	16	17	18	18	15	12	11	9	20	16	9	9	17	17	15	23	15	21	10	22	12	32	19	18	10	19	30	21	20	10	35	17	16	20	22	8	36	17	16	22	27	27	13	4	50
off																																							1												1
on	3	3	2	2	1	1	3	2	2	4	3	3	2	2	5	4	3	2	2	3	5	4	4	5	4	3	3	3	8	4	5	6	6	7	2	4	4	4	4	4	4	7	4	4	2	5	7	9	3	4	50
out						1	1																										1				1			2	1						1		2		8
over	1																			1	1	4	2	2	2	1	1	1	4		1	3	3	1	2	1					1	2	1			1	1	1			23
through	1	1	1				1		1		1	1			1	2	2	1		2	1	3	1	2	1	1	1	1	1	1	2		3	1	2	2	1	1	1	2	1	3	1			1	1	3	1	2	39
to	11	3	6	4	6	3	7	8	4	8	6	14	18	8	7	7	4	5	8	7	9	8	6	6	8	3	6	6	10	6	6	8	5	7	4	6	8	8	7	4	1	4	8	7	5	6	6	7	19	5	50
toward																												2																							1
under				1												1																	1													2		1			5
unto				1	1	1	2		1		1	1	2	2				1																																	10
up																																																	1		1
upon	2	1				1	2		1	1	1	1				1	1							1		2	1	2		1	2	1		4	2		1	1		4		2	2	1		1			2	1	28
with	6	10	6	6	11	7	11	10	7	11	7	5	8	7	12	12	6	6	9	9	9	10	11	8	8	10	6	6	8	7	9	5	5	11	9	6	12	4	8	4	8	6	5	8	4	8	5	7	6	6	50
within		1			1	1											1																1																2		6
without				2			1	1	2	1													1														1												1	1	9
Total	45	47	46	50	64	60	69	59	62	72	54	66	55	49	71	63	46	42	61	64	66	81	65	64	60	68	54	89	75	62	62	68	92	86	63	49	93	57	61	63	64	69	95	66	52	80	84	94	75	57	
Rel. Conj.																																																			
that	5	4	5	11	15	11	11	10	8	10	10	13	5	6	7	7	5	5	3	5	3	4	2	8	3	8	2	4	9	7	7	6	3	3	3	3	16	5	5	12	7	2	12	4	5	4	5	5	8	5	50
what					2	1		2	1	2	4	4	1	1	2	1	2	2	1	1	2	2	1	1	1	1	2	1		2	1	1	1	1		1	2	1	3	2	1			2	2	1			3	3	39
which			2	2	1	11	7	7	2	5	2	10	2	4	7	1	3	3	3	4	2	2	1		1	2		1	2	3	2	4	6	1	2	1		1			1	3		1	1	3		3			39
who		1	1	2	3	4	3	4	2	3	3	7	2	5	6	2	3	2	6	4	2	5	4	2	7	4	7	2	5	2	3	4	3	2		2	4	3	3	2	1	2	5	4	4	3	2	3	1	1	47
Total	5	5	8	15	21	27	21	23	13	20	19	34	10	16	22	11	13	12	13	14	9	13	8	11	12	15	11	8	16	14	13	15	13	7	6	7	22	10	11	16	10	7	17	11	12	11	7	8	12	9	
Prep. Conj.																																																			
after				1																																	1			1	1	1		1							6
and	37	25	23	21	29	32	27	19	23	24	32	46	27	25	27	32	23	34	27	40	30	32	28	26	25	40	31	48	26	30	43	26	39	40	23	23	50	28	30	32	36	36	35	19	32	21	35	30	22	19	50
as	3	4	2	5	6	5	5	3	4	5	7	10	5	4	7	4	6	4	3	3	3	4	2	2	3	5	4	2	5	2	5	5	6	5	3	8	12	5	3	2	4	6	5	5	4	4	6	4	5	2	50
because						1		1				1	1																											1											5
before							1		1		1		1															1				1					1			1					1				1		10
but	5	1	4	6	4	5	8	7	4	7	8	13	7	6	5	4	7	6	8	3	5	1	4	2	2	5	4	4	3	2	4	6	3	4	3	3	5	4	5	4	5	4	7	3	6	3	5	1	4	4	50
either																																																			
ere																1			1																		1														3
for	8	3	8	7	7	8	6	8	5	9	6	9	5	4	5	3	5	4	9	6	5	2	6	2	3	4	5	5	3	5	4	6	3	8	2	7	10	4	4	6	4	3	10	4	6	4	4	3	4	5	50
how			1	1	4	2		1			1	1	1	1	1	1	2	1	1		1		1	1			1				1			1							1		1	2	1				2		25
however																																																			
if	1			4	2	1	1	3	2	3	3	9	3	3	1	1	2		3	1	1		1		1	1	2	1	1	1	1	2	2	2	1	3	3	1	1	3	4	1			2		1		1	1	41
neither																																																			
nor	1	1	1	2	1	3	1	1	1	3	3	5			2	1	1	2	1	2	1	2	3	3	1	2	2	1	1	2	2	3		2	1	1	3	1	1	2	2	1		1	1			2	1		43
now													1								1																														2
or	2	1	1	3	2	3	2	4	3	4	11	9	5	4	2	5	2	4	4	5	7	4	7	2	4	5	4	1	3	3	2	4	3	5	2	3	6	4	7	8	4	1	2	4	2	1	4	2	4	4	50
since (sith)				2	1	1		1	1	1		3		1																		1						1	1										1		12
so			5	1	1	1	2	2	1	1	1	3	3		1		1			1								1									1		2	1	1		1						1	1	22
than	1				1	1	1	1	1	2	3	3			3		2		1	1	1		1		1	1				1	1	1	1	1		2	3	1						1			2		1	1	29
then							1			1		2	4	1																											1										6
therefore			3	1								1																																							3
though(al-)				1		1				1	1	3	1	2	1		1	2	1		1		1		1	2	1		1	1		1		1			1	1		1			1	2	1				1	1	28
thus													1					1	1																																3
unless																																																			
until (till)	1	1					1	1		1	1	2		1		1	1					1	2	1	1		1	1	2	1	1		2		1	2	2	1		1	1	1			1		1		1	1	30
when	2	1	1	1	5	3	3	2	1	6	2	6	4	2	3	2	3	3	3	2	4	1	2		3	2	3	2	4	4	2	2	3	2	3	2	2	3	2	4	2	2	4	2	2	2	2	2	2	2	49
where		1	1	1	5	2	1	2	2	2	1	2	1	1	2	2	2	3	3	2	2	3	3	3	3	2	3	1	2	2		2	2	3	2	1	2	2	2	2	1	2	3	1	3	3	2	1	3	2	48
whether									1				1																																						2
while						1	1	1					1		2	2	1	1	1	2	2	2	2	1	2	1	2	1	2	1		1	1	2		2	1	1	1		1								1	1	30
why																														1																					1
yet			1	2	1	2	2	2		1	2	3	1	3	1		2	1	2		1		2	1	1	1	2	1	2	1	2	1				1	1	2	1		1	1	2	1	1	1	1		2	1	39
Total	61	38	51	65	69	72	63	57	50	71	83	131	73	58	63	59	61	66	69	68	65	52	65	45	51	71	65	70	55	57	69	62	65	76	41	58	105	59	60	70	70	60	71	46	63	42	63	45	57	45	
Total Connectives	112	90	108	130	154	159	153	139	125	163	156	231	138	123	156	133	120	120	143	147	140	146	138	119	123	154	130	167	146	133	144	145	170	169	110	114	219	126	132	150	142	134	184	123	127	133	154	150	144	111	

*Note that a Figure 1 = a use of 10, 2 = a use of 20, 65 = a use of 650, etc.

TABLE 4B SUMMARY OF MAJOR CONNECTIVES IN BRITISH PROSE

	Bible	More	Latimer	Ascham	Holinshed	Hooker	Lyly	Sidney	Bacon	Dekker	Jonson	Donne	Hobbes	Browne	Milton	Clarendon	Bunyan	Dryden	Locke	Burnet	Swift	Shaftesbury	Addison	Berkeley	Johnson	Smith	Burke	Gibbon	Godwin	Alison	Hazlitt	DeQuincey	Carlyle	Macaulay	Darwin	Ruskin	Arnold	Pater	Frazer	Shaw	Churchill	Russell	Joyce	Lawrence	Huxley	Read	West	Connolly	Orwell	Wain	Total Prosists
Prep.																																																			
about									1	1			1					1	1	1																1			2		1	1	1				1		1	13
above					1								1																																					2
across																																																			
against	1	1			1						1				1	1				2		1						2	2			1		1															1		13
amid(-st)																														1																					1
among(-st)	1			1	2			1				1		1	1											1						1		1				1													11
a-round																																							1							1					2
at	1	2	2	2	3	1	2	1	1	3	1	2	3	2	2	3	5	2	4	3	2	3	5	5	4	4	3	2	2	3	3	3	3	4	2	2	2	3	4	3	6	5	4	4	3	3	6	2	3	3	50
beneath																																																			
between							1													2						2		1			2			2	1	1					1	1			2	1	1				13
beyond																																																			
by	8	8	1	7	10	6	5	6	4	4	5	3	9	6	7	6	6	4	6	6	5	3	4	8	9	7	6	10	7	5	5	7	4	11	5	8	3	5	7	5	8	7	1	2	4	5	4	6	5	5	50
during																												1						1																	2
from	3	2	2	1	3	2	1	1	3	3	2	3	4	5	3	4	4	3	3	3	3	1	3	3	4	4	4	6	4	7	4	5	2	6	6	5	1	4	5	3	5	2	1	3	4	4	3	5	3	3	50
in	12	15	16	23	17	15	14	19	16	16	13	20	16	20	11	17	11	18	11	18	14	20	18	18	12	22	19	11	14	21	18	18	16	15	20	18	16	19	21	10	18	22	11	13	16	19	13	12	14	16	50
into	1	1	1		2	1	1	1	2	3	1	1	2	1	3	2	2	2	1	2	1	2	3			2	1		1		2	2	1	1				2	3		1	1	2	1	2	1		1	1	1	40
like							1			4	1																				1	1	1		1	1	1	2	1	1		1	5	2	2	1	2	2	2	1	21
of	30	20	24	24	43	31	21	29	35	24	18	29	35	37	33	31	19	32	29	28	28	28	34	25	30	54	45	61	43	53	36	35	26	49	35	50	37	50	32	21	37	38	13	26	32	45	19	27	21	33	50
off																																											1								1
on	1		1			1				2	1		1	1	1	1	1	2	4	3	2	3	1	3	2	1	4	4	1	1	4	3	3	3	4	3	4	3	7	3	5	4	5	2	2	2	4	3	2	4	43
out					1					1	1				1		1				1		1																				2								8
over	1				1												1																	1									1								5
through	3	1	1							1																	1				1	2	1					1													9
to	11	4	8	8	6	3	9	7	11	7	6	8	9	1	11	11	1	7	10	13	8	7	8	4	9	8	9	10	10	15	11	10	7	11	10	11	6	7	7	6	8	10	4	6	7	9	8	8	6	9	50
toward																																																			
under	1				1																1						1	2	1			2		1	1						1										10
unto	6	2	1		2	6	1		1					4			1																																		9
up																																						1								1					2
upon	1		1		2	1	1	1	1	2	1	3	1	2	1	4	3		1	3	3	1	4			1	1		4	2	2	5				1	1				2										29
with	3	4	6	5	5	3	8	7	4	6	7	3	1	5	4	7	8	4	4	7	6	4	7	3	8	5	6	5	6	7	5	5	8	5	6	4	6	7	6	4	5	5	11	5	4	3	5	4	4	5	50
within					1			1																																											2
without	1	1		2	1	1	2	1	1		2	1		1	1	2		1	2		1		1	5	1		1				2	1				1							1						1		25
Total	85	61	64	73	101	72	67	75	74	77	61	74	81	88	80	89	63	75	76	91	76	73	89	74	79	111	101	115	95	115	96	101	72	112	91	105	78	105	94	58	97	96	66	65	78	95	65	71	63	81	
Rel. Conj.																																																			
that	18	14	13	7	11	6	10	4	14	9	11	13	11	4	11	3	16	7	16	10	6	5	19	13	8	4	7	5	9	9	9	9	6	6	11	10	6	5	5	11	5	11	2	5	6	9	10	5	12	5	50
what	3		2	2		2		1	1	2	3	1	3	1	5	1	3	1	2	1		2	1	4	1	2	2				3	1	3	1	1	4	2			1		3	4	2	1	1	2	1	1	1	40
which	7	1	2	3	5	14	3	7	8	4	4	5	10	6	8	9	5	7	9	8	7	5	6	7	7	9	6	7	8	11	6	6	2	12	4	12	11	9	5	9	7	7	7	1	5	5	3	8	5	4	50
who	8		2	1	5	2	4	3	1	2	3	3		2	6	5	3	4	3	3	3	3	3		5	2	3	1		3	1	2	1	2	1	2	3	3	3	3	2	3	1	1			2	6	2	2	44
Total	36	15	19	13	21	24	17	15	24	15	21	22	24	13	30	18	27	19	30	22	16	15	29	24	21	17	18	13	17	23	19	18	12	21	17	28	22	17	13	24	14	24	14	9	12	15	17	20	20	12	
Prep. Conj.																																																			
after	1			1	2	1				1				1		1	1	1		2	1		1									1		1				1			1	1	3					1	1		20
and	18	34	25	32	22	31	16	22	35	24	28	30	32	31	35	36	28	23	28	27	28	23	23	23	23	24	22	13	24	20	30	20	27	30	22	30	34	24	21	26	27	23	19	21	17	21	27	23	21	18	50
as	5	7	6	6	11	9	7	11	6	8	7	7	10	4	8	6	7	9	11	4	6	4	9	6	5	5	7	4	4	6	7	8	5	5	6	9	9	5	4	6	4	6	3	3	5	6	4	4	4	7	50
because	1	1	1	1	1	2			1	1	1	1	1				2	1	2		1	2									2		2			2	1		1			1	3	1			1	2	1		27
before		4	1		1	1	1	1		1		1		1	1	2	1	1	1	1	1		1				1							1																	19
but	10	6	7	7	4	4	6	7	6	6	12	8	7	6	8	3	8	6	8	7	5	5	3	7	5	4	4	3	3	4	6	4	4	4	4	7	5	3	3	4	6	7	3	6	4	7	6	4	5	4	50
either				2	1	1	2			1			1																	1																					7
ere																																																			
for	16	8	12	9	5	5	6	6	9	8	7	8	9	3	6	4	7	6	6	7	5	8	6	5	5	7	6	4	5	2	5	8	8	4	5	5	7	6	4	5	5	5	6	5	6	5	7	10	4	7	50
how	1	2			1	1	1	1	1	2				1	2	1	1		1		1						1				1			1	1	1	1	1					1								22
however																1											1	1		1											1										5
if	5	3	4	4		2	5	3	3	5	2	3	1	1	3	2	3	3	5	1	1	3	2	3	1	1	2		3	4	4	2	3		2	2	1		2	2		3	3	2	1	1	2	2	4	2	45
neither	1	1		1		1	2		1															1							1																				8
nor	1	1	1	1					1	1	1	1	1	1	1		1		2		1	1		1			1				2					2				1								1			21
now	2																																																		1
or	2	4	2	4	4	3	6	5	9	5	9	3	11	9	6	3	1	4	5	2	4	5	4	13	2	6	5	5	5	13	9	4	4	2	8	10	3	3	5	4	4	4	6	6	5	6	1	8	5	3	50
since (sith)					1			1						1			1		2																							1									6
so	1	1	2	1	1	1	1		2	3	3	1	2	1			3	1	1	5											1				1			1					2								21
than		3	1	3	1	2	5	2	3	4	5	1	2	1	3	2	1	3	2	2	1	2	2	2	3	3	2	2	3	1	2	3	1	2	2	3	2	1		2	2	2		1	3	2	1	1	1	1	47
then	3									1							5														1			3									2								6
therefore	2								1	2					1		2			1	1									1		1				2															10
though (al-)		1	1	1	1	2	1	1	1	2	1	2	2	2	1	1		1	1	2	1		1		1	1	1				1	1			1	1						1	1								29
thus																																							1		1					2					3
unless															1																																				1
until (till)										1					1				1	1			1										1						1				1								8
when	2	1	2	3	2	1	1	1	1	2	3	5	5	1	2	2	2	2	3	2	1		2		2	2	1	1	1	4	2	1		2	4	1	1	1	4	3	2	2	6	3		2	2	2	2	2	46
where			1	1	2			1			1	2		1			1	1												2	1			1		4		1					1					1	1		17
whether		1	1				1	1						1	1																				1																7
while														1		1												1																							3
why																																																			
yet	1	1	1	2	1	1	2	1	1	1	2	2	1	1	2		1	2	1	2										3	1	1		1	1													1			25
Total	72	79	68	79	61	69	69	65	81	79	81	75	85	67	82	64	76	64	80	66	58	53	55	61	47	53	54	34	48	62	76	54	55	58	58	79	64	43	46	53	53	56	69	48	41	52	51	60	49	44	
Total Connectives	193	155	151	165	183	165	147	155	184	171	164	171	190	168	192	171	166	158	186	179	150	141	173	159	147	181	173	161	160	200	191	173	139	191	166	212	164	169	153	135	164	167	140	122	131	162	133	151	132	137	

	POETRY											PROSE										
	Dwight	Bryant	Emerson	Whitman	Dickinson	Robinson	Eliot	Crane	Roethke	Lowell	Total Poets	Edwards	Paine	Emerson	Whitman	Twain	Santayana	Eliot	Hemingway	Lardner	Baldwin	Total Prosists
Prep.																						
about										1	1			2	1		3			1	1	4
above								1	1		2											
across								1			1											
against	1									1	2	1	1							1		3
amid-st																						
among-st					1						1			1								1
around	2																					
at	1	3	2	4	3	3	4	3	2	3	10	3	2	3	3	6	3	3	3	5	3	10
beneath	1		4								2											2
between								3			1						1		1			2
beyond						1		1			2											
by	3	4	2	4	2	2	2	3	2	2	10	3	8	4	4	4	4	4	4	3	5	10
during																						
from	6	8	3	5	2	2	2	6	3	4	10	4	5	3	3	4	3	3	3	3	5	10
in	11	13	9	15	5	9	12	14	11	10	10	17	15	14	19	14	16	15	12	16	14	10
into	1	1				1		2	2	2	6		2	3	10	2	1	2			2	7
like	2	1	1	1		3	1	3	2	2	9						1	1	1		1	5
of	21	24	15	35	11	24	17	26	16	15	10	34	27	38	36	20	32	33	22	24	29	10
off										1	1											
on	4	4	3	6	2	4	4	6	4	7	10	3	4	3	3	5	2	2	3	7	3	10
out			1	1							2					1	1					2
over	2	2	1	1			1	1	1	1	8					1	1					2
through	2	1		3		1		4			5	1			1		1		1		1	4
to	9	5	7	12	5	6	4	7	6	6	10	13	7	1	8	7	8	8	5	8	8	10
toward									1		1											
under								2	1	1	3	1		1								2
unto				1							1											
up								1			1											
upon		2		1	2	1	1			1	6	3			1	1						3
with	13	9	5	12	2	8	5	7	7	6	10	4	5	5	7	4	1	5	5	5	6	10
within								1			1										1	1
without			1		1	1					3	3	2								1	3
Total	74	80	51	104	37	65	60	89	58	62		89	81	74	96	75	73	77	61	74	79	
Rel. Conj.																						
that	4	7	3	5	3	13	2	6	2	2	10	9	8	7	6	6	9	11	8	7	9	10
what	1			2	1	2	1	1	2	1	8	2	1	3	1	3	3	2	1	3		10
which		2	2								2	9	6	5	1	2	6	12	4	3	9	10
who	2	4	2	1	2	2	4	3	1	3	10	2	3	2	1	1	1	2	2	2	4	10
Total	7	13	7	8	6	17	7	10	5	6		22	18	17	11	10	19	28	16	13	25	
Prep. Conj.																						
after			2			1	1	1			4	1			1	1						3
and	39	39	22	55	11	32	28	26	16	27	10	30	25	34	43	32	27	18	24	20	25	10
as	2	4	2	6	3	3	2	5	3	3	10	5	5	5	6	2	4	5	5	5	7	10
because						1					1	1	1				1	1	2			5
before		1		1	1		1	1		1	6	1			1					1	1	3
but	3	1	3	2	4	8	2	3	3	2	10	5	5	7	4	4	4	5	5	3	3	10
either								1			1						1					1
ere																						
for	3	4	4	9	6	8	5	2	3	5	10	7	6	6	8	7	5	7	7	8	6	10
how	1			1	1						3	2		1						1	1	4
however																				1	1	2
if			1	1	1	2	2	2	1		7	2	2	3	1	2	4	2	3	1	1	10
neither														1								1
nor	2	1	2	2	1	3		1		1	8	1	1		1							3
now																						
or	3	2	5	9	4	2	2	3	2	2	10	4	5	6	10	4	5	5	6	2	6	10
since (sith)																				1		1
so				1	1						2	1			2					1		3
than		1	3	2	1			1		2	6	2	2	1	3	1	1	3	2	1	2	10
then				2	1	1	1	2			5	1						1				2
therefore												1									1	2
though (al-)	2			1	1		1				4	1	1	1	1							4
thus																						
unless																						
until (till)		2			2		1		2		4	1										1
when	1	2	1		3	3	1	1	2	3	9	3	2	1	3	2	1	1	3	3	1	10
where	3	3	2	1	1	3	1	2	1	4	10		1	1			1			1	1	4
whether																						
while	3	1		1				2			4				1			1	1			3
why	1										1											
yet	1	1				1				1	4	2	3	1								3
Total	63	63	53	93	44	71	47	53	34	50		67	59	70	84	57	53	47	58	48	57	
Total Connectives	144	156	111	205	87	153	114	152	97	118		178	158	161	191	142	146	152	135	135	161	

93

rather than of time, cause, manner, or choice. With the increase of the verb, we can see how these directional terms fit; they relate action to location. As in reference, the main vocabulary has its strong source in the Bible. And, as in reference, the connective terms of poetry are agreed on more intensively by more authors than in prose. And one may note the characteristic difference between Milton's *ere*, still with a poetic aura, and Clarendon's clearly prosaic or spelled-out trisyllabic *however*.

Connective terms, because they are structural rather than referential, are used so much more intensively that their full pattern of usage may be summarized on a page. Therefore, Tables 4A, 4B, and 4C can make available much interesting material in compact form.

Reading across the top of Table 4A, for example, we see, at the right, for the moderns, the clustering of new prepositional forms that we have just observed in the briefer table. Then we may note the prepositions dominant for almost all poets: *at, by, from, in, of, on, to, with*; of these, *in* and *of* are the strongest in frequencies. Then the relative *which* and *who*, and the conjunctive prepositional *and, as, but, for, or, when, where*; among these, *and* is by far the strongest. These conjunctive-prepositional terms, with their greater flexibility of use — *before dawn*, or *before day dawns* — are in total more frequent than relatives or prepositions, yet reading across the page we see an increase of prepositions to totals of eighty or ninety in Thomson, Blake, Shelley, Swinburne, Sitwell, and later poets, not paralleled in the more conjunctive forms, which are never so strong again as they were for Donne.

In total connective usage, first Donne's strong conjunctives and relative forms make for the largest number; then a good deal later strong totals are presented by Shelley, Keats, Swinburne, Sitwell on the basis of their prepositional uses, their phenomenal *in*'s and *of*'s. Least connective are the poetic extremes early and late: the Ballads, Dunbar and Coverdale, then Jennings and Gunn.

For prose, the details are similar: the increase of *about, against*, and *between*; the fully used *at, by, from, in, of, to, with, that, which, and, is, but, for, or, there, when*. *On* and *where* are used with more unanimity in poetry, despite Lessing's strictures on temporal progression, but *that* and *then* are used in more cursive and subordinate prose.

The totals of prose-use, at the bottom of the page, show that no prose writer is so ardent a user of connectives as the poet Donne. (Dialogue: I suggest that this is a great clue to Donne's difference from other metaphysical poets. The critic protests, but Donne is much more than just a lot of connectives; I reply, true, true.) On the other hand, at least twenty prose writers, from the Bible and Bacon to Locke, Adam Smith, and Macaulay, are as connective as the three or four strongest connective poets. Least connective among prose writers are Lyly early, Lawrence and Orwell late. Major for prose are *of* and *which*; for poetry, *with*; the rest are similar in average usage.

The differences in relative and conjunctive forms are not great either in total amounts or in individuals, except for Donne's and Swinburne's magnitudes in poetry, and the Bible's, Milton's, and Locke's strong relatives in prose. In prepositions, however, the differences are great at first glance: the higher sums from the Bible on, especially for such terms as *by, in, of*. The common usage for poetry is fairly level through the years, with certain exceptions; but for prose it not only begins more strongly but increases more strongly, from the portent in Holinshed to the significant late eighteenth-century increase in Adam Smith, Burke, Gibbon, Godwin, Alison, De Quincey, Macaulay, and Pater, in those *in* and *of* pharases that would make for more nouns and thus also for the possibility of more adjectives. So as early prose had worked with many verbs both free and clausally connected, now later prose worked with many adjectives both free and phrasally connected. The content and form of Smith's major terms *simple, river, sea, society*; Burke's *political, policy*; Gibbon's *modern, strength*; Godwin's *human, institution*; Alison's *beautiful, strong, animal, form, taste*; Pater's *early, element,* represent the prose interest of this era in significant qualification of new concepts in qualifying phrases as well as in central statements. Poetry, meanwhile, with its mere adjectival *pale* and *cold* and with exceptions in Blake, Shelley, Swinburne, and Sitwell, is turning back to verbs, like a few writers in prose also: Shaw, Joyce, Lawrence, West, and Orwell.

In American connectives, similar contrasts are apparent between poetry and prose: more *because* in prose, more *if*, more *than*, more *what, which, about, in, of*. Poetry, on the other hand, shows more *where, until, from, like, on, over, through, with*. That is, considering poetry's lesser wordage, we may especially note its preference for locational over logical terms. But we see no pattern by genre: Whitman and Eliot use fewer *and*'s in their prose than in their poetry; Emerson, more.

A number of terms, in either form, are used quite uniformly by all but one or two authors; for example, Robinson's and Emerson's logical *but*; Robinson's and Eliot's relative *that*, and Eliot's *which*; Twain's *at*, Paine's *by*, Bryant's *from* — all active — with Whitman's less active *in, into, of, or*; Dwight's and Whitman's *with*.

No connective in either form increases much, except for *like* in both.

95

Because these tables are organized by time rather than by type of syntax, it is less easy to see what connective terms characterize the chief types. But, as we have already noted, strongly connective styles are twice as apt to be adjectival or balanced as to be predicative. Almost all highly adjectival styles are also highly phrasal; the balanced, as it balances adjectives and verbs, does so also with phrases and clauses. Of verb-styles, Holinshed's alone is highly phrasal.

Moreover, certain specific connective terms are characteristic of certain styles — the conjunctive of manner and of temporal and causal sequence in *how, so, thus, because, if, though, unless, when, whether, yet,* especially for early verb-writers like Donne; the subordinative of person or direction in *to* and relative pronouns for Bacon, Hooker, Milton, Locke; and the locational *in, among, between,* and disjunctive *either, or, rather, than* for the adjectival Ascham, Browne, Ruskin, Smith, and De Quincey. Time brought changes in emphasis also, from early logic to later location. The great eighteenth-century changes in prose brought decrease of *because* and *though,* increase of *at, by, from, in, of,* the purely phrasal connectives. For many a connective, decline is by half or two-thirds. The victory is for Seneca's *dum, ubi, quando* over Cicero's *enim, ut, autem.* Of the adjectival authors, Smith, Macaulay, Ruskin are strongest in connectives, and only Carlyle and Huxley perceptibly weak.

Great varieties of range are to be seen. For example, in prose, Swift, not a great user of connectives, uses *and* five times as often as Browne; Spenser, *in* six times as often as Sidney. In totals of connectives from Tyndale's, Hobbes's, Milton's, Ruskin's 2000 to Shaw's, Lawrence's, Huxley's 1200 — almost twice as many for some as for others — examples of chief uses are: Browne and Milton, *and;* Hooker, *because;* Ascham, *either, which, in;* Tyndale, *for, therefore;* Hooker, *though;* Donne and Joyce, *when;* Joyce, *about, after;* Macaulay and others, *between, by, during, from;* De Quincey and Gibbon, *under.*

Though predicative writers as a whole are less connective than others, a few are strong in their use of connectives. This strength results from unusual stress on phrasal prepositions; thus Jennings uses *to* in poetry; and, in prose, Tyndale, Holinshed, Dekker, Hazlitt — as, in effect, narrators — put especial emphasis on setting, by using *from, over, through, among, at, on, with, between, to, into.* Others stress one or another of the clausal relations: the relative *that, what, who, which,* for Renaissance poets and for Tyndale, Hooker, Bunyan, Berkeley, Johnson; the alternative, *either, neither, or, nor, rather, than,* for Johnson, Hazlitt, Connolly; the terms of manner, in *how, so, thus,* for Hooker, Sidney, Jonson, Donne, Bunyan; of logic, *because, if, therefore, though, unless, whether, yet,* for poets like Yeats and for Tyndale, Hooker, Dekker, Donne, Bunyan, Hazlitt; of time, *after, before, now, since, then, till, when, while, yet,* for Tyndale, Dekker, Donne, Bunyan, Joyce. In other words, one writer may combine signs of time and logic; another, logic and manner, and so on; Hooker and Dryden are representative of these balanced combinations. Finally to be noted are those predicators who use a minimum of connectives; namely, More, Latimer, Lyly, Sidney, Shaftesbury, Joyce, Lawrence, West — many of them because they are "curt" — focusing upon a temporal sequence of unconnected simple statements. Because of this group, the predicators' average of connectives is less by two hundred. So Lawrence's *Spirit of Place,* sparing of connectives:

> The world doesn't fear a new idea.
> It can pigeon-hole any idea.
> But it can't pigeon-hole a real new experience.
> It can only dodge.

As a whole, then, we may say of the chief English prose style, the predicative, that it drew from two different predicative traditions: on the one hand, the Biblical, as in the plain style of St. Paul, in which, as adjectives were essentially meager, connected clauses were the major type of qualification; and, on the other hand, the Roman, indeed Senecan, style in which adjectives were more freely used and connectives diminished in proportion. In our own day, this less connective style is the one that seems to dominate.

The terms of poetry are not really special to poetry. A prose treatise on colors or on feelings, on scene or attitude, could well emphasize any of these. Frazer's *Golden Bough,* D. H. Lawrence's essays, for example, emphasize many. They are free and common terms. But, on the other hand, we feel that many prose terms will probably not be used in poetry — Why? Certainly *whole* or *real* or *early* might, intangible as they are; also *idea* or *form, become* or *believe.* But possibly not *understand,* and though possibly *state,* not *government?* We begin to note that the question is not so much one of reference as one of sound: the multisyllable word seems not easily repeatable in poetry, though it may perform such a major single service as *multitudinous* does for Macbeth's pentameters. Besides flexibility, too, there is the question of commonness. G. K. Zipf's proposals about the correlation between singleness of syllable and frequency of use have pertinence here. Wilhelm Fuch's "On Mathematical Analysis of Style" [1] assumes

[1] *Biometrika,* XXXIX, Nos. 1, 2 (May, 1952), 125.

the plurisyllabic quality of prose as distinguished from poetry. At least we may see that of the 260 main terms for poetry, about 50 are disyllabic: *golden, silver, father, mother, noble, tender, hearty, flower, nature, eternal, worthy, heavy, power, spirit, desire, fortune, reason, pleasant, winter, delight, behold, gentle, little, happy, shepherd, virtue, divine, mighty, nothing, water, glory, sorrow, garden, people, human, superior, various, country, mountain, silent, distant, pleasure, morning, fancy, body, darkness, shadow, summer, creature, memory.*

Important here is the relation of prose and poetry to the resources of language. Most of the major language is shared in common and comes from the basic stock of the words most commonly spoken, monosyllabic or disyllabic language. Most of the remaining terms of poetry come from this also; many of prose's do not. Prose, not poetry, is the specializer of language in its materials of choice. Poetry's specializations are achieved less by choice than by setting; by enforcing the referential power of the common words in closely controlled referential contexts and, especially, by the devices of sound; the poetic forces of rhythm, rhyme, and other repetitions give sensory, particularly auditory, pattern.

It may be wise to revise some of the critical assumptions of the past decades about the esoteric selectivity, the special connotative powers of the language of poetry. We need not deny any of these powers to poetry, but we do need to be aware that many come into it by the design of the words, not by the nature of the words. The power of the words themselves is the great power of commonness, centrality of use, as the various "word-lists" attest. What distinguishes prose is the greater individuality of its subject matter, its concern with basic topics of education and government, its seeking out and drawing of refinements of special diction into the language, its efforts at conceptualization through the borrowing and re-creating of Latinate forms, as in such terms as *perfection, philosopher, consequence, imagination, understanding, particular, constitution, association* — each a little construct in itself.

It is possible to conclude either that prose was slowly responsive to forces in poetry, or that both were responsive to certain general tendencies in language but at somewhat different rates. The native tongue for both was strongly predicative, as were Ciceronian, Senecan, and Biblical prose, and ballad songs in poetry. But in each of the Renaissance centuries there were poets like Spenser, Shakespeare, Sylvester, Waller, Milton, and Dryden, and prosaists like Ascham, Bacon, Hobbes, Milton, and Locke, who pulled away toward a "classic" or toward a more extreme English style. And in the eighteenth century this style almost completely dominated poetry, from

Pope to Wordsworth, with Thomson, Gray, Collins, and Blake as most extreme; while for prose it worked a little less pervasively, reaching its height in the nineteenth century with De Quincey, Carlyle, Macaulay, Darwin, Ruskin, and Pater, then receding to balance in the last century, as it had for poetry in the last two.

What was this drive toward, and then away from, an extreme adjectival style? Should it be called "poetic?" Perhaps, in that it was strong in poetry earlier than in prose; but perhaps not, in that both forms began without it and have been in agreement in recently abandoning it. Perhaps it was an effort by art to pursue possibilities in the English language previously unexplored? Or perhaps a certain state of mind which required a certain sort of expression?

A factor analysis of seventeenth-century poets and major words, showing statistically the degree to which each poet and word is dependent on each other poet and word, gives a clear picture of these dependencies and casts emphasis on the three strands of predicative, connective, and adjectival style.[2] The strand running throughout and conditioning the whole century is the group of verbs used by the group of poets dominated by Donne. In this view, the chief "sons of Ben" are in fact scholastic sons of Donne, the poets of Donne's "Let us possess one world, each hath one, and is one"; while Ben Jonson's sons are the later, the more substantival, connective, and balanced group — Oldham, Denham, Dryden, and surprisingly, Herbert — in the Horatian-classical order of "What art is thine that so thy friend deceives?" Then, third, there is the mid-century group — Lovelace, Marvell, Waller, Quarles, Sandys, Crowley, Crashaw, Milton, of "Together both, ere the high lawns appear'd" — Biblical, aesthetic, lofty, of *fair* and *bright, high* and *heaven, earth* and *night,* and *hear.*

If Charles Morris, Hanan Selvin, and others are right in their generally agreed-on triad of factors in human relations — activity, judgment, receptivity — then we may see a version of the triad in the seventeenth-century language of poetry. At any rate, of the three tendencies, the first was consumed within the century; of the others, especially the receptive drew greater strength as it moved into the new century. In the poetry of Pound, Crane, Thomas, and the followers of Whitman, we see it flourishing still today — the reception of the material world through the senses: *sweet* and *fair* becoming *deep* and *high,* becoming *long* and *wide,* becoming *dark* and *bright,* becoming *green* and *blue,* becoming *cold* and *dry,* soon to be *wet* and *warm.*

[2] Cf. Jacob Leed, ed., *The Computer and Literary Style* (Kent State University Press, 1966).

As the complex that analysis of seventeenth-century poetry showed us — the ascendance of a sensory and qualitative style out of a pervasive background of concept in predicate structures — is visible in prose also, once the clue of the sensory is given, so the parallels in the displacement of this style may be followed out. The seventeenth-century proportions of both forms were chiefly predicative; in the eighteenth they parted company; in the nineteenth and twentieth centuries they begin to return to likeness.

In vocabulary, the poetry of the seventeenth century brought in much action and feeling, as we have noted, in Jonson's *grow* and *meet*; in Donne's *bad*; Fletcher's *grief* and *sit*; Herrick's *fear, glory, joy, sorrow, feel*; Waller's *care* and *fate*; Vaughan's *sleep* and *weep*; in contrast to Milton's and Marvell's terms of sense. In prose, there is a parallel: Donne's *affection, begin*, and *seek*; Jonson's *reach*; Hobbes's *action, dream, fancy, imagination, motion, sound, thought, understand*; Browne's *hold* and *leave*; Bunyan's *fall* and *meet*; in contrast to the physical settings of Donne's *house* and *bed*; Browne's *fire* and *substance*; Milton's *city*; Clarendon's *court*; and Dryden's *poem* and *verse*. So, a century later, at the turn away from the qualitative eighteenth century, we see poetry's newly specific objects: Wordsworth's *tree*; Coleridge's *body, moon, rock*; Browning's *house*; Swinburne's *shadow*; Hardy's *shape*. And these are paralleled by the also limiting terms of romantic prose: Alison's *animal, form*, and *instance*; Hazlitt's *moment*; De Quincey's *fact*; Darwin's *period, structure*, and *view*; Ruskin's *artist* and *perception*; and Pater's *element*. These most-used new, rather than continued, terms in both forms indicate the steadying agreements of prose thought with poetic, and show as the main differences between the two the abstractness of the new prose language and its ability to hold on to new adjectival structures like *moral, social, ideal*, as in the text of Huxley.

A brief tracing of examples of this form may give context to the proportioning we have already observed. In 1631, we have a fine early statement of the relation between adjective and verse-line, in James Shirley's *The Changes*, noted by Professor Ben Lucow. See that the relation is structural, the demands of the line stronger still than the demands of subject, which in 1631 were still external, even outworn.

> *Goldsworth:* Master Caperwit, before you read, pray tell me, have your verses any adjectives?
> *Caperwit:* Adjectives! would you have a poem without adjectives?
> They are the flowers, the grace of all our language:
> A well chose epithet doth give new soul
> To fainting poesy; and makes every verse

A bride; with adjectives we bait our lines,
When do we fish for gentlewomen's loves,
And with their sweetness catch the nibbling ear
Of amorous ladies; with the music of
These ravishing nouns, we charm the silken tribe,
And make the gallant melt with apprehension
Of the rare word: I will maintain't against
A bundle of grammarians, in poetry
The substantive itself cannot subsist
Without an adjective.
Goldsworth: But, for all that,
Those words would sound more full, methinks, that are not
So larded, and if I might counsel you,
You should compose a sonnet clean without them:
A row of stately substantives would march
Like Switzers, and bear all the field before them;
Carry their weight, shew fair, like deeds enroll'd,
Not writs, that are first made, and after filed.
Thence first came up the title of blank verse;
You know, sir, what blank signifies? when the sense
First framed, is tied with adjectives like points,
And could not hold together without wedges:
Hang't, 'tis pedantic, vulgar poetry;
Let children, when they versify, stick here
And there these piddling words for want of matter.
Poets write masculine numbers.

The metaphor of sinew still held good, for poetry as for prose.

The Renaissance concept of masculine verse, of bare bones or sinews of statement as essential, was in contrast to flesh or drapery as added, as feminine ornament. So Spenser, who used more adjectives than most in his time, was consistently called *feminine, sweet,* and *smooth* because of an idea like Shirley's that the filled-out line, with a regular concord of syllables and stresses, was the smooth line. Inasmuch as adjectives or qualities were considered extras by the Shirleys of the day, they could be added when needed to fill in the blanks, in the accord of line and statement.

Associationist psychology changed this distinction, as we noted in eighteenth-century prose. Qualities became the vital concerns of perception, so that they and not their rather illusory substances carried the significance in the poem. The filled blanks of blank verse then became structurally useful, and structure became subordinate to, as useful to, reference. But the adjective was not dependent upon the waiting metrical blank and burgeoned also in the more freely irregular lines of eighteenth-century odes, piling up long lists of qualifications and then falling back into implicative singularity.

When we look at representative passages from the adjectival poetry of the eighteenth century, in contrast to its less adjectival predecessors and followers, we may see that a similar meter does not make for similarity of reference. The following three passages are all to some degree in iambic pentameter, the basis of blank verse, and contain a similar number of words per line. Yet hear how differently they move. Donne's *Good-Morrow*, with its verbal play over the idea of reflection, of two in one and one in two, and with the characteristic metaphysical adjectives *true* and *good* or *better*, gains the effect of speech, with internal pauses after *eye, north, one, slacken,* and with emphasis on the logic of the *if*, and the consequent verb.

> My face in thine eye, thine in mine appears,
> And true plain hearts do in the faces rest;
> Where can we find two better hemispheres
> Without sharp north, without declining west?
> Whatever dies was not mixed equally;
> If our two loves be one, or thou and I
> Love so alike that none do slacken, none can die.

As the evaluative and figurative adjectives here are part of the argument, they are relatively spare and part of the sinew.

The lines from Cowper's *Task* proceed in eighteenth-century fashion to use proportionately more adjectives, with proportionately more regularity of position and emphasis. Almost every noun is defined by its major *distant, soft, silent, sweet* epithet.

> No less composure waits upon the roar
> Of distant floods, or on the softer voice
> Of neighb'ring fountain, or of rills that slip
> Through the cleft rock, and, chiming as they fall
> Upon loose pebbles, lose themselves at length
> In matted grass, that with a livelier green
> Betrays the secret of their silent course.
> Nature inanimate employs sweet sounds,
> But animated nature sweeter still,
> To soothe and satisfy the human ear.

After a century of such fitness, how drastic the romantic challenge of the ballad, and of Coleridge in *Christabel* and *Kubla Khan* when he suggests that the only seemingly irregular meter is founded on a new principle, that "occasional variation in number of syllables is not introduced wantonly, or for the mere ends of convenience, but in correspondence with some transition in the nature of the imagery or passion." And so we hear in *Kubla Khan*, adjectival in the *bright* eighteenth-century tradition, the flexible lengthening of the line, by which, in terms of the first two lines, the third does not provide a "blank" for *sinuous*, nor the fourth for *bearing*, nor the fifth for *ancient*, nor the sixth for *sunny*.

> So twice five miles of fertile ground
> With walls and towers were girdled round:
> And here were gardens bright with sinuous rills,
> Where blossomed many an incense-bearing tree,
> And here were forests ancient as the hills,
> Enfolding sunny spots of greenery.

When we look at these poetic passages, we may see the relation between observation of single contexts and generalization of whole tendencies. The relation is based upon the fact that writers do, consciously or unconsciously, work together, sharing main emphases in time and type. By dealing with proportions we avoid stressing items out of context and provide, instead, a continuity of relation. The use of adjectives is significant in relation to the number of nouns and verbs, in relation to modifying phrases and clauses. It is significant in relation to subject matter, the sequence from concept to quality to object in English poetry. And it is significant in relation to patterns of sound in word and structure. All these proportions could serve to focus denser and denser clusters of traits, showing how forms, references, and functions reinforce each other in sound, sense, and structure. The poetry of the eighteenth century is not only formally adjectival but functionally adjectival, focused upon the sensory qualification of the natural world. In this concern it differs from seventeenth-century metaphysical concept on the one hand and nineteenth-century symbolization of objects on the other. And in this concern every eighteenth-century poet shares, whatever differences he may achieve, so that a single poem as well as its poet may reveal the choices of its time.

After adjectives begin to seem too literal, too general, another force of interpretation took their place: that of stated feeling. Concern shifted to the bearer of emotion. Older terms of feeling — the enduring *love*, love's location in the *heart*, the evaluative *fair, dear, sweet*, and social or spiritual *noble, gentle, faith, glory* — first gave way in some degree to Wyatt's words of complaint, in carrying on the *pain* of James I of Scotland to *cruel, de-*

sire, tear, woe, please, and then the metaphor of *fire*. The poets of the golden era tempered their *grief* with *hope*, their *proud* and *happy* with *sad*, in classical and pastoral balance. And after them, in the seventeenth century, came the innovations of exuberance, divine enthusiasm: Campion's *joy*, Herbert's *praise*, More's *sense*, Roscommon's partly emotional *wild*, Walsh's *charm*, Pomfret's *delight*. All of these terms were used widely by their fellow poets. Where Wyatt and Surrey had each stressed perhaps a dozen terms of emotion, mainly woeful, and a half-century later, Daniel and Campion had played the full Elizabethan melody of half-again as many, no one until a full century after — not even Crashaw with his *weeping*, nor Roscommon's intensive *sense* — achieved the varied emotional expression of Walsh's and Pomfret's neoclassical literalness: their *charming, fair, happy, fear, breast, heart, joy, love, pain, passion, pity, tear, torment, hate, love,* their *gay, sad, delight,* and *cry*.

Another century later, it was Crabbe who turned emotion into new explicitness by stressing again its more somber variety, in *fair, happy, humble, proud, sad, care, fear, grief, hope, joy, pain, pleasure, pride, woe, to feel*. He began a new sway of emotional explication — for Burns, for Bowles, for Wordsworth, for Southey, for Moore, and Keats — and this, while not quite as strong as in Pomfret's time, is yet rich; in addition to his times' characteristic *happy, sad, joy, love, pain, passion,* with *mournful, weary, fancy, pity, sorrow, woe, feeling,* and *weeping*. Wordsworth's *dear, sweet, joy, pain, loving,* and *weeping,* and Keat's *happy, sad, sweet, joy, love, pain, pleasure, sorrow,* and *woe* thus make a blend of earlier enthusiasms and later moderations. Crabbe's characteristic earlier use of *pleasure* and *to feel*, Blake's *to weep*, Bowles's *sorrow* — these, along with Roger's *memory* and Moore's *dream*, are the last verbal innovations for explicitly named emotion in English poetry. After them comes the tide of natural forces, first appearing hesitantly with Sylvester's *sea* and Milton's *wind*, Vaughan's *cloud* and Blackmore's *land*, Thomson's *mountain* and Warton's *field*; suddenly, in the later eighteenth century, strengthened and filled, with Bowles's *wave* and *wood*, Wordsworth's *tree*, Coleridge's phenomenal *bird, body, moon, water*, Moore's *star*, Keats's *wing*, and then with all the recent terminology of *rain, grass, hill, snow, leaf,* and *stone*, which ends in Auden's *nothing*. Not only in invention but in amount, emotion is subordinate to natural force, so that we see in highly emotional poets like Swinburne or Yeats only two or three recurrent terms of *sad* or *sweet, love* or *sorrow*.

Our era then is like the mid-sixteenth, seventeenth, or eighteenth centuries, when Scottish moralities, or metaphysical metaphors and concepts, or neoclassical scenes and generalities provided modes of feeling other than literal naming. Our future, like theirs, may well be coming around, as we see it in the newest poetry, to passion again.

Those who in the past decade have written of Wordsworth's poetry have emphasized its quality of process, the on-going of experience that we are drawn to share. I would emphasize about this sharing of process that it is a sharing also of interpretation of process; that is, that the poet not only undergoes but remembers the undergoing and, in tranquillity, decides and tells what it has meant to him in terms of joy or sorrow, hope or fear. Therefore the poetic texture is not presentative but interpretive, not implicative and evocative but declarative, in its relation to human feeling. Something new then happens to reduce declaration, in the nature of Lawrence's "The Sea, the Sea":

> The sea dissolves so much
> and the moon makes away with so much more than we know —
> Once the moon comes down
> And the sea gets hold of us
> cities dissolve like rock-salt
> and the sugar melts out of life
> iron washes away like an old blood-stain
> gold goes out into a green shadow
> money makes even no sediment
> and only the heart
> glitters in salty triumph
> over all it has known, that has gone now into salty nothingness.

Prose provides a like contrast. The implicative predicates of Lawrence's prose strongly differ from Huxley's adjectival observations. Lawrence, from "Pan in America":

> Morning comes, and white ash lies in the fire-hollow, and the old man looks at it broodingly.
>
> "The fire is gone," he says in the Pan silence, that is so full of unutterable things. "Look! there is no more tree. We drank his warmth, and he is gone. He is way, way off in the sky, his smoke is in the blueness, with the sweet smell of a pine-wood fire, and his yellow flame is in the sun. It is morning, with the ashes of night. There is no more tree. Tree is gone. But perhaps there is fire among the ashes. I shall blow it, and it will be alive. There is always fire, between the tree that goes and the tree that stays. One day I shall go —"
>
> So they cook their meat, and rise, and go in silence.

Huxley, from "Watching the Courtship of Birds":

> Redshanks, cock as well as hen, are sober-coloured enough as you
> see their trim brown bodies slipping through the herbage. But dur-
> ing the courtship all is changed. The cock-bird advances towards
> the hen with his graceful pointed wings raised above his back,
> showing their pure-white under-surface. He lifts his scarlet legs
> alternately in a deliberate way — a sort of graceful goose-step —
> and utters all the while a clear far-carrying trill, full of wildness,
> charged with desire, piercing and exciting. Sometimes as he nears
> the hen he begins to fan his wings a little, just lifting himself off
> the ground, so that he is walking on air. The hen will often suffer
> his approach till he is quite close, then shy away like a startled
> horse, and begin running, upon which he folds his wings and runs
> after. She generally runs in circles, as if the pursuit were not wholly
> disagreeable to her, and so they turn and loop over the gleaming
> mud. Then she pauses again, and the tremulous approach is again
> enacted.[3]

The contrast is vivified by Marshall McLuhan's contrast between media
of high and low intensity. The highly controlled, assumptive, adjectival
mode is the more objective, more effectively visualizable; while the
aphoristic mode enlists more participation by its readers.[4] Hence the recom-
mendation to move, rather than to tell, of writers from Longinus, from
Fénelon and Arnauld, to our own day. When we know that eighteenth-
century grammarians saw adjectives as constricted sentences, as Priestley
did,[5] and, in turn, Biblical phrases were recognized as being comparable
to English epithets, *the mountain of holiness* paralleling *the holy mountain,* then the controlling economy of the English adjective becomes
clearer. Phrases and clauses function as words, as Whitehall reminds us in
Structural Essentials (p. 58); they function especially as adjuncts, in the
specifying of time, place, manner, and they are therefore the closely controlling establishers of context. So Huxley rather than Lawrence emphasizes them; so some modern poetry moves toward the unreconstructed
verb, to state action but imply value.

As much as the attribution of human feeling to the natural world has
been criticized, its absence in modern poetry may provide some basis for
criticism too. Where has it gone, the feeling world? All into symbol? As the
major poetic vocabulary of the present is mostly terms of natural objects —

[3] *Bird-watching and Bird Behaviour* (London: Chatto and Windus, 1930), p. 62.
[4] *Understanding Media* (New York: McGraw-Hill Book Co., 1965), p. 319.
[5] B. Wackwitz, *Die Theorie des Prosestils* . . . (Hamburg: Crum, 1962), p. 96.

wing, shadow, rain, stone, hill, grass — and as there is no major modern vocabulary of feeling, the objects are unattached, or carry their significance by context. For example, the chief adjectives of Thom Gunn's first book are *dead* and *great*; the chief verbs, *come, feel, find, go, hold, keep, know, leave, lie, make, move, see, take, think, turn, want*; and these work upon chief nouns like *bird, body, bed, ground, head, street, wind,* and *world* — a context for deepest emotion, but perhaps not for attribution of it. Gunn's "Human Condition" begins:

> Now it is fog, I walk
> Contained within my coat;
> No castle more cut off
> By reason of its moat:
> Only the sentry's cough,
> The mercenaries talk.
>
> The street lamps, visible,
> Drop no light on the ground,
> But press beams painfully
> In a yard of fog around.
> I am condemned to be
> An individual.
>
> In the established border
> There balances a mere
> Pinpoint of consciousness.
> I stay, or start from, here:
> No fog makes more or less
> The neighbouring disorder.

So also the first two stanzas of "The Truth the Dead Know" in Anne Sexton's *All My Pretty Ones*:

> Gone, I say and walk from church,
> refusing the stiff procession to the grave,
> letting the dead ride alone in the hearse.
> It is June. I am tired of being brave.
>
> We drive to the Cape. I cultivate
> myself where the sun gutters from the sky,
> where the sea swings in like an iron gate
> and we touch. In another country people die.

107

Or the first lines of A. R. Ammons' "Risks and Possibilities" in *Expressions of Sea Level*:

Here are some pretty things picked for you:

1)   dry thunder
rustling like water
down the sky's eaves

is summer locust
in dogfennel weed

2)   the fieldwild
yellow daisy
     focusing dawn
inaugurates
the cosmos

3)   the universe comes
    to bear
on a willow-slip and
you cannot unwind
    a pebble
from its constellations

In these versions of the natural world, things mean or be not in themselves but as objects which are under pressure from meanings beyond them and beyond us. The meanings therefore carry the labels of our feelings as rarely as they carry the labels of their own qualities. Perhaps this is why the power of verbs is now returning, in poetry as in prose, because now neither concept, quality, emotion, nor object is the bearer of significance, so much as is the human treatment of them, the action upon them.

Many standard contrasts — between adjectival style as static and predicative as active, between poetry as adjectival and prose as verbal, between seventeenth–eighteenth century as prosaic and eighteenth–nineteenth as poetic — seem overly simple in the light of close observation. One great danger in contrasting is to impose a dualism without awareness of alternative dualisms. Do we contrast sweet only to sour, or also to bitter, and is the sweet of one stage the bitter of another, by a progression of degrees?

All is not chaos; when we look, we do indeed find such strong clusterings of traits that we are able to discern nameable centers of style. And there are of course sequences of simple contrasts, which may shift or widen. One main notable cluster is that of usage in the Renaissance: largely predicative and connective in proportional studies, and conceptual and logical in major vocabulary. It could be called, I suppose, "English," in contrast to later classical or Biblical; baroque in contrast to some classical but not to some Greek and Biblical; dynamic in contrast to some classical but not in contrast to romantic. And so on. Then, when we proceed to the classicism of balanced forms in adjectives and verbs, we see also a new vocabulary of essentials, which may be more poised than static and which develop into another classic form in the twentieth century, with newly concrete vocabulary and newly symbolic concerns. And third, when we observe the romanticism of the eighteenth and nineteenth centuries, we see it takes two forms — low and high, predicative and adjectival, implicative and off-center — in two very different ways.

A more effective procedure seems to me therefore to study in the media of expression itself the potentialities for variety, the basic habits possible, and the possible variations upon them, and so to be able to recognize at the outset not just the simple dualistic contrast as it is seen by any one time, but one of many contrasts in a field of possibilities and tendencies. Social scientists speak of a process of disturbance and then adjustment of equilibrium; art histories of a warring between extremes; scholars, such as Chandler, Boder, Fries, Guiraud, Lee, Spitzer, Whatmough, and Whorf, of contrasting functions of nouns and verbs or adjectives and verbs, or long and short sentences, or repetition and innovation, or rhetoric and logic, or time and place, or levels of language; and most of the critics of the twentieth century, of the basic contrasts between prose as informative, or demonstrative, or formal, and poetry as presentative, or connotative, or formal. What chiefly happens is that the critic draws from either hand instances of a contrast on what for him is a significant basis. But a sense of alternatives can do him no harm. And the alternatives within the powers of language are mighty and multiple.

◆《 FIVE 》◆

Rhetorics of Proportion

Critics and rhetoricians, from Aristotle and Longinus to the Renaissance's Thomas Wilson and George Puttenham, to the eighteenth and nineteenth century's Edward Bysshe and George Campbell, to the twentieth century's R. P. Blackmur and Kenneth Burke, have focused upon figures and meters, devices, connotations, and rarities. They have specifically dealt with the special bents and biases of literary art in their use of language; the intensifying of aesthetic pattern by the doubling of literal to figurative, of sentence to verse-line. As I hope to have shown, one may also profitably attend to the usualness of the language in which the arts work — what they accept and use, as well as what they vary. So the art of sentence-making equally underlies verse-making and figure-making in poetry and in prose.

As one would expect of a well-working art, its various parts are not irrelevant to each other. In this chapter, I should like to consider some of the chief relevances. Rhetoric's logos, ethos, and pathos, or principle, action, and commitment, are paralleled by Logic's conjunction, subordination, choice or disjunction; Grammar's word, name, quality; and thus Art's structure, material, proportion. A sense of consistency should lead us to suppose that a writer's use of special literary forms would be related to his use of general linguistic forms.

Granted the words, the word-groups or syntax, the sentence and sentence groups, and the chief functions of these to name and relate; granted, that is, a working language, what are the biases that art can put upon it, and to what effect? The language can be used truly, purposefully, and aesthetically for formal sensory satisfaction. Art can work to strengthen these functions and their interrelations by increase of latent patterns: repetition, comparison, contrast, association, cumulation; it can also distort these patterns by exaggeration, condensation, or displacement.

One major latency which can be drawn into structure is that of verse —
the close patterning of natural accents of syllable, word, or phrase into
meter, strong-stress, or cadence in linear recurrence — which the other po-
tentially repeatable units of sound, assonance, rhyme, and refrain may
then support as aids to formal identity and memorability. Even without
verse structure, the other traits may function in varying degrees of control,
so that in prose progressions the controlled recurrences of sound stress and
quality may range from apparently accidental echoes to the most closely
repeated syllable, word, phrase, and sentence patterns in parallelism, association, and cumulative force, all these working effectively first to establish expectations and then to suspend, prolong, defeat, or satisfy them.

In meaning as in sound, assumptions can be established and then played
upon. So figurative references, that is, figures of thought rather than of
sound or speech, play upon and enrich literal references by combining with
them: by assuming normally essential or characterizing likenesses between
terms or concepts and then stressing the nonessential likenesses, the likenesses with characterizing differences. Thus metaphor plays over the norms
of the lexicon. Indeed all variations upon these norms, both the terms
usually dealt with as diction — foreign terms, borrowed terms, neologisms
and archaisms, slang and distorted terms — and also the terms dealt with
today in the range from denotative to connotative, and image to symbol,
take their power from the assumption of the verbal norms, in the concreteness and abstractness, the particularity and generality of vocabularies.

Accepted sentence structures, like accepted syllable and word structures,
can be intensified, elaborated, or distorted by art to a purpose. A shift from
active to passive, from present to past tense, from positive to negative, from
declarative to interrogative, can work to an upsetting or confirming or
pleasingly varied effect. One of the best-known and most quickly recognized
of such shifts is the rhetorical question, which, like metaphor at the referential level or like rhyme at the level of sound, carries the power of doubleness of form as the question assumes answer.

Without putting more than one foot into the vast territory of the
rhetorician, I should like to make some suggestions about sound, sense,
and structure patterns as they bear upon and make use of the limitations
and probabilities of grammatical structure. That is, I think that the kinds
of choices made between the uses of meter, strong-stress, or cadence; between literal, figurative, or symbolic reference; and between assertions,
questions, and contradictions are like the kinds of choices made also between chief possible structures in the language: predicative, subordinative,
or assumptive. The basis of distinction is that of attitude: of active on-

going process, of subordinated consideration, or of receptive and observational assumption.

A metrist may stress where he steps by favoring alternate steps, by favoring those steps that seem to suit the terrain, or by taking no regular steps at all but rather a stride established by mood or assumption of goal, in which case attention to his steps could be irrelevant or even distortive. A metaphorist may note likeness in great difference, in slight difference close to literality, or in everything, different or not, because of a larger assumption. A sentence-maker may capitalize upon the singular and unreplaceable presence of the verb in the normal sentence, and stress it by repetition, sentence after sentence, stepping with the stress of the time-signal; or he may avoid such parallelism by moving into the more progressive complexity of subordinate levels; or he may shoulder much of the material up into the off-beat adjuncts. He may specifically contradict a statement, a whole subject-predicate, or he may deny or affirm various substantive contraries and contrasts.

I do not mean to suggest by such alternatives that they all add up to a great umbrella-like triad of possibilities. Each of these possible attitudes would have a different effect with different materials or situations. But I do mean to show in a few examples — some in poetry, some in prose — how the artist in language is able to assert directly, to supplement and subordinate indirectly, and by assuming to alter the emphasis of his effect.

IN SOUND AND SENSE

We noted at the outset the traditional gamut of complexity from sound, to sense, to structure, or from phonology and vocabulary to grammar, logic, and rhetoric; it therefore seems important now, having considered vocabulary and grammar, to take at least a look at some of their relations to prosody.

What I should like to suggest about prosody is simple and well known: Sound-stress in poetry and prose works variously with the meaning-stress and often against it.

The famous metrical regularity of Gray's *Elegy* provides an example for traditional poetry:

> The cur/few tolls/ the knell/ of par/ting day
> The low/ing herd/ winds slow/ly o'er/ the lea.
> The plow/man home/ward plods/ his wea/ry way
> And leaves/ the world/ to dark/ness and/ to me.

In the first three lines only one measure,/*the knell*/, coincides with meaning. A satisfaction of the fourth line is, therefore, that all the measures except/*ness and*/ do effectively coincide. The potential corroboration becomes actual.

An example of full coinciding is: (rising) "Preserve/ again/ the fish/ within/ the sea"; or (falling) "Foster/ later/ monsters/ under/ ocean." Slight variation can come with addition or elision of syllables: "Preserve/ (yet) again;/ So fost'r/ again. . . ." Greater variation will bring the two sorts of stress into discrepancy: "Foster/ again/ the fish . . ." or "Preserve/ the lat/er mon/sters and/ their kind . . ." or "Preserve/ the lat/er mons/ters, keep/ their kind . . . ," the rising unit cutting across pause as well as word. When such an ambiguity of choice between metrical and logical stress arises, the rest of the pattern usually guides the emphases; Yeats likes to allow for two possible choices at once.

A strong-stress meter, in contrast to relative alternation, allows for whole phrasal groupings, and therefore its choices and discrepancies are freer: "Foster,/ while you are about it,/ all sorts of monsters/ and other fish."

As words and sentences work with and against syllable units and lines, both the assumed and the imposed patterns have power. The sentence "Blackbirds/ warble" provides a congruence, while "The black/ birds sing" does not. In the sentence and line "Blackbirds/ warble/ joyful/ly," parallel structure reduces the syllable *birds* to the power of the *-ble* in *warble*. Even drawing out its length, *black* bi-i-rds, would not strengthen it, because duration does not provide a significant phonemic contrast in English. But a different verse pattern might tell us that these were black *birds*, not *black*birds; for example, "The bold/ black birds/ still sing," or even "Black birds/ are not/ so si/lent as/ black trees," in which the possible alternative of a reversed first pair is countered by the parallelism in meaning: Black *birds* . . . black *trees*.

For poetry, then, we have the play of metrical stress upon and around the basic lexical stresses, and the reader hears in his mind the relation of the two sequences. When he reads aloud, he must decide which to emphasize, the meter's beat or the meaning's beat, without losing the one he subordinates. Some will read, "The plow/man home/ward plods/ his wea/ry way"; others, more selectively, perhaps, "The plowman homeward plods/ his weary way." But the important fact underlying the choice of emphasis in performance is the persistence of the two frames in relation to each other; they are not to be reduced to one, rather they are set up by the coinciding of two separate expectations: rhythmic or irregular lexical recurrence and metric or regular recurrence.

Different poets make different uses of the coinciding. Some make it as close as possible, emphasizing the exact fit of pronunciation and measure. Others maintain the fit in order to break it with strong effect, to provide a balance of ambiguity. And others underplay the fit so that discrepancy just loosely happens, without particular significance. In the following examples of all three of these possibilities — close, alternative, and free fit — I italicize the regular metrical stress, leaving the reader to supply the stress of word or phrase. Note that my italics serve to scan the meter only, and that they ignore such commonly recognized concepts as "truncation" and "reversed foot," because these, according to my proposal, make a confused blend of lexical and metrical stress by conceding one to the other. Strictly, the progress of "Brave as he was, he fell," stresses *as, was, fell,* however the stress of sense falls on *Brave.* Let the reader supply this second sort, the *should* of sentence in relation to the *should* of meter, so that the sparks may fly. Let the lexical reinforcement of Blake's metrical *"Tiger, tiger"* provide a guide by parallel when we come to the fourth line, *"Could* frame *thy* fear. . . ."* The double possibility is often part of the poetry.

But often it is not. Many poems create an effect of correspondence of phrasing and metering. Yvor Winters and his students, for example, have been much concerned with achieving such an effect of the right accentual place for the right meaning, with a kind of moral as well as formal force. And many Elizabethans, followed by such eighteenth-century poets as Gray and Collins, sought this effect of rightness. We have heard it obviously in the "The plow/man home/ward plods/ his wear/y way," subtly in Collins' "Evening," and expertly in poems like Winters' "By the Road to the Air-Base," ending

> Yet fruit/ grows on/ the trees;
> Here schol/ars pause/ to speak;
> Through gar/dens bare/ and Greek,
> I hear/ my neigh/bor's bees.

The only discrepancy here is at *on,* and note how slight it is. No other word is robbed of the stress that *on* receives from the regularity of meter; rather, the weighted *on* gives importance to the whole phrase. It is characteristic of such controlled poetry that its few discrepancies call attention to phrasal structures.

But, secondly, work of such measured inevitability may yet make more complex use, in the metaphysical tradition of Donne, of the discrepancies it develops. Marvell's "The Garden" begins:

> How vain/ly men/ themselves/ amaze,
> To win/ the palm,/ the oak/ or bays,
> And their/ incess/ant la/bours see
> Crown'd from/ some sing/le herb/ or tree . . .

Notice how neatly, with what apparent pleasure, the stresses of sound and sense coincide: "How vain/ly men/ themselves/ amaze." Meter and statement agree on what is important. In the four lines, only one exception appears: "Crown'd *from*/ some sing/le herb/ or tree," in conflict with a more meaningful "reversed" "*Crown'd* from/ some sing/le herb/ or tree." Marvell likes the effect of building his lines from the blocks provided by the structure of language. His units are accepted whole: most simply, them*selves,* a*maze,* to *win,* the *palm;* a little more completely in How *vain,* by *men,* some *single herb,* where the basic unit of measure cuts across a word but still fits its second part into a natural place. With really long words this takes some doing, as in Shakespeare's "The *mul*/*titu*/di-nous *seas*/ incar/na*dine.*" In such company, the fit can be part of the pleasure; yet the small variations may provide good possible doubleness of meaning or emphasis. For example, a few lines later, Marvell allows,

> No white/ nor red/ was ev/er seen
> So am/orous as/ this love/ly green.

Either a ripple of unimportant syllables comes together in a suitable, breathless way after the intensive *so;* or the comparison itself is important in *as.* Whichever the reader reads, he can keep both in mind to good effect. This is the useful sort of ambiguity of which William Empson has written in *Seven Types of Ambiguity,* where his emphasis is on meaning rather than on sound.

See how well such alternatives work for Dryden also, at the beginning of *Mac Flecknoe:*

> All hu/man things/ are sub/ject to/ decay,
> And when/ Fate sum/mons Mon/archs must/ obey.
> This Fleck/noe found,/ who, like/ August/us, young
> Was called/ to Em/pire and/ had gov/erned long;
> In prose/ and verse/ was owned,/ without/ dispute
> Through all/ the realms/ of Non/sense, ab/solute.

The accented linking of phrasing "Fate *sum* mons *Mon* archs *must*" makes the summons all the stronger, and the fit of the "In prose and verse" line makes the wrenching of the next — the "of *Non* sense, *ab* sol *ute,*" with its linking across a pause and a comma — the more forceful, as *sense, ab* is an odder unit than *and verse.*

> Shadwell/ alone,/ of all/ my sons,/ is he
> Who stands/ confirmed/ in full/ stupidity.
> The rest/ to some/ faint mean/ing make/ pretence,
> But Shad/well ne/ver de/viates in/to sense.

The first accent on Shad*well* seems dubious, so that the second *Shad*well comes as the more downright, like the two stresses in stu *pid*/i *ty*, and the balanced stresses on *some* and *nev*/er.

Pope, too, capitalizes upon odd units:

> Slight is/ the sub/ject, but/ not so/ the praise,
> If She/ inspire,/ and He/ approve/ my lays. . . .
> In tasks/ so bold,/ can lit/tle men/ engage,
> And in/ soft bo/soms, dwells/ such might/y Rage?

Donne is much like Pope in cleverly crossing caesuras and in accenting his own meanings:

> There I/ should see/ a sun,/ by ri/sing set,
> And by/ that set/ting, end/less day/ beget;
> But that/ Christ on/ this cross/ did rise/ and fall,
> Sin had/ eter/nally/ benight/ed all.

Christ and *sin* here, like *Fate* in Dryden's lines, are suspended between two stressed syllables, so that there is a constructed hovering of choice over these important words.

Spenser's is another matter, a third kind of discrepancy. In his "Epithalamion," meter does not play across phrase or lexicon meaningfully.

> Ye learn/èd sis/ters,/ which/ have oft/entimes
> Been to/ me aid/ing,/ others to/ adorn,
> Whom ye/ thought wor/thy of/ your grace/ful rhymes,
> That even/ the great/est did/ not great/ly scorn
> To hear/ their names/ sung in/ your sim/ple lays,
> But joy/èd in/ their praise.

Here is simple pattern of stress after pause, which emphasizes minor words not for the words' sake but for the pattern's sake, even doubling the stress in many of the large refrain lines. Milton wrote similarly in "Lycidas"; and later, as in Keats, we find an extension of the freedom. The last lines of Keats's "Elgin Marbles" read:

> So do/ these won/ders a/ most diz/zy pain,
> That ming/les Gre/cian gran/deur with/ the rude
> Wasting/ of old/ Time — with/ a bil/lowy main —
> A sun/ — a shad/ow of/ a mag/nitude.

The measured reading here is not a possible alternative; it is just bad. No possible variety of thought or nuance is brought out by this regularity; so it is subordinated to the irregularity which is provided by the sense and which is indeed beautiful: a *sun* — a *shad*ow of a *mag*nitude, each stress followed by its lengthening shadow, in the dash, the prepositional phrase, and the length of the final word. Now Keats is doing even more than Spenser and Milton did to subdue the metrical structure to the substance. And note, for example, Arnold's lines of substance in "Dover Beach" in contrast to Swinburne's lines more metrically adapted.

Modern free verse extends the possibilities of this Spenserian and Miltonian measure, which does not foster ambiguity in its freedoms. See, for example, Henley's "London Voluntaries":

> St. Mar/garet's bells,
> Quiring their/ innocent,/ old-world/ canticles,
> Sing/ in the stor/ied air . . .
> O the low,/ ling/ering lights!/ The large/ last gleam . . .
> And the cal/low, gray-faced/ Hospital. . . .

Like Arnold's "Dover Beach," it makes scansion fall apart! This is true too of Whitman's verse and even of H.D.'s:

> The light/ passes
> from ridge/ to ridge,
> from flower/ to flower —
> the hypaticas,/ wide-spread
> under/ the light
> grow/ faint —
> the petals/ reach inward,
> the blue/ tips bend
> toward the blu/er heart
> and the flow/ers are lost.

In this cadence, such regularization of the stresses to any two in a line, though it is possible, does no good to the poem. The essential effect is the free play of reference and sound, not to be related either correlatively or ambiguously to any steady measure. Instead of setting sentence against meter, free verse sets phrase against line, achieving its own sort of discrepancy by line breaks that serve to counter phrases. The line "To the *end* of the *town*, the *world* came and *went*" may become

> *To*
> the end of the town, the world came and *went*

or, among other possibilities,

> To the end of the town, the *world*
> *came*
> and *went*

the line-ends providing stresses where the natural phrasing would not.

Along with the other uses of stress, this use is more important to the contemporary poet than syllable count, which ignores stress. The light, little ripples of extra syllables, so liked by nineteenth-century poets after Coleridge's encouragement in his preface to "Christabel," have become stronger in their number and power of irregularity; but still, as a whole, our verse is a stressed-verse, concordant, ambiguous, or freely cadenced as the poet wishes. In the past century, in the work of Blake and Yeats, we may see wonderfully complex developments of the ambiguous use. In Blake's *Tiger*, as we have noted, the shift from falling to rising pattern yet retains the expectation of falling, so that *"Tiger"* in the first line will be paralleled by *"Could* frame" in the last, against the lexical and phrasal importance of *frame* and *fear*.

> Tiger,/ tiger,/ burning/ bright
> In the/ forests/ of the/ night,
> What im/mortal/ hand or/ eye
> Could frame/ thy fear/ful sym/metry?

But after the stress imperatives of the first line, simple meaning leads to a reading very different from this. In the second line, *in* and *of* would not be stressed; in the fourth, the whole measure would turn iambic; but note how effectively and importantly *Could* and *thy* and *ful* can receive the stress of meaning when the measure demands it. Here again there is the hovering ambiguity of combination we have seen in the earlier colloquial poets, here much heightened. Similarly in the third stanza, and throughout, the lines that could well be read iambically are heightened by the metric pressure toward trochaic so that we come effectively to the final "Dare frame/ thy fear/ful sym/metry?"

Yeats's usage is still more complex, because he adds stress in a way which reverses expectation. In "Her Praise":

> Though she/ had young/ men's praise/ and old/ men's blame,
> Among/ the poor/ both old/ and young/ gave her/ praise.

Or in "Self and Soul":

> When such/ as I/ cast out/ remorse
> So great/ a sweet/ness flows/ into/ the breast
> We/ must laugh/ and we/ must sing,
> We/ are blest/ by ev/erything,
> Ev/erything/ we look/ upon/ is blest.

Here even the number of beats is held in suspension. The pattern is iambic, the beat four or five, so we feel that initial syllables have been withheld; at the same time it is possible in some lines to suppress one beat rather than add initially. Thus, possibly,

> So great/ a sweetness flows/ into the breast . . .
> Ev/erything we look/ upon is blest.

This power of alternatives makes Yeats a marvel to me. For others, other powers of sound are more valuable: the containment of certain classicists; the rising-above-it-all of the poets of cadence. At any rate, it is in the small breaks in poetic pattern that we may discern the philosopher behind the poet. Discrepancy may be minimal and of minor significance; it may be maximal and irrelevant; it may be moderate and important. So we see different kinds of integrations into wholes, when we are willing to read literally both the sound and the sense.

Such a merging is less possible for prose because its sound stresses are never so separated. The use of patterns like the Latin *cursus* — certain expectable units of stress setting up tensions between rising and falling rhythms, as in the final accent patterns of sentences, *went to Chicago; went to Connecticut;* or *went to South San Francisco* — did achieve in prose some effect of triumphant coincidence by merging not counter but merely infrequent measures with meanings, while avoiding trochaic beat. And in underlying ways, though without such formulas, our prose still moves in and out of expectable units of phrasing; the Biblical parallel, for example, or the "poetic" suspensive participial construction. But most inventive in our day is the concept of American idiom, held by William Carlos Williams and others, which establishes the phrase as a poetic unit and lets stress play across it by use of line structure. At the end of the nineteenth century, Robert Louis Stevenson wrote in his "On Some Technical Elements of Style in Literature" that the two contrasting units of poetry are the foot and the group, or unit of sense, and that in prose "the phrase is the strict analogue of the group." This analogue Williams carries over into poetry, keeping it from prosaicness by the counter-stress of the line.

Autumn

A stand of people
by an open

grave underneath
the heavy leaves

celebrates
the cut and fill
for the new road
where

an old man
on his knees

reaps a basket-
ful of
matted grasses for
his goats

As in the foot-measured *Elegy*, in this phrase measure the units at times coincide, at times do not. A *stand of people* is like *the knell* in "The curfew tolls the knell of parting day," while *grave underneath* is like *-few tolls*, or *of par*. As Williams later, in *Asphodel*, for example, experimented with longer phrases, he kept them firm with closer correlation to line stresses.

Looking at prose with its phrasal divisions written as if in lines, we may see the contrast:

> I cannot praise a fugitive and cloistered virtue,
> unexercised and unbreathed,
> that never sallies out and sees her adversary,
> but slinks out of the race
> where that immortal garland is to be run for,
> not without dust and heat.

Without counter-measure, there is nevertheless the variety, the rhythm that comes from pattern, in the adapting of one phrasal unit to the next. First, the basic statement, subject, verb, and object with modifiers; then additional modifiers in participial form; then a doubled relative clause as new modifier; then a clausal modifier of the last noun in that preceding clause; then a negative modifier of its predecessor, now phrasal rather than clausal and thus returning to catch up the non-clausal as well as the rhythmic pattern of the earlier participles. This is strong patterning, and it is autonomous; it does not rely upon, or work against, the counter-pattern of a meter.

Lacking the interest in double measure, prose accentuates, by repetition, its singleness of design. Without cutting across the accents of word and phrase, prose takes a larger breath and adapts itself to them, then stresses the adaptation. Proverbs and aphorisms are good examples of design in prose. *A rolling/ stone/ gathers no moss,* without close measure, shows nevertheless a pattern of recurrence, in *s* and long *o* sounds, and in the final stresses. *Give me liberty/ or give me death* accentuates the contrast between *liberty* and *death* by setting them in parallel structures. The *Gettysburg Address* is a structure of the greatest prosaic intricacy, beginning by contrasting the long temporal phrase *Fourscore and seven years ago* to the short and immediate *now,* by contrasting the chief verbs *brought forth* and *now we are engaged,* and by contrasting the past qualifiers *conceived* and *dedicated* to the present *testing;* ending with cumulative contrasts *of, by,* and *for,* moving toward the final locating phrase *from the earth* in contrast to the beginning *on this continent.*

Such designs of sound in structure, whether double or single, are further heightened by their counterplay with logic and reference. The fabric can grow more and more richly complex or more and more starkly simple. But its main lines run clearly and distinguishably throughout, in their patterns of recurrence.

In prose, there is less possibility of play of one frame across another, because the frame of measure is not so firmly established. Not foot-foot-foot-foot as in marching, but the swing of leg in hip and knee, as in less regular, more variable, walking. Nevertheless, the differences of tone we have noted in metrics may still be seen in prose, if we take meter as simple free measure. If we take the essential verb as the beat or the stride, then the three structurally contrasting passages with which we began this study may be scanned in contrast also. With / marking verbs and x nouns, adjectives, and phrases, in Lawrence's passage, the beat would move

$$
\begin{array}{l}
\text{x x x /x. x x. x / x x. / x x x} \\
\text{/ x x x / x x. / x / x x. x x x x x / x.} \\
\text{x x x / x. x x / x x x. / / / x x.}
\end{array}
$$

The variation is upon the recurrent end-pattern of / x x, or verb-object.

Then Russell's passage would be

$$
\begin{array}{l}
\text{x x x / x x: x x (/) x x x x, x x x (/) x x (/).} \\
\text{x / x x, / x x x (/) x (/) x x. / x x x x.} \\
\text{/ (/) x x x x.}
\end{array}
$$

Only the first part of the first sentence is like Lawrence's — with verb-phrase-phrase. But the colon makes it and the others work with substresses under long sustained statements with long phrasal sequences.

Huxley's prose, like Keats's poetry, makes even less of periods:

x x x x x x x / x x x x x x x x
x x x. x x / / x x x. / x / x x x x / x x.
/ x x x / x x x x x x / x x x x.

The piling up of adjectives and phrases is eloquent in the first sentence; for which the other sentences are, in effect, minor echoes or appositions. The beat therefore provides the focus for the multiple phrased endings: too large . . . too small; animal . . . human; too much . . . a little lower . . . , the final unit swelling back toward the beginning fullness.

In summary: Lawrence steps with short strides, Russell controls substrides by longer strides, while Huxley minimizes their significance to "A sun — a shadow of a magnitude."

IN METAPHOR AND LEXICON

As for figurative language: What is it trying to figure? When you look up the definition of *dove* in Webster's *Dictionary*, you find: "(dŭv) n. 1. A pigeon — applied specifically to many of the smaller species, as the turtle-dove, mourning dove, etc. 2. One regarded as pure and gentle. 3. The emblem of the Holy Spirit." The primary definition here serves to do what *de-fin-ition* purports to do, to draw the limits around the reference, to put the bird first in the pigeonhole and then in the special section, for smaller pigeons, marked *doves*. A more extended description would list the necessary (pigeonlike) and sufficient (dovelike) traits of the family Columbidae. Then, a printed reference to a dove would give us at least a minimal image of a dove, that is, an imagined likeness or representation; and a listing of qualities such as color, size, sound, shape would make the image more and more specific. "The fat, gray dove sits on the branch and coos." We say we can "see" it and "hear" it, as the word calls up a "concrete" image.

Then also we may associate certain other images, qualities, and concepts with this dove. Webster lists two possibilities: pureness and gentleness, which the dove suggests; and a concept, Holy Spirit, with which it is associated as an emblem or symbol, that is, as a visible sign of an idea. I myself also associate the dove with the concept of peace. Webster's definition of *peace* is "1. A pact or agreement to end hostilities; 2. A state of tranquility or quiet . . . 3. Harmony in personal relations . . . 4. Freedom from fears. . . ." These meanings, even the first, are less concrete, less imageable than a dove; they are more abstract, more conceptual; they draw qualities out of objects, drawing the qualities of tranquillity, harmony, freedom, for example, out of the specific situations that include them, as doves today in political argument are drawn in contrast to hawks.

Concrete and abstract references thus interact; not only may the object *dove* suggest the concept *peace* with its various qualities of concord and tranquillity, but the concept *peace* may suggest the object *dove* and other objects: olive branches, by traditional symbolization, or hammocks, firesides, or fishing rods by more personal, seasonal association. So references to things and to qualities support each other in our language; and, when we are particularly conscious of their artful use and relation, we stress them: the "vivid imagery" of a poet like Keats, the "complex abstractions" of a poet like Donne, or the specific embodiment of concept in image through the "profound symbols" of a poet like Blake. All of these rest in definition plus association or connotation; that is, in the extension of primary or ordinate qualities by secondary or subordinate qualities, as the image of the dove may support the quality of tranquillity, and the concept of tranquillity suggest the presence of the bird.

Metaphor is not so simple. While image and concept present, and symbol uses image to stand for concept, metaphor, as its own reference indicates, carries across or transfers, and that action is not simple. Why not? Because qualities usually combined one way are recombined in another. The dove is taken out of its pigeonhole and transferred to, let us say, a cabbage-hole. "The dove is a cabbage" — not a stringbean, not an avocado, but a cabbage. It is not long and thin but relatively round and fat. It has not a smooth, slick surface but a ruffled surface. It is among birds, we may suggest in this context, as a cabbage is among vegetables.

What have we done by this transference? It is a relatively superficial one, lacking depth of context, except for the endearment of *le petit chou*, yet it is characteristic in structure. We have reversed the ordinate and subordinate qualities in the definition of *dove*, emphasizing those of shape and texture, which do not appear essential in delimitation, and underplaying those of bird and pigeon, which set it apart from the vegetable world. By putting the dove in the cabbage côte, we have given it vegetable traits — a round and solid leafiness — and have taken away part of its birdiness — its Columbidae characteristics of beak and claw — yet have retained, with the leafiness, its feathers and its round puffed profile, for the sake of the metaphor's own newly created relevance. In considering the dove-cabbage range — the relatively plump and ruffled within bird and vegetable worlds — we have based upon an *ad hoc* relation or proportion (more than a simple property) an *ad hoc* class, which, were it to be extended beyond this special context, might become a generally usable class. It is like the *foot* of table or mountain, now a dead metaphor, but one which, as live metaphor, works directly for its one created purpose. So the famous King Richard the Lionhearted takes the stout, royal heart of the king of beasts — that lion which is generally a large, carnivorous mammal of the cat family, having a tufted tail and a shaggy mane. This is the pride and pathos of metaphor: for its moment we are not bound by lexical boundaries.

Can it do as much for concept as for image — for peace as for dove? Most modern writers on metaphor suggest not; but I think this is because they are thinking of metaphor as a device for more vivid imagery in the fashion of our day. The many books on Shakespeare's, Milton's, Shelley's "imagery," which are in fact chiefly concerned with images created by metaphors, attest to this emphasis. But for the Elizabethans, and for some moderns like Emily Dickinson and W. H. Auden, the metaphors of concept are equally strong: Bacon's "Revenge is a kind of wild justice," Yeats's Love as "The supreme theme of Art and Song," Roethke's "We think by feeling," Frost's "Ah, when to the heart of man/ Was it ever less than treason/ To go with the drift of things . . ." For our own *peace*, our own *cold war* is not a bad metaphor; or, one of the more drastic dove-cabbage sort, "Peace is the anarchy of the good."

What is vital in both concrete and abstract metaphor is the sense of relative position within a group or class — the sort of position which, when carried out through the other implied places, yields allegory. If the dove is a cabbage, then the tanager is a carrot, and the parrot is a squash. It is only by maintaining the sense of relative place within the new category that the metaphor can keep, in such alien territory, the vestiges of its place in the old and thus have the best of both worlds — best, at any rate, as the context creates a value for it.

This transferral is what Aristotle means when he talks about genus to genus, species to species, and genus to species; and it is at the basis of his idea that extreme metaphors make riddles. In the Sphinx's riddle of man, for example, a wooden bird is bundled into the dovecote — the old man's cane or wooden leg. So also a fabric bird in that fine riddle:

> As I was going over the Bay Bridge,
> I saw something on a ledge.
> It had four fingers and a thumb,
> But was not made of flesh and bone.

By the same token, we may look at metaphors in English poetry. A ship is a large sea-going vessel, according to a dictionary definition; that is, like a dish or a truck or a boat, it is a container; then like a truck but not a dish, it goes; then like a boat but not a truck, it goes to sea; then unlike a boat, it is large. George Gascoigne in the final chorus of his *Glass of Government*, 1559, wrote of offspring,

> We care for them to keep them from the shelf
> Of such quick sands as we ourselves first found,
> When heady will did set our ships on ground.

Do we then ask: Our *what* on ground? and get for reply: *Our large sea-going vessels?* If so, it is not an adequate answer, because the context here shows a different interest, a subordinate characteristic, the way the vessel is steered and what human quality may misguide it. That heady will may ground a ship is not a fact essential to its definition, nor yet a fact contradictory or even contrary to it, but rather is a fact, generally irrelevant, made specifically relevant by the context, by the transfer of ship traits to character traits.

Similarly, when George Herbert writes of "Sweet spring, full of sweet days and roses,/ A box where sweets compacted lie," both *full* and *box* establish a context relevant to the container — like qualities of spring; though, in the dictionary, spring's essence is to leap up, to spurt, and thus, through derivation, to be the source or first stage of something, as of seasonal growth. Spring as a box, in turn, makes days and roses as candies possible; indeed, the two aid each other: *days* by preserving some of the temporality of *spring, roses* by emphasizing some of the object-quality of *sweets,* the parallel plurality of the two suggesting a qualitative by a quantitative likeness.

By the same token, in Henry Vaughan's

> I saw Eternity the other night,
> Like a great ring of pure and endless light,
> All calm, as it was bright,

eternity can be given substantiality by *ring* because it was *seen,* on the one hand, yet *endless,* on the other; the relevances it includes are in precarious balance. That a *like* is present here, to suggest a simile, seems not important; though sometimes, if the *like* really represents greater definitive likeness, a simile may carry us closer to simple analogy without much transfer. Herrick says, "The leaves will strew/ Gems in abundance upon you." Taylor asks, "Shall I be made/ A sparkling wildfire shop?" Swift predicts, "In your own heart you'll reap the fruit." Browning, "And thence ye must perceive the world's a dream." Meredith, "Lengths down our road each fir tree seems a hive/ In swarms outrushing from the golden comb." Frost, "A snow-drop spider, a flower-like froth." (Webster, "Froth: the bubbles caused in liquids by fermentation or agitation.") Auden, "Great buildings jostle in the sun for domination." ("Jostle [dimin. of joust]: To run against and shake; to elbow; to hustle; to crowd.") Each of these, even in the fragmentary unit quoted, establishes a context that makes shop, buildings, fruit, and dream relevant to human traits; makes gems, swarms, and froth relevant to natural ones. The essence of jostling is what buildings cannot do, and so the daring of the diminutive. And almost the most daring is the one that crosses the boundaries merely between two natural categories — the *snow-drop spider*. Fearful! And it is the fearfulness of the poem as a whole: "If design govern in a thing so small."

Other poets give us other types of metaphors: Spenser's body as palace, stars as lamps of love; Milton's eyelids of morn, flowers' gay wardrobe or sad embroidery; Cowley's bird with painted oars; Thomson's aerial magazines; Gray's Conquest's crimson wing; Collins' bright-haired sun; Smart's lily's silver bell; Keats's morning's eye; Tennyson's hungry heart; Lawrence's flowers like comets; Pound's sun fulvid as a lion; Crane's dice of bones and calyx of death's bounty; Thomas' green fuse. These are as a whole more sensuous, less conceptual, than the ones first quoted; that is, the context of relevance is more often sensory, especially visual, and especially in relation to human anatomy. But like the first group they move in time toward more and more emphasis on nature. Earlier, nature was put to establish a context for man; now it is put to clarifying contexts for itself in its multiplicity. Contemporary poets who see in the images of nature the symbols of man are apt also to seek in the cross-categories of nature the possibility of metaphors obliquely relevant to man.

Least metaphorical of the poets are the classical describers, the essentializers. For them metaphor's wrench from essence into context is too far-fetched. For all Shakespeare's scythes of time, and bare ruined choirs, he is more easy in phrasings closer to analogy, as in "Like as the waves make toward the pebbled shore/ So do our minutes hasten to their end." Shelley's vale of tears, Bryant's prairies, Arnold's sea of faith, come as near as they can to the naturalness of their transfer. As Wallace Stevens writes, "There are men of a valley/ Who are that valley." This is the spirit of the intensive figure — a kind of part for whole — metonymy or synecdoche. "Love is more thicker than forget/ more thinner than recall." Cummings, by wrenching the grammar, keeps the figures close to comparison. Or consider in Jeffers' *Lovely Rock*, "The star-color precipices." Webster says of *star:* "Any of the luminous bodies seen in the heavens; specif. Astron., any self-luminous celestial body . . . as distinguished from the much smaller bodies, known as planets, that shine by reflected light." Jeffers is ignoring the distinction; he is giving us the transfer from earth to heaven so easily, as if by analogy in terms of color, that we do not feel the metaphysical or sublime, romantic wrench. We accept rock self-luminous as if by reflected light, because of the intense and pure naturalness of the categories.

> . . . [I]t was the rock wall
> That fascinated my eyes and mind. Nothing strange: Light-gray
>   diorite with two or three slanting seams in it,
> Smooth-polished by the endless attrition of slides and flood; no
>   fern nor lichen, pure naked rock — as if I were
> Seeing rock for the first time.

Like poets, prose writers of a certain syntax would tend to prefer a certain sort of metaphor, and earlier writers would use it more than later. Metaphor, as a proportion, is a partial yet double statement, an *as* and an *if*. It accords best in the minds of those who delight in sentence, as Emerson does, for example. The qualifiers can do well with epithets, the symbolizers need the simplest nouns; but the verb of the predicate of relation is implicit if not explicit in metaphor. So Joyce is verbalist, figurist, in a way that a patient and receptive observer like Darwin or Huxley is not; so metaphor in our day is often secondary to image and symbol, as the play upon categories is secondary to the play upon senses and associations.

Our recent metaphors for metaphors, namely, *vehicle* and *tenor* from one point of view, *paradox* and *tension* from another, seem to me not very helpful. What kind of duck are we now trying to make of the art of trope? Trope, figure, metaphor — all suggest artistic action, doing some special shaping, turning, transferring of the language, for some effect. In proverbs, with their close shaping, we may see the best examples of all the old sorts of trope and figures of thought and speech, now nameless. Or, indeed, in George Puttenham's *Art of Poetry* (1584) we may see the names. But the present names, *vehicle* and *tenor*, mislead us. They make us, or me, think, "That singer shouldn't be riding in that rickshaw"; whereas what I should be thinking is "Where is he going?" or "Where has he gone, and to what effect?" *Vehicle* does mean a carrier, indeed so does the *-phor* in *metaphor*, like the *-fer* in *transfer;* but it is also the *meta,* the *trans,* that is important: Carried to where? to an alien land. This is foreign trade, as Aristotle makes clear in his list of odd uses in the *Poetics.*

127

But *foreign* need not necessarily mean hostile or opposed; that is, the alien category need not be contradictory, or contrary, thus setting up paradox or tension by negation; but is, rather, simply different, irrelevant until made relevant by context. That is, again, the extraordinary transfer is not based on central, ordinate characteristics, but on peripheral, subordinate characteristics in relatively similar or proportionate position; not from dove to anti-dove or to hawk, but from dove to cabbage. The world of metaphor is not so much a world of vehicular tension as a world of holiday, of variety, of free-wheeling, where within the familiar limitations of every day a word can move and transport us, making first qualities last and last first, in the crosscurrent of values. Like Hopkins' Peace, wild wood dove is metaphor's dove.

> He comes with work to do, he does not come to coo,
> He comes to brood and sit.

IN CONTRAST AND CONTRADICTION

The power to state is also the power to negate. *The boy is building the boat. The boy is not building the boat.* One whole sentence contradicts the other whole sentence. To the degree that the boy is building the boat, the contradiction is false; or there may be a middle position, the boy *may be building* the boat. The truer the statement, the falser the contradiction, but paradox may allow for a mixture of degrees or of meanings — the boy is building in one way, though not in another.

As we have seen, the analyzable parts of a statement may be treated separately from their whole, and negatives when so applied make for denials other than contradictions; that is, they deny an adjective, a noun, or a verb, but not a whole statement. Notice for example, the contrasting pairs:

> *The boy* is not building the boat.
> You are building the boat.
>
> The boy *is* not building the boat.
> The boy was building the boat.
>
> The boy is not *building* the boat.
> The boy is destroying the boat.
>
> The boy is not building the *boat*.
> The boy is building the boats.

The contrasts can apply to any of the terms and to time, person, and number as well as to reference.

In application to terms, then, negatives may be simple denials, *not a boat* or *non-boat*; or antithesis, *anti-boat*; or contrasts, *a car, not a boat*; or just differences, perhaps even irrelevant, *a statue, not a boat*. These are separate and distinguishable enough; but, because of current confusions about phenomena in the physical world, we seem to confuse the language for them also. A geographic pole, a magnetic field, a strained muscle, an electric current, a plant cell, a political election — all offer examples of opposition and tension that we do not clearly discriminate.

A central metaphor is that of a circle. "Diametrically opposite" would mean a contrast; two positive poles with a neutral midpoint; or a positive mean, as in Aristotle's mean between an excess, prodigality, and a defect, parsimony.[1] "Antithetical" then would represent a positive and an opposing negative pole with a neutral midpoint. "Polarization" would tend to suggest a directional increase in degree from negative to positive pole, with midscale at the midpoint. "Difference," irrelevant difference, would be represented by a perpendicular to the diameter, a right angle at the center.

Here metaphor functions, in the relating of unrelateds — *bicycles are artichokes*. As David Hawkins says: A green logarithm or an unhappy molecule seem incongruous because we think of differentiating traits as being well defined only with respect to the genus that they differentiate.[2]

It is useful to distinguish *American* from *non-American*, from *anti-American*, from *Australian*, from *fat*; yet constantly we find such non-discriminations as the following: "Dewey's educational theory was formed in the hope that a proper educational synthesis would overcome certain ancient polarities and dualisms in educational thought. The antitheses between the child and society, interest and discipline, vocation and culture, knowledge and action, must all be resolved and ultimately harmonized . . ."[3] Or, ". . . some great styles are characterized by a profound polarity — an inner contradiction that springs from the experience upon which they are built. These are the styles of "open" form — the Gothic, the Romantic, as well as the Baroque. The experience of power on the one hand, and of utter lack of it on the other."[4] Dangers lie along these verbal crossways, and Morris Cohen clarifies them well: "Logic enables us to organize fields of experience by providing us with relations like exclusion and inclusion whose recognition constitutes sanity. A day cannot become a piece of butter and a color cannot become a sneeze. . . . Everything is connected

[1] *Nicomachean Ethics*, II, 7.
[2] *Daedalus*, Summer, 1962.
[3] Richard Hofstadter, *Daedalus*, Summer, 1962, p. 522.
[4] Carl Friedrich, *Horizon*, II, 6.

in definite ways with definite other things, so that its full nature is not revealed except by its position and relations within a system. . . . While the application of the principle of causality thus implies the genuine existence of constant class properties, it is well to note that in order that these classes be recognizable there must be discontinuities in nature. . . . Opposites such as immediacy and mediation, unity and plurality, the fixed and the flux, substance and function, ideal and real, actual and possible, etc., like the north (positive) and south (negative) poles of a magnet, all involve each other when applied to any significant entity. . . . A type is an ideal configuration of distinguishable but not always separable features. It has scientific value in that it enables us to look for and identify certain characters after we have recognized others that co-exist with them in a given type." [5]

What shall we make of the seeming identifications of *anti's, non's*, and *contra's*? Suppose we try to disentangle them. A simple assertion is, *It is so*; a simple negation, *It is not so*. Such a negation is the most easy-going possible; we may call it permissive: it lets the subject be a multiplicity of anything except *so*. A more extreme, basically dualistic form of negation is antithesis, or negative correlation; in these terms, the two statements *It is so* and the contradictory *It is not so* make up the total of possibilities. *So* and *non-so* or *not-so* constitute the total positive and negative ranges; here is basic dichotomy, binarism, symmetry, anti-matter, in polar positive and negative. A third sort of negation is more limited; it works within the others' extremes, setting up its negative opposite on an axis of likeness; here, *It is not so* means *Rather, it is this*, the contrast being set up between the two positives *this* and *so*.

For each of these negatives, the graphic picture of the circle tends to be used, with its terminology of *center* and *nucleus, periphery* and *circumference, diameter* and *diametrically opposite, pole* and *polarity*. We see that we may call negation or denial diametrically opposite to affirmation, along an axis of degree, with *It may be so* in the middle. Similarly for terms: *non* or *un interested* is opposite to *interested, non* or *un moving* to *moving, non* or *un sweet* to *sweet, non* or *un American* to *American*, along an axis of degree, with one positive and one negative pole, toward the positive, from zero or minimum to maximum.

Negative correlation or antithesis then builds a whole negative dimension on this zero point. The more something is present for the positive, the more it is absent for the negative. The two ranges of degree move

[5] *Reason and Nature* (Glencoe, Ill.: The Free Press, 1953), pp. 144n, 150, 154, 165.

symmetrically away from each other, across from a zero center. The anti side, as negative mirror of the positive side, would move to destroy it if they coincided. Anti-interest-sweetness-moving-American as active opposition in which the whole negative half has power to annihilate the positive half may be sometimes, especially today, confused with simple negative, on the grounds that he who is not for me is against me. *Non* or *un-Republican* does not tend to be confused with *anti-Republican* any more than *uncertain* tends to be taken for *anti-certain*; yet *un-American* may be taken for *anti-American*, and, as in Mr. White's article, *unintellectualist* may be taken for *anti-intellectualist*. These are two very different sorts of opposition: one across a simple diameter with a moderate center; the other across a double diameter with a neutral center. A grade of 70% on the first is a grade of -70% on the second.

The third sort of negation is that of contrast in the classical sense, implying a positive center as basis or axis for the contrast, and poles not so extreme, but both positive extremes to the more positive center. Interaction on a double axis provides the dynamics of this relation of contrast. In *not so* but *thus, thus* is the positive contrasting term, as *red* contrasts with *green*, or *Republican* with *Democrat*: unlikes on the basis of some sort of like, such as color or political party. What Aristotle calls the excess, *prodigality*, and the defect, *parsimony*, of the mid-virtue, are such contrasting positives with a double positive center which partakes of the qualities of each. In *not sweet, but sour, sour* is the positive opposite contrasting to *sweet*, as is *bored* to *interested*, *blocked* to *moving*, *Australian* to *American*; each provides in its denial a limited alternative with positive qualities of its own.

To complete the relation, we must consider in addition to the three sorts of negatives a fourth relation, that of simple difference — *not so, but another; not bicycle, but artichoke* — what is called statistically irrelevant and indicated by a perpendicular. In these two we get *difference, disinterest, de-*sweetened, *dis*affiliate, *dis-American*; that is, separate from, to be distinguished from. So graphs may relate age and height, for example, along a curve between two axes, as Pythagoras noted the relating of heat and dryness at their circumference. And in language, metaphor functions by asserting likeness or identity of these two: *age is weight*; that is the identifying of irrelevant entities, on the basis of characteristics irrelevant to their definition.

It has been suggested that certain of the distinctions I have been making here are related in language to the functions of certain parts of speech. For example, in "Comparisons of Word-Association Responses in English,

French, German, and Italian," [6] Mark Rosenzweig reports not only the likeness of responses but also that about seven-eights of responses by opposite were to adjectives by adjectives, like *high . . . low*; and that coordinate responses tended to be substantive, like *chair . . . table*. Such distinctions are not surprising when it is considered that we think of different coordinate or subordinate objects, but of qualities in a single scale of degrees from high to low. But we may also find that parts of speech are not limited in usage to one or another of the negatives. So we may have the adjective *sweet*, with a gamut of degrees of sweet, a general negative *not sweet*, an antithesis *anti-sweet*, a contrast *sour*, a difference *tall*. Or a noun, *justice*, general negative *not justice*, antithesis *anti-justice*, contrast *mercy*, difference *imagination*. Or a verb *go*, negative *not go*, antithesis *anti-go* or *obstruct*, contrast *come* or *stop*, depending on the axis of likeness, and difference *see*. Perhaps the main difference lies in the complexity of reference, inasmuch as complexity, a combination of like and different qualities, is needed for contrast, while one simple quality is basic to a scale of gradation. So *house* and *garage* easily contrast. But they can also, nevertheless, be thought of on respective scales of *houseness* and *garageness*. "Out in the West where men are *men*" provides a colloquial example. But, on the other hand, such simple qualities as sweet and sour can contrast, not merely range on a scale, when they achieve the complexity of substance in cooking — in a sweet-sour sauce, for example. And actions may be seen as progressive along a scale, or as contrasting complexes: *Stop-Go*, or *Come-Hesitate-Stop-Go*, for example.

A negative can, then, be neutral, emphasizing degree; opposing, emphasizing totality; contrasting, emphasizing parts; or disassociating, another sort of whole. With reference to games: a race, with one goal and a series of winners; a boxing-match with a knockout; a two-goal game like football; and one not in the same league.

Some negatives can provide a false choice in disguise — weak or strong, a middle between extremes. Contrast provides true choice.

The question of evil too is pertinent. For a pluralist, evil is failure, is a step in the gradient toward good, or a variety of contrasts or differences. For a dualist, it is one half of an encompassing contrast of two major positives; as in Manicheanism, evil is a positive force. For a monist, it is obliterative, unless it itself is obliterated — a war to the death, he who is not for is against, because there is only one positive position.

The contrast or antonym to *bad* or *mal* — as to *dis* and even *anti* or *contra* — is not *yes*; rather it is, for *mal*, *well* or *good*; yet many modern

[6] *American Journal of Psychology*, September, 1961.

critics confuse the two contrasts by identifying *mal* with *non* by saying, for example, that poetry they consider bad, like the eighteenth century's, is really not poetry at all. There is neither Aristotelean nor modern evolutionary basis for this usage, but only the totalitarian *all or none* basis of complementaries. When Hoffa was indicted for "malfeasance, disfeasance and nonfeasance," a good strong totalitarian might well have added anti-feasance to the list to signify the destructive force of the other negatives. The yes-yes–no-no of contrast, the yes-no of degrees of some, are carried further by the yes-no complementarity of *all-none*. *No Parking*, for example, often implies a contrast to *No Unloading*, or degrees of negation like "No Parking from 5–7 P.M."; but sometimes, if parking is one's only and total motive, it may be absolute.

Why are we running into so many difficulties with these concepts? There are reasons both ideological and linguistic, I think. Ideologically we have moved away from interest in categories and contrasts, with one sort of negative; to interest in degrees, scales, with another; to the recent interest in absolute positives and negatives, in anti-matter, complementarity, negative correlation, with a third meaning for *not*; and all too easily those have run together, without thought of their radically differing implications. Further, technically, dictionaries of synonyms and antonyms have confused us by using inconsistent principles of definition, mixing sometimes contrastive, sometimes negative, only infrequently real *anti* meanings. They deal with "opposites," yet opposites as we have seen on our circles may be opposite in various ways, generally or specifically (diametrically), positively or negatively. The whole lot gets mixed up together. An "opposite" may be a friendly "opposite member," or an "opponent." Paul Henle talks about pairs of opposites like day and night, war and peace, as contrasts.[7] Morris Cohen talks about opposites like ideal and real, actual and possible, again as contrasts.[8] Note then the difference from Amerigo Castro's dialectic of possible and impossible: can we have a dialectic with a mere *im*, not a *contra*? Is not the actual a part of the mere impossible, as a contrast to the possible? How about a dichotomy of presence-absence: does not a dialectic like a dichotomy have a zero-center, and what then about half-present, not-all present? I am playing colloquialisms against potential graphs consciously here because I think sometimes they have been played unconsciously (not, I hope, anti-consciously). What of Jakobson's dichotomy of the relation of similarity to the relation of contiguity, and his

[7] *Language, Thought, and Culture* (Ann Arbor: University of Michigan Press, 1958), p. 49.
[8] Cohen, *op. cit.*, p. 165.

twelve polarities, as of interruption-continuance? What about Bruner's antinomies of detachment and commitment, deferral and immediacy,[9] his reference to "Bohr's now famous dictum that you cannot know somebody at the same time in the light of love and the light of justice," and his reference to "two traditions almost as antithetical as romanticism and nineteenth-century scientism," [10] in relation to his praise of Freud's resolution of polarities, child-adult, rational-irrational, art-science, the all-or-some distinctions replaced by continuities? [11]

In our increased interest in relations rather than part-wholes or atomism, we have not been careful enough to help our vocabulary keep sharp. We *do* have a good set of relational terms to help us: positives, as . . . as, so . . . that, if . . . then; disjunctives, either . . . or; negatives, neither . . . nor; mixed, and, but, yet, however. But too often we use the easy abbreviation *vs.* for all distinctions. The lecturer says salt should be distinguished from cinnamon; and the student writes *salt vs. cinnamon*, making an opponent out of what is not even a negative but a mere difference. *Versus* means to turn, turn back, confront, face, in the sense of to be opposite, even as mildly as one line of poetry faces another by turning again to the left margin. Various *versus* words are available to us: *con*verse, *con*vert, like *con*trast, *with; a*verse and *contra*vert, inimical to; *di*verse, different from; these parallel the distinctions we have been considering, except that there is no simple negative *non* or *un* verse except in the specialized sense of unpracticed, not "with it." There are also *extro, intro, in, ob, per, re, sub, trans*, of which at least *inverse, obverse, reverse* have to do with kinds of symmetries or reproductions of symmetries. Deep as our language will take us then, we find emphasis on multiplicity of uses, a narrowing only by a kind of selectivity, by a kind of evaluative focusing, from negative, contrast, and diversity to the simple dualism of the all-none, pro-con contradiction. Indeed, a strong value judgment seems needed to reduce to this form. As we have seen, of all our negatives, the denial, *no*, is the simplest; that is, it asserts nothing: no contrasting positive, no diverse other, no complementary negative. *No-yes* are the working pair for negation-assertion; for contrast, they are *yes-no–no-yes*; for contradiction, the *no* means *contra*, and the *yes*, not merely affirmation, but *pro*; thus there is, as in *mal* and *bon*, a judgment involved. And judgments need wary relating to, not unwary identification with, descriptive statements.

What then of those approbative terms *tension* and *polarity* in modern

---

[9] Jerome S. Bruner, *On Knowing* (Cambridge, Mass.: Belknap Press, 1962), p. 23.
[10] *Ibid.*, p. 152.
[11] *Ibid.*, p. 154.

critical judgment? To what relations or attributes do they refer? What are the strains on the rope, the muscle, the nerve, the purpose, the social or artistic structure? Most probably they would seem to be the pulls of contrast, or diversity, or of two different positive forces, between mercy and justice, between tennis and golf, between rhyme and reason, between stability and change. As Winifred Nowottny says of poetry, ". . . there are, at every level of poetic organization, features of language which can be structured in more than one way at a time, so as to set up tension between the various structurings; metaphor is not the only source of multiple relationships." [12] Other so-called tensions, between positive and negative, or between pro and con, would be only momentary; the first, moving to other alternatives; the second, quickly obliterative.

Polarity is today taken to be axial and directional; it is not dialectical or dichotomous; it does not establish tensions of contrast, though these might exist along the axis; it provides, as we might say, focus as well as direction for the spiral of symmetries round its helix. Between rotation and direction, between antimony and polarity, then, there may be tension, when these are looked at together, in contrast.

For human beings, metaphorically, the same distinctions need to be made. A good model for productive tensions can be a marriage, with its contrasts of two individuals and so of traits and function masculine and feminine; another is a work of art with its tensions and contrasts between reference and medium. Polarities and antitheses are not so productive; for them, moves directional, dichotomous, or counter are apt to remove the tensions as rapidly as possible, as competition becomes monopoly. Two nations or two political parties can create strong tensions in contrast, but not in head-on, all-or-none relations. The Hegelian dialectic, which I suppose we misunderstand, sets a Dionysus against an Apollo; the Marxists, one economy against another; the Coleridgean fusion of opposite or discordant qualities, "the novel and the familiar," "a more than usual state of emotion with more than usual order." All these are productive contrasts, not negatives or antinomies. Note too that Coleridge's *discordant* is not, as it is usually taken, a mere synonym for *opposite*; rather, it is an alternative, meaning different — the perpendicular to opposition's diameter. The opposite of discordant is concordant or harmonious, and *harmony*, the arm and the elbow, means *jointed*, the joining, at right angles, of differences. So Coleridge's *novel* and *familiar* are opposites; his *emotion* and *order*, discordances or differences.

Not our classic sources but ourselves are confused about relations in our

[12] *The Language Poets Use* (University of London, 1962), p. 97.

135

fields of action. Our language has not pressed our variety of just distinctions, and our desire to keep these distinctions clear has not pressed our language. It is dismaying to try to list the many places one may find a mixing of terms. The footing is commonly precarious. My fear is that we keep letting negatives, contrasts, and even differences fall into antinomies because we wish to, because we wish a simple dualistic pro or con evaluation with us on the good side and nobody worth anything on the bad. We destroy plurality, multiplicity, variety by a verbal sleight-of-hand which reduces *some*'s to *all*'s or *none*'s and reduces directions and interplays to final confrontations. Etymologically our *anti*'s were once *and*'s, and our *contra* mere *con*; even our disjunctions allowed for positive choices, while the positive-negative choice is merely *this* or *anti-this*.

I wish that our language might do its best for our thought; with *non*, *un*, *not* as negatives; *anti* or *contra* as complementary antitheses or contradictions; *dis* as difference; and two contrasting differences along an axis of likeness called contrasts or opposites. Then we should prevent the sorts of mixtures of negatives and contraries we get, for example, in Osgood's *Measurement of Language*, and should rather build on Stanley Payne's wise warning that open, dual, and multiple questions get very different answers. To ask "What you allow or not allow?" then, gets a very different result from asking "Would you allow or forbid?" [13]

Perhaps our underlying wisdom about these differences persists in revealing itself in humor. There are countless jokes based on each of the discrepancies we have here observed.

For antithesis, for instance, hypostatization of absence: The customer says, "I'll have my coffee without cream." The waiter replies, "You'll have to have it without milk, we didn't get any cream today."

For variety: The ticket buyer in the railway station asks, "Why do you have two clocks at opposite ends of the station, telling different time?" The stationmaster replies, "Sure and if they told the same time, why would we have two?"

For direction: The man asks the worm, "Which end of you is which?" And the worm replies, "Which end are you talking to?"

And for contrast: A man asks his friend, "Do you believe in baptism?" The friend replies, "Believe in it? I've seen it done!" — a double contrast, and full of tensions, for those who like tensions!

This humor of ambiguity in subject or predicate recalls by contrast the humor of confusion between predicate and adjuncts that we noted in Chapter One. The stress here is on logic; the stress there was on syntax

[13] *The Art of Asking Questions* (Princeton: Princeton University Press, 1951).

and rhetoric; there as here the motive is to call attention to the simple norms by laughing at the absurdity of departure from them. The guru: "Life is a tree." The disciple: "It is?"

Syntactic choices move at the heart of logic, of metaphor, of measure, of modes and times of style. Negation of a noun is a choice different from negation of a verb. Metaphor capitalizes upon statement and concept more than upon phrase and thing. Measure relies heavily upon the movable portions of phrase. Certain purposes are aided by certain structures: the effect of shared process by the quickness of sentence; the effect of deliberate and judicious consideration by subordinate structures; the effect of impersonal and objective distance by the naming of quality and substance. Of all these the English language is equally capable, but about them its writers have not been equally enthusiastic: the majority over the years having chosen the structures and tones of process; the majority now choosing a balanced combination with subordinate objectivity in both poetry and prose.

Poetry and prose draw upon the same resources of grammar and meaning, and even to some degree of measure. The repetitions that establish design are closer for verse than for prose, in the unit of measure; in the focus on single image, concept, or figure; and in the units of sentence, as they comprise the larger makings of pattern. Given the bases of similarity in the medium of language, we should then be able to distinguish more precisely the varieties of division that make for likeness and difference.

Meter, metaphor, contradiction, like many other discriminable characteristics of art in language, are matters of proportion. Recurrence of stress, recurrence of analogy, recurrence of denial are proportioned how regularly, where, in what relation? Any repetition of any element may be so considered in relation: alliterative or rhyming sounds as well as stresses; metaphor and other figures of speech as well as figures of sound; figures of statement, question, exclamation, subjunction, as well as contrast and negation. The arts of rhetoric make use also of the arts of grammar and logic to give shape and form in sensory effect. Passions, feelings, thoughts, purposes — all can be grounded and strengthened in sense and the designs of sense.

The basic designs of sense that the material of language makes possible are not many, though the varieties of their combinations may be. The language settles into certain structures of apprehension; and individual styles are those that not so much change the norms as make use of them. Because the individual artist is dealing with whole and habitual structures, the isolation of elements in his work — of a word, a phrasal form, or a beat — is less relevant to his art than the sense of such elements in relation to each other. So proportion is relevant; so syntactic and referential relations.

It is not accidental that metrists of easy flow are often symbolists, not figurists; that figurists, on the other hand, use strong negatives, paradoxes, and counter-measures, creating a tension in meaning as well as in sound; and that strong external formalists in structure and measure prefer to subordinate than to set up the inner tensions of contradiction. As we might expect, then, for these three types of writers, the proportioning of chief parts of speech will differ accordingly. Nor does it appear to be accidental that preferences differ from time to time as well as from person to person, as Yakov Malkiel has suggested for the study of style.[14] Purpose of expression and of effect appears to draw upon the potentialities of the medium in certain basic ways for certain ends.

The advantage of attempting in one view to relate qualities of grammar, logic, and rhetoric to each other in quantitative or proportional terms is the advantage of a whole view though a superficial one. Such studies as I have suggested here raise more questions than they answer, and do not cope with crucial problems of linguistic on the one hand and of literary values on the other. Neither a grammatical nor a rhetorical system comes clear, nor a system of preferences; but rather, at best, some suggestions for the basis of preference, that is, for the available possibilities of choice and intent. Especially for prose I think the possibilities of art should become more and more recognizable with the simplifying of terminology of the grammar of English. An easy recognition of most connected phrases and clauses as qualifying words will allow us to appreciate the basic minimal, and thus the more complex, patterns of predicates with their adjuncts, which make up our designs of statement.

As Richard Foster Jones wrote, "To determine the prevalence and importance of a thought pattern in a climate of opinion, the first test is obviously the frequency with which it or its constituent elements occur. If, however, this test is carried too far, it degenerates into mere statistics which ignore the fact that repetition may evince conventionality only. In its life cycle an idea may begin as a thought, proceed as an emotion, and expire as a habit." [15] So we saw in the sequence from adjectives to nouns

[14] "A Tentative Typology of Romance Historical Grammars," *Linqua*, IX, No. 4 (1960).
[15] *The Triumph of the English Language* (Palo Alto: Stanford University Press, 1953), p. ix.

in the nineteenth century. So John Holloway shows us in the change from Addison's noble metaphor which "casts a kind of Glory around it, and darts a lustre through a whole sentence" [16] to Emerson's luster of sentence, and then to Carlyle's and Stein's rich single word. So Francis Bacon inversely regretted that "men began to hunt more after words than matter; and more after the choiceness of the phrase, and the sound and clear composition of the sentence, and the sweet falling of the clauses, and the varying and illustration of their works with tropes and figures, than after the weight of matter, worth of subject, soundness of argument, life of invention, or depth of judgment." [17]

Whether literary style is simply a means by which one personality moves others,[18] or "the message carried by the frequency-distributions and transitional probabilities of its linguistic features," [19] it is "largely a matter of density of information, and this covers to a large extent the subject-matter of the experience, real or fictive, which is communicated, since the understanding and appreciation of literary communication implies previously shared experience, and shared experience implies familiarity with a certain vocabulary." [20] It is, as Matthew Arnold said of Newman's style, "his syntax, the mode in which his thought is evolved." [21]

The long line of theorists in the language of literature, from Aristotle and Demetrius to Richards, Empson, Barfield, and Burke; and the long line of theorists in language from the Greek grammarians to Firth, Fries, Wittgenstein, Jakobson, and Chomsky tend often to run steadily parallel, or counter, not to meet. Supposedly, in our day, the difference is a difference between art and science; probably it is rather a preoccupation with complexities seemingly too great to allow for more than precise, elemental discriminations. In regretting the imprecisions and oversimplifications of this study, I nevertheless hope that its suggestions about whole forms may precede greater precisions by others in these wider fields, by the guiding lines of relevant typologies.

The progress from small to large via type and category is a precarious one; and one particularly out of favor at present because it seems imposed, formal, static, external. The large realms of the categorizers, of Wölfflin, for example, of Charles Morris, Wylie Sypher, and Northrop

[16] *Spectator*, p. 421.

[17] Krapp, p. ix.

[18] Frank L. Lucas, *Style* (New York: Collier, 1962), p. 47.

[19] Bernard Bloch quoted in S. R. Levin, *Linguistic Structures in Poetry* (s'Gravenhage: Mouton, 1962), p. 14.

[20] André Martinet, *Elements of General Linguistics*, trans. Elizabeth Palmer (London: Faber and Faber, 1964), p. 157.

[21] *Essays*, p. 253.

Frye, do indeed have an awesome inevitability yet rigidity about them, as if in telling all they tell less of immediacy. So an alternative of playing by ear and by impact becomes the more favorable. Yet one reason we may be impatient with old guidelines is that new ones are overdue — lines that follow more closely our contemporary concern with the relation between structures external and internal, and that can carry a burden of significance from synthesis into analysis and back. My rebellions have been against the twentieth-century synthesizers who imposed, as it seemed to me, their interests upon the interests of the literature they read. Many rebellions now are against the twentieth-century analyzers who take apart more than it seems they can ever put back together again. My hope is that the analyzers will have provided new lines of relevance for the synthesizers, so that we may be able eventually to learn more about the relation of audience to art, reader to read, without having lost either one to the other.

The texture, the textures, of English poetry and prose are firmer and clearer and more various than we yet know. The texture of the English language is more simply describable than we have yet managed to see. Yet all the while, the studies of linguists, of psychologists, of social and physical scientists, of historians, and of artists are providing glimpses, ways and means, toward such recognitions.

Appendix

Tables A.1 and A.2 together show the proportions and references of major terms in fifty British and ten American poetry texts of six to eight thousand words, and in the same number of prose texts of eight thousand words each, in order of their authors' birthdates, ten in each of five centuries. The authors are those generally accepted as leading writers. The texts are taken as generally representative of their work; but though most authors seem to persist in one style, some do not, and no assumption should be made beyond the single text.

A third as many texts are presented here as in earlier work on poetry (in *Eras and Modes*), where I studied ten texts for each generation, thirty for a century. Inasmuch as summaries for fifty poets are not unlike those for a hundred and fifty, the economy in number seems warranted for comparative generalization. The limit of eight thousand words has been chosen because it equals or exceeds the largest poetic texts studied, and often amounts to a chapter, just as the poetic text often amounts to an *oeuvre* or collection. Order by birthdate provides more stability than order by publication, on the premise that writers born from about 1470 to 1570, for example, published their representative work in the sixteenth century.

Major terms are taken to be those adjectives, nouns, verbs, connectives repeated at least ten times (seven to twelve times) in the eight thousand words, or about one in a thousand. A writer seems to use about sixty such referential terms and a nearly full range of the sixty or so chief connectives. The terms considered therefore amount to nearly half the total text — the rest being made up of the frequent pronominal, adverbial, and determiner particles, and auxiliary verb-forms not counted separately.

When at least two writers in fifty agree on a major term, it is included in the period-table summary. Categorization as adjective, noun, verb, connective is based on formal convention and does not discriminate borderline usages. The applicability of the standard affixes for comparison, person, number, or tense provides the criterion by which *iron hand* is taken as two nouns, *rustling tree* as adjective and noun, *hope to go* as two verbs. Limiting, participial, and descriptive forms are taken as adjectives, gerunds as nouns, auxiliaries as part of the verb, and all conjunctions, prepositions, and adverbs on which grammatical units depend as connectives. Referentially, different numbers and tenses are taken as parts of the same form, so *good-better-best*, or *go-went*, or *man-men* are counted together. Proportions in parentheses represent a simple convenience, division by ten in order to see more easily comparable figures. In the introductory table on p. 16, I have used even a smaller denominator — the minimal four, to minimize differences for the sake of contrast.

Differences of detail in these tables represent, it is hoped, corrections of earlier errors. The most fully corrected tables in addition to these are to be found in *Eras and Modes in English Poetry*, Berkeley: University of California Press, 1964, to which acknowledgment for the adaptations here; and in the revised edition of *Continuity of Poetic Language*, New York: Octagon Press, 1966. Further corrections by those using the books are most welcome. As a postscript of interest, I note the results of a recent study of poetry written in America by poets born since 1930, a study in which I was aided by Mr. John Crawford. Proportions for the work are about 2–4–2–2, confirming the decline of the connective. The only adjectival poet is Gary Snyder, who perhaps follows Allen Ginsberg in this characteristic. Major terms for the poetry are black, dark, long, old, white, air, eye, day, face, hand, leaf, light, love, man, moon, night, shadow, sun, thing, time, tree, come, hear, know, love, make, see, stand, think. Again, this list suggests a confirmation of nineteenth-century poetic vocabulary, as less complete lists for prose do also.

TABLE A.1 TEXTS, MEASURES, PROPORTIONS, AND MAJOR WORD LISTS*
FOR 50 BRITISH AND 10 AMERICAN POETS

Major words occurring approximately ten times or more in a thousand lines; twenty times or more indicated in parentheses. Specific omissions here, though counted in totals, are: numerical adjectives, proper names, auxiliaries and to be, to have, to do, to say.

BRITISH

Poet Birth Date	Work and Edition (first 1,000 lines)	Measure	Total Words	Adjectives	Nouns	Verbs	Connectives*
Ballads 1470	Ballads, first 18. (Ed. W. M. Hart, 1916.)	4' stanzas	7,800	570 (6) bonny dear fair golden good green handsome old red silver young (20)	1,340 (13) bed child church day father (20) hand heart home king lady life lord (30) love man (30) mother (40) sister son steed time word	1,090 (11) come (70) die go leave lie (30) look make (30) play see (30) sing speak take (30)	1,180 (12)
William Dunbar 1470	Thistle, Targe, Synnes, Makaris. 700 lines (Scottish Text Soc., 1919.)	5' - 4' stanzas	4,850	550 (8) awful bright clear fair full fresh green lusty noble red sharp shene sweet tender white	1,130 (16) beam beast beauty bird dame dance day death field fowl flower (20) god lady leaf light love May morrow nature queen rose sky	500 (7) affray come go hail make rise see (20) sing take think	920 (11)
Miles Coverdale 1488	Ghostly Psalms, through XLVI. "Psalm of David." (Ed. Pearson, 1846.)	4' stanzas	6,100	480 (5) dear eternal free good great (30) holy (20) strong sweet worthy	1,230 (12) Christ day (20) death (20) enemy evil faith father (20) flesh god (80) the good grace heart (20) heaven hell hour law life lord (50) love man (30) mercy (20) might mind name need night pain power right saviour sin (20) son (20) spirit tentation thing (20) verity will (20) word (20) world	940 (9) bear believe break bring call come (20) deliver die fall forgive fulfill give (20) go help keep live love make (20) pray put rejoice rise see sin show stand take trust	1,110 (11)
Thomas Wyatt 1503	Songs. Rondeaus. Odes. (Works. Boston. 1854.)	5' stanzas	7,430	700 (7) blind cruel dead dear fair good great true	1,200 (12) cause death desire faith fire fortune grace heart (50) life love (20) man mind pain (30) place reason sigh tear thing time woe	1,060 (11) find go hear know love make please see seek take think (20)	1,380 (14)
Henry Howard, Earl of Surrey 1517	Sonnets, etc. (Poems. ed. Padelford, 1920.)	5' stanzas	7,840	740 (7) good great green pleasant secret sweet true woful	1,750 (18) beauty breast (20) day death desire eye face fire flame heart (40) heat lady lord love (40) man (20) mind (20) nature night pain place sun thing thought (20) time winter woe year	1,320 (13) bring come find (30) give go know (30) lose make (20) methinks see (40) seek serve show take teach think (20)	1,640 (16)

* For major connective lists see Chapter IV, Table 4, in which totals do not include miscellaneous as they do here.

Poet Birth Date	Work and Edition (first 1,000 lines)	Measure	Total Words	Adjectives	Nouns	Verbs	Connectives
George Gascoigne 1542	The Steele Glas. (Works, ed. Cunliffe, 1912.)	5' bl. verse	8,110	850 (9) common (20) filthie foul good (20) great high pleasant strange trusty worthy	1,800 (18) cause day deed (20) delight eye glasse (40) god (20) gold heart king (20) knight life lord (30) love lust man (40) mind (20) priest (30) prince steele thing time soldier world youth	1,210 (12) behold come (20) find give go keep live make (30) pray (20) see (60) seem serve show sing speak tell think	1,750 (18)
Edmund Spenser 1552	Faerie Queene, Amoretti, 500 lines each. (Oxford, 1910.)	5' stanzas	8,100	1,150 (12) black blind dear fair (20) foul full gentle good great (20) little naught new proud sad sweet (20)	1,590 (16) day eye (30) heart (20) heaven lady life (20) love (30) man (20) night thought word world	1,100 (11) come find give hear know lie look make (20) see (20) take tell think	1,750 (18)
Philip Sidney 1554	Eclogs, and Astrophel, 500 lines each. (Cambridge ed., 1912-26.)	5' stanzas	8,950	1,030 (10) fair gold good (20) great (20) happy high inward long old own poor rich sweet (20) true wise	2,090 (21) beauty being breast day desire eye (30) fool fortune friend hand heart (30) heaven hell life love (60) man mind muse nature praise sight shepherd soul sun thing thought virtue wit word	1,290 (13) behold come find give go know learn love make (40) run see (20) seek seem show speak take think yield	1,400 (14)
Joshua Sylvester 1563	Divine Weekes. (Ed. Grosart, 1880.)	5' couplets	7,160	1,060 (11) bright divine eternal fair glorious good great high immortal sweet mighty proud pure sacred (30)	1,900 (19) air (20) art beauty day earth eye fire god (30) heaven light lord nature night nothing power sea soul spirit sun time water work world (30)	850 (9) give make see seem	1,300 (13)
William Shakespeare 1564	Sonnets, 1,050 lines. (Cambridge ed.)	5' stanzas	8,520	1,000 (10) bright dear fair good great happy old sweet (30) true	1,780 (17) beauty (30) day (20) eye (50) love (80) time (30) world heart (20) life man nature night (20) thing thought (20) sun youth	1,130 (10) bring die find give (20) go (20) know lie live (20) look love (20) make (30) see (20) take	1,730 (17)
Ben Jonson 1573	Underwoods, through XV, 1,070 lines. (Oxford edition.)	5' - 4' stanzas	7,580	630 (6) good great poor proud sweet true	1,470 (14) day eye face fire friend god grace hand heart life love (30) man (40) name nature son thing world	1,230 (12) call come find fly give go grow hear know look love make (40) meet see take tell think	1,660 (16)
John Donne 1576	Songs and Sonets, 1,010 lines. (Random House.)	5' - 4' stanzas	7,100	660 (7) bad false good new poor true	1,300 (13) day death eye face fear heart love (110) man name soul sun tear thing world year	1,230 (12) come die fall find give go keep know love make see show take (20) tell think	2,380 (24)
Robert Herrick 1591	Hesperides, 1,090 lines. (Poems, ed. Grosart, 1876.)	5' - 4' stanzas	6,750	770 (7) dead good poor rich small sweet (20) true white	1,410 (13) bed day eye flower heart lip love (40) man night part rose	1,180 (11) bring call come (30) die fall find fly give go grow hear keep kiss know lie live look love make see show sing stand tell think	1,500 (15)

144

Poet Birth Date	Work and Edition (first 1,000 lines)	Measure	Total Words	Adjectives	Nouns	Verbs	Connectives
George Herbert 1593	The Church, through "Mattens." (Oxford ed., 1941.)	5'-3' stanzas	7,260	600 (6) good great (20)	1,450 (15) art blood day (20) death dust earth eye faith fear glory god grace grief (80) heart heaven (20) joy king life (20) light lord love (20) man (20) name part place praise sin (30) sorrow soul (20) stone sun way (20) world (20)	1,060 (11) bear bring come die drop feel fly give go know let make rise see seek show sing take write	1,246 (12)
Edmund Waller 1606	Poems, 1,050 lines. (Works, ed. C. Clarke, 1862.)	5' couplets	7,700	1,180 (11) bold bright fair (30) good great high just new noble old proud sweet	1,940 (19) care eye fate fire god heart heaven (30) love (40) man part power sea thing world	1,030 (10) bring come find give grow hear know make (30) see seem sing stand tell	1,620 (16)
John Milton 1608	Nativity, L'Al., Il P., Lyc., Comus. (Minor Poems, ed. M. Y. Hughes, 1939.)	5'-4' lines	6,720	*1,200 (12) dark fair good great high holy old sad sweet	1,550 (16) air day ear eye god heaven light night star sun wind	770 (8) bring come (20) give go hear (20) keep know lie live make see sing sit	1,420 (14)
Andrew Marvell 1621	Poems, 500 lines through Coy Mistress, 500 lines, Appleton House. (Poems, ed. MacDonald, 1952.)	5' couplets	7,700	660 (7) fair great holy sweet (20)	1,360 (14) day eye (20) flower (20) foot garden grass hand head heaven (20) lily love man (20) rose soul sun tear time world	900 (9) die find go grow know lie live make (20) meet see (20) seem show take	1,300 (13)
Henry Vaughan 1622	Silex Scintillans and Poems, 1,050 lines. (Ed. Grosart, 1871.)	5'-2' stanzas	7,120	750 (7) dark fair full quick	1,300 (13) blood cloud day (30) death earth eye god heaven hour life light (20) lord man night sin soul star sun tear thing thought time wing year	950 (9) bring come fall find give go know make see shine sleep take think weep	1,300 (13)
John Dryden 1631	Absalom and Achitophel, 1,030 lines. (Ed. Noyes, 1950.)	5' couplets	7,800	1,020 (10) bad good high long old public true wise	1,950 (19) arm day eye fate father friend god hand heart heaven (40) king (40) law (20) life love man (20) name time nature people (20) power (20) prince soul (30) youth	1,060 (10) bring find give (20) know love make (30) please rise see think	1,500 (15)
Richard Blackmore 1655	Wit, 350 lines, Nature, 500 lines. (Collected Poems, 1718), "Vanity," "Happiness," "Morning Thought," 150 lines.	5' couplets	6,970	1,185 (12) bright divine fine good great happy high human pure superior vain various wild	1,990 (20) brain day god head heaven land law learning life man mind (20) muse nature power pride race reason sense (30) sky soul spirit sun thought (20) town virtue wit (50)	1,010 (10) fill give grow know make (20) raise see take	1,530 (15)

*at least one third participial

145

Poet Birth Date	Work and Edition (first 1,000 lines)	Measure	Total Words	Adjectives	Nouns	Verbs	Connectives
Alexander Pope 1688	Rape of the Lock and Eloisa, 200 lines. (Vol. II. Poems. ed. Tillotson, 1939.)	5' couplets	8,200	1,090 (11) bright fair new sad silver soft various	2,020 (20) air (20) beauty (20) breast day eye (40) fate god hair hand (20) head (20) heart (20) heaven (20) king lock lord love (30) maid man (20) name night nymph (20) power prayer queen sky soul spirit star sun sylph thing	1,110 (11) fall find fly give know lie make rise see (20) speak take think	1,470 (15)
James Thomson 1700	The Seasons, Winter. rev., 1749. 1,070 lines. (Works. Oxford ed.)	5' bl. verse	7,704	*1,660 (16) deep fair fierce gay great happy long mighty pure sad wide wild	1,880 (18) air cloud country day death eye flood friend hand heart heaven hill land life (30) man (20) mind mountain nature night (20) power scene sky (20) snow soul (20) storm sun thought wind winter world year	800 (7) come fall hear know rise see stand swell	1,580 (16)
Samuel Johnson 1709	London, Vanity. Prologues, plus 7 poems ff., 1,020 lines. (Poems. ed. Smith and McAdam. 1941.)	5' couplets	7,380	*960 (9) gay general great new vain	2,110 (21) age air art (20) day eye fate foe friend gold heart heaven king land life (20) love (20) man nature (20) power (20) pride scene time virtue voice wealth woe world youth	1,060 (10) behold come die find fly give know leave make please rise see	1,350 (13)
Thomas Gray 1716	Poems, 1742 ff., 1,090 lines. (Oxford, 1937.)	5' stanzas	7,818	*1,090 (10) golden human little solemn sweet wild	1,870 (17) air day eye (20) fate flower friend god hand head heart joy king love man muse night soul sun wine way	890 (8) come fly give go hear know leave rise see (20)	1,240 (12)
William Collins 1721	Poems, 1742 ff., 1,060 lines. (Oxford ed.)	5' stanzas	7,703	*1,260 (12) divine fair gentle golden green happy royal sad silent soft sweet (20) tender wide wild (20)	1,800 (17) air day eye (20) flower hand (20) heart heaven hour love (30) maid (30) man mind nature power scene shepherd son song soul thought truth virtue way youth (20)	920 (9) bless call come find (20) hear (20) know lead leave love make rise see (20) sing teach	1,310 (13)
William Cowper 1731	The Task. (Poems. London, 1931.)	5' bl. verse	8,000	*1,130 (11) distant good soft sweet	1,730 (17) air art beauty country day earth eye foot god heart life man (20) nature (20) scene sofa wind world	840 (8) fall feel find love make see seem stand	1,600 (16)
George Crabbe 1754	Village, 500 lines. Eustace Gray, 200 lines. Parish Register, 200 lines. (Poems. ed. Carlyle, 1908.)	5' couplets	6,800	1,010 (11) fair great happy humble own poor proud rude sad	1,750 (19) age care child day eye (20) fate fear field friend grief hand heart hope hour joy labour (20) life man (20) mind muse nymph pain peasant pleasure power pride scene song sun swain thought time view way woe year youth	1,030 (11) ask behold come die feel find give go hear know lie live look make reign see (20) stand think	1,340 (13)

Poet Birth Date	Work and Edition (first 1,000 lines)	Measure	Total Words	Adjectives	Nouns	Verbs	Connectives
William Blake 1757	America, etc. (Poetry and Prose, 1939.)	5' lines	7,700	1,200 (12) beautiful black bright dark divine eternal (20) gentle golden great happy human little (20) old pale red silent soft starry sweet terrible wild	2,400 (24) air bosom child cloud (30) daughter day (30) death (30) earth eye fire flower foot furnace god hand head heaven (20) joy (20) lamb land life love (20) man (20) morning mountain night (20) son sun time valley (20) voice wheel worm	1,030 (10) awake bring come fall find give go know hear hide live look love make pass rise see sing sit sleep smile stand take turn walk weep	2,380 (24)
William Bowles 1762	Sonnets and Other Poems. (8th ed., London, 1802.)	5' stanzas	7,600	*1,310 (13) beauteous bright cold (30) dark distant fair high mournful pale poor sad (30) silent soft sweet vain weary white wild	1,860 (19) charm cliff day (30) delight ear earth eye fancy fate friend (30) heart (30) hill hope (20) hour (30) life (20) man morn (20) mountain pain pity scene (20) sense shade shore sight song sorrow sound spirit sun tear (20) thought tide time vale view virtue wave wind woe woods world year youth	1,000 (10) bear behold bid come feel fly go (20) hear (20) love mark meet pass see seem think turn wait weep	1,520 (15)
William Wordsworth 1770	Lyrical Ballads, omitting groups between "Anecdote" and "Old Man." (Complete Poetical Works, Cambridge ed., 1904.)	5' - 4' stanzas	6,596	*940 (9) cold dear deep green little old poor sweet warm wild young	1,560 (16) day heart joy love mountain nature pain spirit sun thing thought tree wood year	940 (9) love pray stand weep	1,400 (14)
Samuel Taylor Coleridge 1772	Ancient Mariner and Christabel, 1,300 lines. (Rinehart ed.)	4' stanzas	8,170	790 (6) black bright holy little poor sad strange sweet white	1,750 (13) air bird body cloud day eye love mist moon (20) night rock sail sea ship sky sun water wind wood	1,200 (9) blow fly love pray sing	1,500 (12)
George Gordon, Lord Byron 1788	Hebrew Melodies, 500 lines ff. plus 200 lines each, Manfred, Childe Harold, Don Juan. (Oxford ed., 1921.)	4' stanzas	8,000	700 (6) blue bright cold deep good own	1,620 (15) blood bosom day (20) earth eye (20) father god hall hand heart (20) hour king land love man mother soul spirit tear thought voice wind year	1,020 (9) appear behold come die feel give go know lie look love make pass see stand tell weep	1,400 (13)
Percy Bysshe Shelley 1792	Poems, 1820, through "Arethusa." (Random House.)	5' stanzas	7,980	960 (10) blue bright deep dim fair golden sensitive sweet (20) white	1,970 (18) air breast child cloud day earth (20) eye flower garden grace heart heaven (30) life light love man night plant power sky soul spirit star sun wind world	870 (9) arise bear come die hear lie make see	1,780 (18)

Poet Birth Date	Work and Edition (first 1,000 lines)	Measure	Total Words	Adjectives	Nouns	Verbs	Connectives
John Keats 1795	St. Agnes, Odes, etc., and Hyperion I, 1,210 lines. bl. verse (Random House, 1951.)	5' stanzas	9,040	1,470 (12) bright deep divine fair (20) full golden happy little old (20) pale sad silent silver soft (20) sweet (20) wide wing'd	2,200 (18) air beauty cloud day (20) door dream ear earth eve eye (20) face fancy flower foot forest god (20) hand head heart heaven honour hour joy light love man moon night (20) pain pleasure sorrow soul star thing thought time tree voice wind wing woe world	940 (8) bear come (20) die fall find give go know lie look make rise see (20) seem stand tell	1,800 (10)
Alfred Lord Tennyson 1809	Poems, 1842, Vol. I, first 21 poems, "Claribel" and ff. (Oxford ed.)	4' stanzas	6,080	1,000 (10) aweary clear dead deep dreary golden (20) good (20) great silver sweet white wild	1,380 (14) day death earth eye (20) flower heart (20) hour life (20) light (20) love mind moon night (20) prime star sun time	640 (6) come (20) fall go hear kiss lie look see sing	1,120 (11)
Robert Browning 1812	Pippa, 500 lines, Dramatic Lyrics, "Cavalier" through "Laboratory," 500 lines. (Works, 1887.)	5' stanzas	6,980	760 (8) black bright good great little white	1,580 (16) day (20) eye friend god (20) hand heart heaven horse house king life love (20) man morning mother night song sun thing time wine word world	1,210 (12) bring come (20) fall feel gallop give (20) go know laugh lie live look love make ride (30) see (20) speak take think	1,070 (11)
Algernon Charles Swinburne 1837	Poems and Ballads, II, through "Ave," I, 230 lines. (McKay ed., 1910.)	5' stanzas	10,490	1,320 (11) bitter bright dark dead (30) fiery full great green high last long old (20) pale sad soft strange sweet (20) white whole wild	2,380 (19) air bed brother darkness day (50) death (30) dream dust earth eye (30) face father field fire (20) flower (20) foot (20) god (30) hand head heart (30) heaven (20) hope hour king leaf life light lip love man (40) moon night (40) place rose sea (30) shadow sky sleep song soul (50) speech spirit star summer sun (40) sunflower sunrise sunset tear thing thought time wave way (30) wind wing word world year	1,100 (9) come die fall find give go grow hear know leave lie look make (30) rise see (20) sleep stand take touch watch (20) weep	2,200 (18)
Thomas Hardy 1840	Poems of Past and Present. (Macmillan, 1925.)	5' stanzas	6,240	550 (6) dear fair good old sweet	1,150 (12) creature day dream earth heart hope joy life lord love (20) man (30) shape soul thing (20) time woman word world	810 (8) bear call come (20) find go hear know (30) look love make see show sing stand think	1,350 (14)
Gerard Manley Hopkins 1844	Poems, "Pool" through "R. B." (Oxford, 1948.)	5' stanzas	8,430	990 (10) black blue bright dear fresh grey lovely sweet (20) wild	1,960 (20) air (20) beauty (20) child Christ comfort day death earth eye fire flesh foot glory god grace hand heart heaven home life light lord love man mind mother nature night patience peace pool self spirit sun thing thought time way world year	1,030 (10) come (20) fall go hear keep know lie live look man see tread	1,380 (14)

Poet Birth Date	Work and Edition (first 1,000 lines)	Measure	Total Words	Adjectives	Nouns	Verbs	Connectives
William Butler Yeats 1865	The Tower, 1,100 lines. (Collected Poems, Macmillan, 1952.)	5' stanzas	7,350	960 (9) ancient great long old (30) wild young	1,760 (16) bird body child day dream eye god heart (30) life love man (40) mind moon mother night song soul stone sun thing thought time tree wind woman year	980 (9) break bring call come cry find give go grow know lie make run seem sing stand take tell think	1,510 (15)
D. H. Lawrence 1885	Pansies, through "Touch," 1,030 lines. (Complete Poems, London, 1957.)	5' - 3' lines, stanzas	7,200	*1,000 (10) black dark dead dear dirty gold good great (20) little (30) living long new (20) old superior white wild young (20)	1,560 (15) beast bird body bourgeois child creature day the dead (20) death eye flame flesh foot god (20) hand heart house life (50) machine man (60) mill mind mist money moon night people (20) sea sex sin soul sun swan thing water woman (20) work world worm	1,120 (11) come (20) die feel fight find get (20) give go (30) know (20) leave live look make (20) put rise see think turn want work	1,470 (14)
Edwin Muir 1887	First Poems and Labyrinth, through "Good Town," 1,070 lines. (Collected Poems, Faber, 1952.)	4' stanzas	7,290	800 (7) good great little long old small strange	1,570 (15) air (30) body day (20) dream earth end eye face father field flower friend grass ground hand head heart (20) hill house land life (20) light man maze memory mound peace pity place (30) plain road (30) rock sand sea shadow silence sky stream thought time (20) tree wall war way world year	980 (9) come (30) die end fall (20) find go (20) grow hurry know (20) lead lie look make pass run see (40) seem sit stand (20) take tell turn walk watch	1,390 (13)
Edith Sitwell 1887	Green Song and Other Poems, 750 lines (New York, 1946), and Street Songs, 350 lines (New York, 1942.)	5' stanzas	9,060	*1,060 (10) bright (20) cold dark dead gold (30) great (20) green last long old (30) young (30)	2,510 (23) air day death (30) eye hand head heart (110) heaven life light love (40) man (60) night (30) rose sun (50) time water world (70)	960 (9) come (40) fall feel give go grow (20) hear know (20) lie (20) love make see (20) seem	1,930 (19)
Robert Graves 1895	Poems, 1938-1945, 750 lines (London, 1948), and Collected Poems (1938), last 11 poems.	4' stanzas	6,460	*900 (9) little old own	1,500 (15) air day dream death eye god hand head heart love man moon night snow sun time	780 (8) come die fall give go know make see	1,300 (13)
W. H. Auden 1907	Poems, through "Trouble," 630 lines (Collected Poetry), and In Time of War, 380 lines (Random House, 1945.)	5' stanzas	7,220	750 (8) good great last little new old	1,590 (16) child (20) day death earth (20) eye father fate heart home life (20) love (20) man (20) mother nothing thing time truth word world	1,030 (10) come fall feel find give go grow know (20) learn look make (20) see (20) seem speak take	1,370 (14)
Stephen Spender 1909	The Still Centre, through "Two Kisses," (Faber, 1939.)	5' stanzas	7,640	*900 (9) deep great little white young	1,890 (19) child day (20) death dream eye (40) hand (20) head heart life (20) light (20) love man mind night sky sun thought time (20) word world (20)	740 (7) fall lie live look make seem stare	1,470 (14)

149

Poet Birth Date	Work and Edition (first 1,000 lines)	Measure	Total Words	Adjectives	Nouns	Verbs	Connectives
Norman Nicholson 1914	The Pot Geranium, through "Turn for the Better." (Faber, 1954.)	5' stanzas	7,010	*770 (8) black dead dry free old	2,140 (21) air bed bird bone child cloud day earth (20) eye (20) finger fire foot grass the green head heart leaf light (20) love man (20) night rain rock (20) roof sand sea (20) shadow shape sky (20) slate smoke stone street sun tide time tree wall (20) water (20) wind (30) window world	680 (7) come fall hear know look make see (20) seem take watch	1,600 (16)
Dylan Thomas 1914	Selected Writings, first 29 poems. (New Directions, 1946.)	5' stanzas	7,960	1,020 (10) black dead golden green red white	2,300 (23) bell bird blood (20) bone boy child day death (20) eye (20) face grave hand (20) head heart (20) heaven house land light love (30) man (40) moon mouth night sea (30) sky sleep stone summer sun (20) time (30) tongue tower tree voice water weather wind (20) word world	790 (8) break drive drop fall hold lie make (20) turn	1,540 (15)
Elizabeth Jennings 1921	A Way of Looking, plus Poems, through "Adopted Child." (London. 1955.)	5' stanzas	7,050	*610 (6) deep new simple strange true	1,450 (15) being child (30) city country death dream (20) eye foot (?) hand heart hill image (20) journey kind landscape legend life light love (30) man (30) meaning mind (50) nothing (20) passion place power (20) room self shadow something sun symbol thing time thought (40) vision water way word world	1,130 (11) bring build feel (20) find go grow hold keep know look love make (30) move (20) play see seem show speak stand take think turn watch	1,500 (15)
Thomas Gunn 1922	Fighting Terms, 1954, plus Sense of Movement, through "Motorcyclist's Vision," 1,020 lines.	5' stanzas	7,540	*860 (8) dead great	1,630 (16) all bed bird body boy day death ground head man miracle nothing street thought time wind world	1,100 (11) come (20) feel find (20) go hold keep know (40) leave lie make move see (20) take think turn want	1,210 (12)
AMERICAN							
Timothy Dwight 1752	Greenfield Hill, 1794, through II. 430 lines. (Conn. Wits, ed. Parrington.)	5' - 4' stanzas	7,830	1,190 (12) bright dark fair happy little lovely mild pure rich sweet	2,190 (22) earth eye (25) field god grove hand heart heaven hill joy (20) land law life (30) man (20) mankind manners mind (20) peace pride sky son soul stream sun swain toil truth virtue world (20) year	1,050 (11) call fill hail look know rise see (30) smile turn	1,520 (15)

Poet Birth Date	Work and Edition (first 1,000 lines)	Measure	Total Words	Adjectives	Nouns	Verbs	Connectives
William Cullen Bryant 1794	Later Poems, 1,045 lines. (Poems, Philadelphia, 1851.)	5'-4' stanzas	7,760	*920 (9) bright dark fair (20) free gentle green little mighty old soft sweet white wild	1,790 (17) air (20) breast child day day death dust earth (20) eye father flower god hand heart heaven hour life light love man night sky star stream sun thought world	900 (9) come die fall grow hear know lie (20) look love rise see seem take	1,520 (15)
Ralph Waldo Emerson 1803	Poems, 1,005 lines. (Boston, 1899.)	4' stanzas	6,140	660 (7) good old proud sweet wise	1,530 (15) beauty day earth eye (20) god (20) heart heaven home love man (20) morning nature (20) rose sea sky sun thing thought time world	820 (8) bring come fall find go hear know lie love make see seem	1,070 (11)
Walt Whitman 1819	"Song of Myself," 500 lines, "Exposition," 250 lines, "India," 250 lines.	6' lines	11,050	*1,330 (13) good great long old white young	2,790 (28) blood child day death earth (30) eye god grass hair hand house land life man (40) mother night passage place poet sea soul (30) sun time water woman wood word work world year	1,040 (10) behold come fall go guess hold know make pass see (40) sleep stand wait	2,070 (21)
Emily Dickinson 1830	Poems, 1863, Nos. 700-780, 1,020 lines. (Harvard, 1955.)	4'-3' stanzas	4,880	440 (4) good small sweet	1,130 (11) bird day death face heaven hill life man nature night sea soul sun world	720 (7) come die go know pass see stop	880 (9)
Edwin Arlington Robinson 1869	Children of the Night. (Collected Poems, Macmillan, 1948.) 950 lines.	5'-4' stanzas	7,600	660 (7) dead (20) desolate good human lonely lost old sad	1,380 (15) day dream eye (20) faith flame friend gleam glory god hand hell life light love man music night place shame song star thing thought time touch truth wall way wind wisdom woman word world year	850 (9) break call come (40) fall feel find give go grow hear know look make read see shine sing tell think	1,020 (10)
T. S. Eliot 1888	The Waste Land, and ff., through "Marina," 900 lines. (Macmillan, 1944.)	5'-3' lines	6,620	*640 (7) blue broken brown dead dry empty good lost white	1,490 (17) air birth city day death desert eye face foot garden hair heart hour king-dom land life light man (20) mountain night people place rock (20) sea shadow silence stair time voice water way wind winter word (20) world year	730 (8) hope know look make pray sing speak think turn walk	1,300 (13)
Hart Crane 1899	The Bridge. (Collected Poems, ed. Frank, 1946.)	5'-3' stanzas	6,890	*1,030 (10) bright green long new white	2,030 (20) arm day dream eye (30) fire god hand heart heaven hill light man night sea sky snow star time (20) water wind wing	800 (8) come go hear keep know (20) see (30) take	1,600 (16)

151

Poet Birth Date	Work and Edition (first 1,000 lines)	Measure	Total Words	Adjectives	Nouns	Verbs	Connectives
Theodore Roethke 1908	The Waking, 1933-1953, 1,060 lines. (New York, 1953.)	4' lines, stanzas	6,680	*800 (8) cold dark dead great long old small soft	1,580 (16) air bird bone cloud day dirt ear eye face fish foot grass ground hand hat head heart house leaf life light (20) moon mouth night nose place rain root rose stem stone sun time tree water (20) weed wind (20)	800 (8) come (20) go (20) hear keep know (20) let look make move sleep see sing stand stay	1,040 (10)
Robert Lowell 1917	Lord Weary's Castle. (New York, 1946.)	5' lines	7,460	*740 (7) black blue dead great old red	2,130 (21) blood body bone child Christ day death eye (20) face father (20) fire glass god hand head heart house ice king life light lord man night sea snow stone time tree water (20) wind world year	1,010 (10) break come cry die fall go hear make see walk	1,240 (12)

TABLE A.2 TEXTS, PROPORTIONS, AND MAJOR WORD LISTS* FOR 50 BRITISH AND 10 AMERICAN PROSE WRITERS

Major words occurring approximately ten times or more in 8,000 words; twenty times or more indicated in parentheses. Specific omissions here, though included in totals, are: numerical adjectives, some proper names, auxiliaries, and to be, to have, to do, to say.

BRITISH

Prose Writer Birth Date	Text (8,000 words)	Adjectives	Nouns	Verbs	Connectives*
William Tyndale 1473	St. Paul to the Romans, through 13.	380 dead free good holy own	1,670 Abraham all another body branch brethren child Christ (20) circumcision commandment day the dead death (20) evil faith (30) father flesh (30) Gentile gift glory God (140) the good gospel grace (20) heart hope Israel Jesus Christ (20) jew judgment law (80) life lord (20) love man (50) member mercy mind offense one (20) people power promise righteousness (40) seed servant sin (50) son spirit (20) thing (30) time truth unbelief uncircumcision unrighteousness word work world wrath	1,170 become believe (20) call come die forbid give impute judge justify know (20) let live love (5) make (30) may (40) obey raise receive save see work write	2,150
Thomas More 1478	The Apology. (EETS, London, 1930, p. 1-23.)	810 bold false good (30) great long (20) new own (20) plain short such (20) true whole wise unwritten written	1,420 answer (20) book (30) brother brotherhood Christ chapter (20) church (50) day deed faith fault (20) folk God (40) gospel heresy man (50) matter need part people place point reader (20) reason sermon scripture (20) thing (30) truth (20) word (100) work (20) writing (20)	1,090 beget (30) believe boast find give hear look make (40) perceive prove put read (20) rehearse show see (20) take teach use write (30)	1,780
Hugh Latimer 1485	The Fifth Sermon. (Sermons, Cambridge, The University Press, 1844.)	570 good (30) great guilty holy such (30)	1,720 bribe faith father fault God (50) judge judgment justice king (60) law man (95) matter (30) office (30) place prayer sin son (20) thing (30) time way word world	1,360 allow answer (20) ask bear come find give go hear look know let make put see speak take (30) think walk wish	1,660
Roger Ascham 1515	The Scholemaster. (Engl. Works, ed. Wright, Cambridge, The University Press, 1904, p. 182-203.)	1,300 learned common (20) fair fond good (70) great (20) hard (20) ill noble old own quicke (20) ready right same such (20) sure true very wise (30) young (20)	1,670 beauty body book (20) child (60) choice deed end England English experience father fault fear gentleman God goodness judgment (20) labor Latin learning (70) lesson life love (20) man (40) manner master (20) matter memory mind nature (30) note order part place pleasure rule scholar (30) school (20) schoolmaster (20) sentence Socrates speaking teaching thing (20) time (20) tongue Tullie use way will wit (50) word (20) youth (9)	1,010 ask beat breed bring (20) choose come find give go keep know learn let love make prove receive serve speak take teach think use wish write	1,760
Raphael Holinshed 1530	Chronicles, Vol. I, Book I, and Book 2, Ch. 1. (London, 1807.)	680 called (20) ancient British divers good great (20) such (20) sundrie whole	2,000 battle Britaine (20) country (20) day daughter earth father giant god history isle (30) island kind king land life man (30) name (30) people reason son (40) thing time water wife word world	900 call (30) come find (20) get inhabit know make pass take think write (20)	2,120

* For major connective lists see Chapter IV. Table 4, in which totals do not include miscellaneous as they go here.

Prose Writer Birth Date	Text (8,000 words)	Adjectives	Nouns	Verbs	Connectives
Richard Hooker 1554	The Laws of Ecclesiastical Polity, VI, 5. (Everyman ed., p. 148-169.)	660 being according concerning able divine eternal good great high natural (30) own present perfect such	1,490 agent angel (20) art cause creature course degree earth end God (90) the good heaven kind knowledge law (80) man (50) manner matter means name nature (40) nothing order other part perfection reason (20) sort spirit thing (80) time way will work (30) working world (20)	890 attain come consider give keep know let make (20) observe see seem serve set speak take work (20)	1,800
John Lyly 1554	Euphues, The Anatomy of Wit. (Rinehart, 1953, to p. 111.)	910 being (17) seeing black cold fair good (20) great hard like little own (20) small such (20) sweet young	1,730 beauty conceit courtesy Euphues (30) father friend friendship gentleman gentlewoman god hard heart love man manner mind nature (30) one (30) other Philantos pleasure quality shadow thing will wine wit (30) woman word youth	1,080 believe bring cause come follow give go know love make (30) see seem show think use (20)	1,550
Philip Sidney 1554	The Defense of Poesie. (Comp. Works, 3 Vols., Cambridge, The University Press, 1923, to p. 21, line 4.)	810 learning divine excellent good (20) great high notable own poetical such (moral natural noble old right 6)	1,790 Aeneas all art beast both cause conceit end example force Greek historian knowledge learning man (50) matter mind name nature one other part philosopher (30) picture poesy poet (50) poetry question reason science skill sort teaching thing (20) verse virtue (20) way wisdom wit word world	1,030 bring call come delight find follow give (20) go hear know (20) let make (30) move see (20) seem set show speak stand take teach (20) tell think	1,640
Francis Bacon 1561	Advancement of Learning, (Everyman ed., Book I, to p. 22.)	660 learned (20) good (20) great (20) like own same such true	1,660 age body business cause conceit duty end error example eye fault fortune God (20) government (20) hand knowledge (30) learning (40) life man (120) manner matter mind (30) nature (20) person philosopher philosophy place pleasure point reason sense state (20) thing (20) time (30) work	770 give (20) let make (30) receive see take	2,060
Thomas Dekker 1569	The Gulls' Hornbook. (Bristol, 1812, to p. 124.)	820 being excellent fair good (20) great (20) such whole	1,770 body cloth(es) day gallant gentleman hair hand head man (30) mean name none nothing one ordinary other Paul some time world year	1,080 can (30) come (13) go know let (20) looke make (30) (may 30 must) observe put see set stand take (20) walk	1,860
Ben Jonson 1573	Timber. (Ed. Herford Oxford, The Clarendon Press, 1947, to p. 590.)	750 (participls—none over twice) good (30) great old own (20) such true	1,780 all (20) another art book counsel courtesy good judgment kind life man (80) mind (8) nature (20) nothing (20) one other (20) person reason study thing (40) time truth vice way wisdom wit word writing	1,350 can (40) come (20) die find give go hear know (20) make (30) reach receive see (20) speak take (20) think (20) write	1,860
John Donne 1576	Sermon at Denmark House, December, 1617. (Sermons, ed. Potter and Simpson, University of California Press, 1953, I, 5 and 1,200 words of #6.)	600 good great old own same such	1,560 affection bed beginnings book Christ (50) church creature (20) day (20) father God (80) grace house Jesus (20) life lord love (80) man (40) nothing one part person place scripture sin soul (20) text thing will wisdom (20) word (30) work world	1,010 begin bring come express find (40) give know lose love (70) make (20) seek (50) take think	1,840

Prose Writer Birth Date	Text (8,000 words)	Adjectives	Nouns	Verbs	Connectives
Thomas Hobbes 1588	Leviathan, I, Chs. 1 through 4. (Everyman)	960 being made past making divers false great infinite like own present same (20) such (20) true	1,830 accident account action affirmation angle another body (30) brain cause conception consequence creature discourse dream ear eye fancy (20) God image imagination (20) invention kind man (80) manner matter memory mind motion (20) name nothing object one organ part (30) place (20) reckoning sense (40) sign sound speech (20) thing (80) thought (40) time (30)trayne triangle understanding use (20) way word (40)	920 call (20) cause come conceive consider find know make (30) observe proceed produce see (20) seem signify take think understand	2,060
Thomas Browne 1605	Hydriotaphia, Ch. III. (Works, ed. Keynes, London, 1929.)	1,060 according found ancient good great (20) high large long noble old (20) Rome sepulchral such	2,070 account antiquity ashes (20) body (30) bone (40) Britain burial burning (20) conjecture country coyne costome day dead death earth fire (20) friend grave (20) ground habitation interrment king life man monument name nation part (20) peece person place practice (30) pyre Romans Rome sepulchre substance time (20) urne (50) way wood year	710 burn (30) bury decline find (40) hold leave lie make (30) seem	1,790
John Milton 1608	Areopagitica. (Prose, ed. Hughes, New York, 1947, to p. 237.)	900 good (20) great (20) new same such (20) whole	1,700 age another book (80) city commonwealth evil God (20) good kind law learning (20) licensing (20) life (20) magistrate man (60) order reading reason sin state thing (20) time (20) truth virtue wisdom world writing	1,040 bring find give hear know (20) leave make read see take think (20) write	2,090
Edward, Earl of Clarendon 1609	History of the Rebellion, I. (Oxford, The University Press, 1839, p. 5–32.)	760 being good great (30) high new own same such (20) whole	1,680 affair affection court (20) crown day duke (30) end highness house journey (20) king (50) kingdom law lord majesty man (30) marriage matter mind nature occasion other parliament (30) part peace people person (20) power prince (50) reason son Spain (20) thing time (20) treaty year	800 believe conclude find give know (20) make (40) pass see take tell think	1,870
John Bunyan 1628	Pilgrim's Progress, through "Eternal Glory". (9,000 words).	520 saying good (30) little next own such	1,420 back book burden (30) child city counsel death door dream fire gate (20) gentleman glory hand head heart heaven house (20) life man (80) name neighbor (20) one other place (30) reason sir thing (30) time truth way (60) wife word world world (+ Christian (50) Despond Evangelist Interpreter Legalite Obstinate Passion Patience Pliable Slough Worldly Wiseman)	1,350 answer ask begin (20) bid call come (60) direct fall find get (20) give go (60) know lead look make meet read run see (60) seek set slew speak stand (20) take (20) tell (20) think turn	1,870
John Dryden 1631	Preface to Fables (7,500 words). (Penguin ed., p. 226–248.)	720 being former good great (20) little old own present same (20) such (30)	1,460 age another beauty book character countryman language man manner nature number opinion part press poet (20) poetry reader reason sense tale thought time (20) verse word work (+ Chaucer (50) Homer Ovid Virgil)	900 call come find follow give (20) know let live make (20) take think (20) translate understand write	1,730

Prose Writer Birth Date	Text (8,000 words)	Adjectives	Nouns	Verbs	Connectives
John Locke 1632	Essay on Human Understanding, 1st 8,000 words. (Everyman ed.)	720 being certain (20) equal evident general (20) great impossible innate (60) necessary own same (20) such (20) universal (20)	1,270 assent (30) child (20) certainty degree demonstration discovery extent faculty hearing idea (20) impression knowledge (30) man (50) mankind maxim (20) mind (40) nature nothing notion object one (20) opinion other principle (30) proposition (30) proof reason (50) term thing (30) thought time truth (50) understanding (30) use (30) way word	840 assent (30) come (30) discover find give know (30) make (20) observe perceive prove receive suppose take think (20) understand	2,020
Gilbert Burnet 1643	History of the Reformation, Vol. I. (Oxford, 1809, p. 1-28.)	820 being (20) civil French good great (50) new own same such	1,840 age all (n) bishop cardinal child church clergy clerk council crown day duke emperor (20) England (20) father (20) favor France (20) (Francis) government house (20) interest king (110) (King Henry) law (20) learning liberty lord lord-treasurer man matter-money one order parliament (20) part peace person place pleasure pope (30) power prince reign (20) Rome son Spain thing time war (20) word year (30)	890 appear begin come fall find get give (30) go keep make (40) raise seem take	1,920
Jonathan Swift 1667	Tale of a Tub, 1-2. (Everyman ed., p. 43-63.)	880 being (20) certain (20) complete farther gold good (20) great (20) long true	1,610 author body brother coat fashion father nothing number point reader shoulder-knot time treatise will (20) work world	830 find (20) think wear	1,600
Anthony Shaftesbury 1671	Characteristics, III. (Ed. Robertson, London, 1900, p. 103-122.)	710 certain good (30) great (20) own same such (30) young	1,510 author (20) fancy interest man manner (20) nothing occasion person poet practice prince (20) reason thought time way world	920 allow appear call find fire make see take think	1,580
William Addison 1672	Spectator 1, 3, 5, 7, 9, 10. (Everyman ed.)	700 good great (20) little same such (20) whole	1,860 audience club (20) day (20) house lady life man (20) member might opera paper part person reader scene self time (20) year	1,000 come fall fill give hear know make (20) see (20) take tell	1,850
Bishop Berkeley 1685	Principles of Human Knowledge, 1-44. (English Philosophers, Modern Library 39, p. 523-536.)	750 perceived (also unperceived and perceiving) unthinking certain corporeal different distinct evident external like possible real same sensible (20) such	1,530 being (20) body (20) cause color existence (20) extension figure (110) idea (110) man manner matter (20) mind (70) motion (20) nature nothing object power principle quality (30) reason sensation sense (40) spirit (20) substance (20) thing (50) thought truth will word (20)	950 acknowledge call (20) conceive (20) excite exist (40) find give know make mean perceive (40) produce see (20) show take think understand	1,500
Samuel Johnson 1709	Life of Pope. (Works, Vol. II, 1910.)	820 being English great (20) little (20) own same such (20)	1,810 Addison author book copy criticism Dennis Dryden gentleman Homer Iliad knowledge life line man money nothing opinion part performance poem (20) poet (30) poetry Pope (60) power praise time (30) verse version volume wit work year (20)	1,000 begin feel find know make (20) print publish read seem show tell think write (20)	1,640

Prose Writer Birth Date	Text (8,000 words)	Adjectives	Nouns	Verbs	Connectives
Adam Smith 1723	Wealth of Nations, I, 1-4. (Everyman ed., to mid-page 23.)	1,110 employed ancient common considerable different (40) good great (50) inland own (40) particular peculiar same (40) simple small (20) such (20) whole	2,040 art branch business commerce corn country (30) day (20) dexterity difference division (20) employment exchange goods improvement (20) industry labour (50) machine man (40) manner manufacture (20) metal (20) money nail nothing number (20) occasion (30) operation (20) part (50) pin pound power produce quantity (20) river sea society sort time (30) trade use weight work (20) workman (20) world	890 carry employ exchange give (20) make (30) oblige perform	2,000
Edmund Burke 1729	Reflections on Revolution in France. (New York, Liberal Arts Press, 1955, p. 4-27.)	870 civil good great (20) hereditary lawful national new old own political public same such whole	1,800 act (20) assembly authority body choice circumstance club constitution England France gentleman government house King (30) kingdom law (20) liberty (20) life majesty man nation nothing one opinion part (20) people (20) person policy power principle (40) proceeding revolution (30) rights (30) sermon society (20) sort state suggestion (20) time (20) title world	780 appear (can) choose come (do) find follow give have (20) hear know make owe see take think	1,870
Edward Gibbon 1737	Decline and Fall of the Roman Empire, Ch. I. (Cincinnati, 1859.)	1,000 ancient (20) military modern Roman (50) whole	2,330 Antoninus Augustus arms (30) auxiliaries barbarian Britain conquest (20) country (30) discipline Danube emperor (30) empire (30) frontier general government Hadrian legion (30) mankind Mediterranean mile monarchy name ocean part (20) province (40) Rhine the Roman Rome soldier strength state Trojan troop valour war	760 become consider divide from receive	2,100
William Godwin 1756	Political Justice. (3rd ed., London, 1798, Vol. I, to p. 37.)	860 great human (20) innate (20) political (20) same	1,760 action cause circumstance character country evil existence government institution idea man (20) mankind mind nothing opinion principle (20) property society species war world (20)	880 consider find make render	1,680
Archibald Alison 1757	Nature and Principles of Taste, Essay II. (Ed. A. Mills, New York, 1854, p. 114-143.)	910 affecting following interesting signified beautiful capable common (20) different (20) expressive (20) external fair great indifferent material (20) obvious particular (20) productive same (50) similar simple strong sublime (60) such (90) various	1,880 animal (20) association (30) beauty (30) being bell case (30) character color connection consideration constitution country danger difference earthquake effect (20) emotion (80) expression form idea image instance (20) kind (20) man (30) manner (20) matter (20) means mind (20) mistake nature (30) noise note (20) object (20) other people power producing quality (100) scene sensation sense sign (30) situation some sound (170) strength sublimity (40) such taste thunder use voice wind	870 affect arise associate (20) become (can 10) consider distinguish feel find fit know make (may 30) observe occur produce (50) seem signify	2,070

157

Prose Writer Birth Date	Text (8,000 words)	Adjectives	Nouns	Verbs	Connectives
William Hazlitt 1778	"Past and Future," "Genius and Common Sense," Table Talk. (Everyman ed., p. 21-40.)	900 certain common (20) different good great last little own real same strong whole	1,840 action all (20) another association case character circumstance (20) day existence eye face fancy feeling (20) future (20) heart hope idea imagination impression interest life (20) man manner matter mind (20) moment nature nothing (30) object one opinion other pain part passion past (20) pleasure prejudice principle reason (20) rule (20) sense (30) subject (20) thing (20) thought time truth valve will year	1,100 (can 50 do 20) come feel give (20) go (have 40) know look make (may must) pass (say 20) see take think (20)	2,020
Thomas De Quincey 1785	Confessions of an English Opium Eater. (Everyman ed., p. 13-34.)	910 great own (20) same such (20) true	1,430 case child Coleridge (20) fact father guardian (20) man (20) opium (20) opium-eater power sermon time wife year	560 become find make stand	1,330
Thomas Carlyle 1795	Past and Present. (New York, 1897, p. 1-23.)	1,210 enchanted (60) deep English good human just little noble old poor strong such (20) true (note negatives: (50) impossible inarticulate insupportable inner ignoble unjust)	1,680 approximation court day (30) English (20) eye fact God (20) heart insurrection interests justice (20) law man (60) Manchester nation (20) nature question soul sphinx success thing (30) time (20) truth wages work (20) worker workhouse world (20) year	1,000 answer come get know make sit stand	1,440
Thomas Macaulay 1800	History of England, Vol. I. (Everyman ed., p. 1-20.)	1,000 ancient chief common English (30) good great (40) Norman Roman Saxon such	2,110 age (20) Britain century (20) conqueror constitution continent country (30) crown distinction empire England (30) English Europe events evils France history (20) house institution islanders king language law length men (20) nation Norman one other part people (20) power (20) prince province race (20) revolution sea society spirit such time (20) year	820 become begin (can) find (have) make (may) regard rise seem take	1,960
Charles Darwin 1809	Origin of Species. (Hutchinson's Classics, 1906, p. 7-30, line 5.)	1,100 domesticated aboriginal black certain common different direct distinct domestic (40) due good great (20) large like little long same (30) slight such white whole wild (30)	1,600 amount animal (30) beak bird breed (60) breeder case (30) carrier change character (20) condition (20) confinement country degree difference dog domestication effect feather form generation habit individual inheritance instance law length life man nature number offspring parent part peculiarity period pigeon (30) plant (20) production race (30) rock-pigeon selection sheep size species state stock structure subject tendency tumbler variability variation variety view wing	720 affect appear (20) attribute become believe (20) breed compare cross descend (20) differ exist find give keep know make produce revert see seem show think vary	1,340

Prose Writer Birth Date	Text (8,000 words)	Adjectives	Nouns	Verbs	Connectives
John Ruskin 1819	Modern Painters, I, 1, 1. Chs. 1-6. (New York, 1858, p. 1-27.)	910 beautiful capable certain cognizant false good great (40) high impossible like material mere necessary noble own perfect real right simple true same such	1,800 art (50) artist (20) beauty bough color deception degree difficulty dignity evidence excellence (20) exertion expression eye fact faculty feeling form (30) ground idea (60) imitation (40) impression intellect judgment kind language (20) man (20) mind (30) nature (20) number object painter painting part perception picture pleasure (40) power (40) resemblance sense source subject (20) taste term thing time thought (20) truth (40) word (20) work (20)	620 become call convey depend feel give (20) imitate look receive (20) require see seem speak understand	2,230
Matthew Arnold 1822	Culture and Anarchy. (New York, Macmillan, 1925, to p. 22, line 18.)	810 increased complete good great (30) harmonious human (40) intelligent immoral large moral necessary new own religious (30) same spiritual such true	1,850 all(n) being beauty character coal condition country culture (50) curiosity desire end England expansion fault force future God (20) good greatness Greek having idea (30) ideal language literature life light machinery (20) making man (20) middle-class (20) mind mister movement nature (20) one organization (20) Oxford passion people (20) perfection (70) Philistine poetry population power race reason religion (30) side sweetness (20) thing (20) thought time view way wealth (20) will word (20) world (20)	940 call (can) come fail find give judge look make (30) point prevail see (20)	1,780
Walter Pater 1839	The Renaissance. (Macmillan, 1888, p. 1-45.)	880 beautiful early fair famous French great (20) human (20) like middle (20) new old own religious strange	1,800 Abelard age (20) Amile (40) amis (30) angel art Aucassin blood body century child (20) church comrade cup Dante death element expression eye God (20) hand heart interest king lord love (20) man (20) mind Nicolette people piece place poetry (20) quality religion Renaissance (20) revival sense sentiment servant song (soul 5) spirit story (30) subject thing time way word world	730 answer become begin carry come (20) find (20) give (20) go hear (20) know make (20) pass see seem speak take weep	1,830
Sir James Frazer 1854	The Golden Bough, I. (Macmillan, 1894, p. 1-29.)	740 certain (20) high long modern old own sacred	1,820 air branch charm cloud custom day Diana drought example fire (20) god ground grove hair head hint image indian king (20) lake magic making man (30) mode one (20) people person power priest (20) priesthood rain (50) river rule sky some spring stone (30) sun (30) sunshine time (20) tree (20) village water (40) way wind (30) woman	1,010 believe blow call catch fall go keep make (30) place see suppose take think throw. (20) use wish	1,680
George Bernard Shaw 1856	Preface to St. Joan. (Penguin ed., through p. 21.)	910 being mad (6) masculine (6) military sane social (6) such	1,830 fact fear imagination Joan (70) life (20) man (20) mind nothing saint (20) soldier vision voice woman (30)	940 believe call come know live make (20) see throw understand	1,620

159

Prose Writer Birth Date	Text (8,000 words)	Adjectives	Nouns	Verbs	Connectives
Winston Churchill 1871	The Second World War: The Gathering Storm. (Houghton Mifflin, 1948, p. 3-28.)	1,020 American British (20) conservative French (20) German (30) great large military new whole	2,090 all ally army Baldwin Britain country debt election empire end Europe fact form France (20) Germany (50) government (20) Great Britain Hindenburg leader life Lloyd George majority man million office one party (20) payment peace people (20) policy power Prime Minister process result Russia scale state time (20) treaty United States (20) victory victory war (30) world (20) year (40)	860 become find fight give make pay remain seem stand	1,760
Bertrand Russell 1872	"Philosophy and Politics." "Philosophy for Laymen," Unpopular Essays. (New York, Simon & Schuster, 1940, p. 1-27.)	1,020 different general good (20) great human liberal modern necessary obvious political practical present same scientific such (20) theoretical (true 5)	2,120 answer authority belief consequence democracy doctrine dogma government history idea (20) knowledge matter philosopher philosophy (70) problem question reality religion science (20) system theory thought way	1,140 accept become (20) believe call consider develop give hold know (20) lead (20) make (20) produce show think (20)	1,850
James Joyce 1882	Ulysses. (Modern Library, p. 723-737.)	670 bad big good great lovely new nice old (20) sure	1,480 all(n) anything bed bit child course (20) day eye face father fool god hand husband kind(n) love man (30) money night nothing one (20) room something thing (20) time (20) way (20) woman (30) world	1,330 ask call come (20) feel find get (30) give (20) go (30) hate keep know (40) leave let like (20) look (20) make (30) put (say 40) see (30) suppose take tell think (20) use want (20) wonder	1,440
D. H. Lawrence 1885	"Spirit of Place." Classic American Literature. (New York, Doubleday Anchor, 1953, p. 11-36.)	950 barbed American (40) dark deep different free (20) great (20) little (20) masterless moral new (30) old (40) pure (60) real vast whole	1,850 artist forest freedom (20) Benjamin (30) Europe (20) God (30) ideal liberty man (50) master (20) nature (20) people self (20) slave soul (30) thing (20) truth wire world	1,160 come (20) get (30) go (20) hate know (20) like make (20) put read think try want work	1,360
Julian Huxley 1887	"Uniqueness." Man in the Modern World. (New York, Mentor, 1949, p. 7-26.)	1,330 animal (20) biological (30) conceptual dominant early evolutionary great (20) high human (40) large some social such unique (30)	2,060 analysis animal (50) action (20) activity brain by-product characteristic consequence control development difference dominance evolution (22) experience group laughter life (20) man (80) object primate process progress period (20) species (20) speech thought (20) tool tradition (20) type (30)	880 appear acquire become (20) develop evolve provide reach	1,740
Herbert Read 1893	Anatomy of Art. (New York, Dodd Mead, 1932, p. 3-39.)	1,000 abstract aesthetic certain classical common formal geometrical good great Greek human intellectual plastic psychological same simple such (30)	2,020 arrangement art (160) artist (30) beauty (30) colour degree element (20) expression feeling (20) form (40) harmony ideal mass mind object part pattern (20) perception period picture (20) portrait (20) pottery process purpose rhythm section sense sensibility shape space structure theory volume word work (60)	910 become define express find give look make (20) take	1,680

160

Prose Writer Birth Date	Text (8,000 words)	Adjectives	Nouns	Verbs	Connectives
Rebecca West 1893	Black Lamb Grey Falcon. (New York, Viking, 1943, p. 27-46.)	860 (tired 5) afraid beautiful German good great (20) little old second-class such young	1,620 (being 6) business (20) carriage food German hand head husband (30) manufacturer man) might nothing people (20) state ticket-collector time train wife (20) year Yugoslavia	1,210 begin come fall go (30) get know leave like look make (30) meet run see seem (20) take (30) think understand	1,650
Cyril Connolly 1903	Enemies of Promise. (New York, Doubleday Anchor, 1960, p. 125-146.)	800 bed early English good great literary long new old own (20) social such young (20)	1,970 admirer age all art article artist (20) author book comedy Congreve creation critic (20) failure form (20) kind life (20) literature love man masterpiece moment money novel one other past people perfection poetry poet (20) prose reader reality short-story society standard success (30) talent thing time (20) word world (20) winter (70) year	1,110 become bring (can) feel find (have) live make (30) (may must) (say) see seem (should) write (30)	1,740
George Orwell 1905	"Politics," "Gandhi," Essays. (New York, Doubleday, 1954, 9,000 words.)	1,060 bad (20) British clear English good human modern political (20) possible same true	1,680 effect English kind language life man meaning metaphor people phrase (20) sentence thing time war way writer writing word (50)	1,200 (be 200) become choose feel get give make (40) take think (20) use (20) write	1,600
John Wain 1925	Introduction to Contemporary Revolutions of Romantic Poetry. (Barnes & Noble, n.d., p. 11-31.)	900 English (20) good great (20) literary (20) long modern political same such young	2,070 article author century (20) critic (20) criticism (20) editor magazine (20) review (30) reviewer time work (20)	920 become begin find give make reach take write	1,540

AMERICAN

Prose Writer Birth Date	Text (8,000 words)	Adjectives	Nouns	Verbs	Connectives
Jonathan Edwards 1703	Sermon I, 1740, in Works VI (New York, 1830, p. 5-22.)	770 approaching difficult divine eternal good great (60) long (20) mighty necessary old (20) own such (30) vast very wicked	1,740 account all (20) ask (40) billows building business (40) care (20) Christ command day (20) deluge destruction difficulty door (20) duty earth end expense family fire flood (40) God (80) heart heaven labour (20) life man (70) mountain need neighbor Noah (50) none nothing order (20) place religion salvation (50) something (30) time (20) undertaking (20) in vain warning water (20) way (20) the wicked word (20) work (50) workman world (40) wrath (30)	1,190 appear believe come (40) employ engage find give go (20) harken know make (20) obtain save (20) see (20) seek stand (20) strive take tell undertake warn	1,890
Thomas Paine 1737	"Common Sense" in Complete Writings I, p. 4-23.	840 being different English good hereditary (20) natural new present same (20) true whole	1,910 America argument authority being (20) Britain case children colony Commons connection constitution (20) continent country (20) distinction England (30) Europe evil at first form France government (90) Great Britain house interest king (60) life man (40) mankind means monarchy name nation nature nothing number one others parent part (20) people posterity power (20) prejudice rest right scripture state succession time title war world year	960 come happen know make suffer suppose	1,790

Prose Writer Birth Date	Text (8,000 words)	Adjectives	Nouns	Verbs	Connectives
Ralph Waldo Emerson 1803	"Self-Reliance," in Essays (Everyman ed., pp. 29-51.)	860 divine good (20) great (20) new (20) own (20) same strong such true	1,870 act action all being brother cause character child day duty eye face fact force friend genius God (20) heart history law life (20) light love man (100) mind (20) moment name nature (20) nothing one perception person power prayer relation right society soul (20) thing (20) thought time (20) truth (20) virtue (20) way word work world	1,290 call come feel give go know (20) let (20) live love make (20) see (20) seem speak (20) take think	1,740
Walt Whitman 1819	"Democratic Vistas," in Complete Poetry and Prose. ed. Cowley, 1948, pp. 208-226.	1,340 American certain common general good great (30) high important main material moral new old own (20) political (20) religious such true vast	2,090 aggregate all (20) American art business character city day democracy (30) field form freedom future history humanity idea land law (20) life literature (20) man (30) mass nation nothing one part past people (20) person personality point power present quality question race result right sense state (30) suffrage thing (20) time (20) United States war woman world (20)	720 come give know make remain see (20) stand	1,840
Samuel Clemens 1835	Life on the Mississippi. (Bantam ed., pp. 114-142.)	980 good (20) great late long new old same such	1,940 application association (50) boat (40) business Cairo captain (30) course current cut-off day (30) dollar (30) eclipse end everybody fact forecastle freight head hour information man (20) member miles (40) Mississippi moment month New Orleans night one (30) organization outsider owner passenger people pilot (50) place race river (30) St. Louis steam (20) steamboat steamer (20) Stephen thing (20) time (40) trip wage (20) water way week Yates year	1,060 begin (20) come (30) get (20) go (30) keep look make (20) pay see seem take (20) try use	1,550
George Santayana 1863	Three Philosophical Poets. (Anchor ed., 1953, pp. 25-53.)	900 great (20) human moral new same such	1,750 atom (20) consciousness death (20) Democritus Epicurus (20) experience fear force form ground life (50) love Lucretius (30) man (20) materialism mass matter mind movement nature (40) nothing (20) part philosophy poem poet poetry power science soul space (20) substance (20) system thing (40) time truth Venus way world (30)	1,050 arise call conceive fear live make pass produce prove seem think	1,620
T. S. Eliot 1888	The Ideas of a Christian Society. (Faber, 1939, pp. 7-34.)	950 Christian (80) conscious (20) different great modern negative pagan particular political (20) present positive religious (20) small social (20) such (20)	1,590 behavior (20) belief change Christian (20) Christianity (20) church community (20) culture democracy (20) faith form idea individual liberalism life (30) mind organization philosophy point problem relation religion society (60) state subject system view	980 accept become believe concern live make mean see take think	1,720
Ernest Hemingway 1898	Death in the Afternoon. (Scribners, 1932, to p. 22.)	770 comic fundamental good (20) great such	1,510 animal (20) danger death (20) emotion foot horse (40) man (30) people (20) ring (30) spectator thing (40) time wine bull (80) bullfight (40) bullfighter (30) bullfighting (20)	950 feel (20) go (20) give happen identify kill know (20) make remember see (40) try (20) write (20)	1,510

Prose Writer Birth Date	Text (8,000 words)	Adjectives	Nouns	Verbs	Connectives
John Lardner 1912	It Beats Working. (Lippincott, 1947, pp. 110-141.)	730 good new same	2,230 ball baseball boy (20) Brooklyn (30) champion club day (40) Dodger (20) dollar Eddie fight game (20) hand man (30) manager (20) New York one other pitcher player ring style syndicate team time way work year (+ Durocher (37) Mac (15) Hickey (30) etc.)	1,000 call find get (20) give go know (20) make (20) play see take use win	1,500
James Baldwin 1924	Notes of a Native Son. (Beacon Press, 1955, pp. 13-41.)	920 able American (20) black (20) good more own (20) same (20) such social (20) white	1,910 all American Americans being Bigger (20) blacks book death darkness face fact hatred image life (30) man (20) Mrs. Stove murder Negro (50) nothing (30) novel (20) one (40) part people protect question reality relationship society something story time truth whites woman world	1,110 accept become believe come consider feel (20) find give know live make (30) mean seem speak tell	1,790
Cicero	Additional figures are: De Senectute. Loeb ed.	1,030	2,080	1,470	2,060
Seneca	De Brevitate Vitae; De Consolatione (200 words), Loeb ed.	1,280	1,920	1,730	1,800
Tacitus	Ab Excessu Divi Augusti Liber I. Loeb ed., Vol. II.				
	first 1000 wds: (projected)	150 1,200	410 3,280	120 960	120 960)
Henry David Thoreau 1817	Walden (Houghton Mifflin, 1957, pp. 1-18.)	880	1,710	1,120	1,740
Abraham Lincoln 1809	"First Inaugural Address," and Annual Address of 1862 in Selected Speeches. (Rinehart, 1958, pp. 138-148.)	870	1,670	730	1,510

* Note: Among verbs, infinitives may be as few as 50 for Tyndale, De Quincey, Darwin; as many as 150 or more for Ascham, Sidney, Dekker, Addison, Arnold, and many others; with about 130 most usual.

In no English prose do participles amount to a third of the adjectives.

163

Works on Style

The works in this selective list are helpful in studying style, both for general theory and for the particular authors. The assistance they give is so varied, though, that the most useful arrangement seems the alphabetical. Concordances are also of use, though chiefly in studying poets. See also, for references on poetry, the earlier *Continuity of Poetic Language* bibliographies.

Abell, Walter. *The Collective Dream of Art*. Cambridge, Mass.: Harvard University Press, 1957.

Abrams, M. H., ed. *Literature and Belief*. ("English Institute Essays," 1957.) New York: Columbia University Press, 1958.

————. *The Mirror and the Lamp: Romantic Theory and the Critical Tradition*. New York: Oxford University Press, 1953.

Ackerman, James S. "A Theory of Style," *Journal of Aesthetics and Art Criticism*, XX, No. 3 (Spring, 1962), 227–237.

Adams, Henry. *The Degradation of the Democratic Dogma*. New York: The Macmillan Co., 1919.

Adams, Robert Martin. *Ikon: John Milton and the Modern Critics*. Ithaca, N.Y.: Cornell University Press, 1955.

————. *Strains of Discord, Studies in Literary Openness*. Ithaca, N.Y.: Cornell University Press, 1958.

————. *Surface and Symbol: The Consistency of James Joyce's Ulysses*. New York: Oxford University Press, 1962.

Adams, Robert Pardee. *The Better Part of Valor: More, Erasmus, Colet, and Vives, on Humanism, War and Peace, 1496–1535*. Seattle: University of Washington Press, 1962.

Albrecht, W. P. *Hazlitt and the Creative Imagination*. Lawrence: University of Kansas Press, 1965.

Alexander, Christopher. *Notes on the Synthesis of Form*. Cambridge, Mass.: Harvard University Press, 1964.

Alison, Archibald. *Essays on the Nature and Principles of Taste*, 6th ed. 2 vols. London, 1825.

Allen, G. W. *American Prosody.* New York: American Book Co., 1935.

Allen, H. B. *Readings in Applied English Linguistics.* New York: Appleton-Century-Crofts, 1958.

Alpers, Paul. *Spenser.* Princeton, N.J.: Princeton University Press, 1967.

Alonso, Amado. "Stylistic Interpretation of Texts," *Modern Language Notes* (November, 1942), pp. 489–496.

Alvarez, Alfred. *The School of Donne.* London: Chatto & Windus, 1961.

Andersen, Johannes Carl. *The Laws of Verse.* Cambridge, Eng.: The University Press, 1928.

Anderson, Edgar. "Natural History, Statistics, and Applied Mathematics," *American Journal of Botany,* LXIII, No. 10 (December, 1956), 882–889.

——. "Efficient and Inefficient Methods of Measuring Specific Differences," *Statistics and Mathematics in Biology.* Ames: Iowa State College Press, 1954, pp. 93–106.

——. *Plants, Men, and Life.* Boston: Little, Brown and Co., 1952.

Anderson, Warren D. *Matthew Arnold and the Classical Tradition.* Ann Arbor: University of Michigan Press, 1965.

Andrews, Edmund. *A History of Scientific English.* New York: R. Smith, 1947.

Arbusow, Leonid. *Colores Rhetorici.* Göttingen: Vandenhoeck & Ruprecht, 1948.

Aristoteles. *Aristotle's Treatise on Rhetoric, with Hobbes' Analysis.* London: G. Bell & Sons, 1878.

Arnauld, Antoine, and Pierre Nicole. *The Port-Royal Logic.* Trans. Thomas Spencer Baynes. Edinburgh: William Blackwood & Sons, 1890. Trans. James Dickoff and Patricia James. Indianapolis, Ind., 1964.

——, and Claude Lancelot. *Le grammaire générale et raisonné.* Paris, 1660.

Arnold, Thurman W. *The Folklore of Capitalism.* New Haven: Yale University Press, 1937.

Aronson, Alex. "Eighteenth Century Semantics of Wit," *Etcetera,* V, No. 3 (Spring, 1948), 182–190.

Arrowood, Charles F. *Theory of Education in the Political Philosophy of Adam Smith.* Austin, Texas: Privately Printed, 1945.

Arthos, John. *The Language of Natural Description in Eighteenth Century Poetry.* Ann Arbor: University of Michigan Press, 1949.

Ascham, Roger. *The Whole Works of Roger Ascham.* Collected and revised, with a life of the author, by the Rev. Dr. Giles, Vol. 3. London: John Russell Smith, 1864.

Aschenbrenner, Karl. "Aesthetic Theory — Conflict and Conciliation," *The Journal of Aesthetics and Art Criticism,* XVIII, No. 1 (September, 1959), 90–109.

Atkins, John Alfred. *George Orwell: A Literary Study.* London: J. Calder, 1954.

Atkins, J. W. H. *English Literary Criticism: The Medieval Phase.* Cambridge, Eng.: The University Press, 1943.

——. *English Literary Criticism: The Renaissance.* London: Methuen, 1957.

——. *English Literary Criticism: Seventeenth and Eighteenth Centuries.* London: Methuen, 1951.

Auerbach, Erich. *Mimesis: The Representation of Reality in Western Literature*. Princeton, N.J.: Princeton University Press, 1953.

Aurner, Robert. "Aspects of the Structure of the English Sentence," *Philological Quarterly*, II (1923).

Babbitt, Irving. *The New Laokoon: An Essay on the Confusion of the Arts*. Boston: Houghton Mifflin Co., 1910.

Bacon, Francis. *The Advancement of Learning and New Atlantis*, with a preface by Thomas Case. London: Oxford University Press, 1960.

Bagby, Philip. *Culture and History*. Berkeley: University of California Press, 1958.

Bailey, John. "Grand Style," in *Essays and Studies by Members of the English Association*. Oxford: The University Press, 1911.

Bailey, Richard W., and Sister Dolores Marie Burton. *English Stylistics: A Bibliography*. Boston: Emmanuel College, 1965.

Bailyn, Bernard. *New England Merchants of the Seventeenth Century*. Cambridge, Mass.: Harvard University Press, 1955.

Bain, Alexander. *Manual of English Composition and Rhetoric*. London, 1866.

Baker, H. C. *William Hazlitt*. Cambridge, Mass.. Harvard University Press, 1962.

Baker, James V. *The Second River: Coleridge's Theory of the Imagination*. Baton Rouge: Louisiana State University Press, 1957.

Baker, William E. *The Grammar of Modern Poetry*. University of California, dissertation, 1964.

Balakian, Anna. *Literary Origins of Surrealism*. New York: King's Crown Press, 1947.

Bald, R. C. *Donne's Influence on English Literature*. Morpeth: The St. John's College Press, 1932.

Bally, Charles. *Le Langage et la Vie*, 3rd ed. Zurich: M. Niehans, 1935.

―――. *Linguistique Générale et Linguistique Française*, 3rd ed. Berne, 1950.

Bamborough, J. B. *Ben Jonson*. London: Longmans, Green, 1959.

―――. "Joyce and Jonson," *Review of English Literature*, I, No. 4 (October, 1960), 45–50.

Bandy, William T. *A Word Index to Baudelaire's Poems*. Madison: University of Wisconsin Press, 1939.

Barber, C. L. "Some Measurable Characteristics of Modern Scientific Prose," *Contributions to English Syntax and Philology*, by C. L. Barber *et al.* "Gothenburg Studies in English," ed. Frank Behre, Vol. XIV, Göteborg, 1962.

Barfield, Owen. *Poetic Diction: A Study in Meaning*, 2nd ed. London: Faber & Groyer, 1952.

―――. *Saving the Appearances: A Study in Idolatry*. London: Faber & Groyer, 1957.

Barish, Jonas. *Ben Jonson and the Language of Prose Comedy*. Cambridge, Mass.: Harvard University Press, 1960.

―――. *Ben Jonson: A Collection of Critical Essays*. Englewood Cliffs, N.J.: Prentice-Hall, 1963.

Barkas, Pallister. *Critique of Modern English Prosody*. Halle, 1934.

166

Barnett, H. G. *Innovation: The Basis of Cultural Change.* New York: McGraw-Hill Book Co., 1953.

Barry, Liam. *Our Legacy from Burke: A Survey of Some of His Works, and a Broad Analysis from the Literary Aspect.* Cork: Paramount Printing House, 1952.

Barzun, Jacques. *Darwin, Marx, Wagner: Critique of a Heritage.* Garden City, N.Y.: Doubleday and Co., 1958.

———. *Romanticism and the Modern Ego.* Boston: Little, Brown and Co., 1943.

Basler, Roy. *Symbol and Psychology in Literature.* New Brunswick, N.J.: Rutgers University Press, 1948.

Bate, Walter Jackson. *The Achievement of Samuel Johnson.* New York: Oxford University Press, 1955.

———. *From Classic to Romantic: Premises of Taste in Eighteenth Century England.* Cambridge, Mass.: Harvard University Press, 1946.

Bateson, F. W. *English Poetry and the English Language: An Experiment in Literary History.* Oxford: The Clarendon Press, 1934.

Baudouin, Charles. *Psychoanalysis and Aesthetics.* Trans. Eden and Cedar Paul. London: Allen & Unwin, 1924.

———. *Contemporary Studies.* Trans. Eden and Cedar Paul. New York: E. P. Dutton and Co., 1925.

Baugh, Hansell, ed. *General Semantics.* "Papers from the First American Congress," 1935. New York: Arrow Editions, 1940.

Baum, Helen W. *The Satiric and the Didactic in Ben Jonson's Comedy.* Chapel Hill: University of North Carolina Press, 1947.

Baum, Paull Franklin. *The Principles of English Versification.* Cambridge, Mass.: Harvard University Press, 1924.

———. *. . . the Other Harmony of Prose: An Essay in English Prose Rhythm.* Durham, N.C.: Duke University Press, 1952.

Bayley, John. *The Romantic Survival: A Study in Poetic Evolution.* London: Constable & Co., 1957.

Beach, Joseph Warren. *Obsessive Images: Symbolism in the Poetry of the 1930's and 1940's.* Minneapolis: University of Minnesota Press, 1960.

Beardsley, Monroe. *Aesthetics: Problems in the Philosophy of Criticism.* New York: Harcourt, Brace and Co., 1958.

Beaumont, Charles A. *Swift's Classical Rhetoric.* Athens: University of Georgia Press, 1961.

Beckwith, Martha Warren. *Black Roadways: A Study of Jamaican Folklife.* Chapel Hill: University of North Carolina Press, 1929.

Belknap, George N. *A Guide to Reading in Aesthetics and Theory of Poetry.* "University of Oregon Publications," Vol. IV, No. 9 (July, 1934).

Bennett, James R. "Annotated Bibliography of Selected Writings on English Prose Style," *College Composition and Communication,* Vol. XVI (December, 1965).

Bentley, Eric F. *Bernard Shaw, 1856–1950.* Norfolk, Conn.: New Directions, 1957.

Bentley, G. E. *Shakespeare and Jonson: Their Reputations in the Seventeenth Century Compared*. Chicago: University of Chicago Press, 1945.

Berelson, Bernard. *Content Analysis in Communication Research*. Glencoe, Ill.: Free Press, 1954.

———. *The Media of Communication*. Chicago: University of Chicago Press, 1937.

Berenson, Bernard. *Aesthetics and History*. New York: Doubleday and Co., 1959.

Berger, Monroe, *et al. Freedom and Control in Modern Society*. New York: D. Van Nostrand Co., 1954.

Bergson, Henri. *The Two Sources of Morality and Religion*. New York: Doubleday and Co., 1955.

Berlin, Isaiah. *Historical Inevitability*. London: Oxford University Press, 1954.

Berlyne, D. E. *Conflict, Arousal, and Curiosity*. New York: McGraw-Hill Book Co., 1960.

Berry, Edmund G. *Emerson's Plutarch*. Cambridge, Mass.: Harvard University Press, 1961.

Berry, Francis. *Poet's Grammar*. London: Routledge & Kegan Paul, 1958.

Bethell, S. L. *The Cultural Revolution of the Seventeenth Century*. New York: Roy Publishers, 1951.

Bewley, Marius. *The Complex Fate*. London: Chatto & Windus, 1952.

Bidney, David. *Theoretical Anthropology*. New York: Columbia University Press, 1953.

Bischoff, Dietrich. *Sir Thos. Browne als Stilkünstler: ein Beitrag zur Deutung der englischen Barockliteratur*. Heidelberg: C. Winter, 1943.

Black, Max. *Critical Thinking*. New York: Prentice-Hall, 1946.

———. *Language and Philosophy*. Ithaca, N.Y.: Cornell University Press, 1949.

Blackall, Eric. "The Imprint of Herder's Linguistic Theory on His Early Prose Style," *PMLA*, LXXVI, No. 5 (December, 1961), 512–518.

Blackmur, R. P. *The Double Agent: Essays in Craft and Elucidation*. New York: Arrow Editions, 1935.

———. *The Expense of Greatness*. New York: Arrow Editions, 1940.

———. *Form and Value in Modern Poetry*. Garden City, N.Y.: Doubleday and Co., 1957.

———. *Language as Gesture: Essays in Poetry*. New York: Harcourt, Brace and Co., 1952.

Blair, Hugh. *Lectures on Rhetoric and Belles Lettres, 1762 et seqq.* London, 1813.

Blair, Walter, and Clarence Faust. "Emerson's Literary Method," *Modern Philology*, XLII (November, 1944), 79–95.

Blake, Ralph, C. Ducasse, and E. Madden. *Theories of Scientific Method, the Renaissance through the Nineteenth Century*. Seattle: University of Washington Press, 1960.

Blanchot, Maurice. *L'Espace Littéraire*. Paris: Gallimard, 1955.

Blanshard, Brand. *On Philosophical Style*. Manchester, Eng.: Manchester University Press, 1954.

Blench, J. W. *Preaching in England in the Late 15th and 16th Centuries.* Oxford: Blackwell, 1964.

Bloomfield, Leonard. *Language.* New York: Henry Holt and Co., 1914, 1933, 1938.

Boas, George. *A Primer for Critics.* Baltimore: Johns Hopkins University Press, 1937.

————. *Philosophy and Poetry.* Norton, Mass.: Wheaton College Press, 1932.

Boder, David P. "The Adjective-Verb Quotient: A Contribution to the Psychology of Language," *The Psychological Record* (Bloomington, Ind.: The Principia Press, 1940), III, No. 22 (March, 1940).

Bodkin, Maud. *Archetypal Patterns in Poetry: Psychological Studies of Imagination.* London: Oxford University Press, 1934.

————. *Studies of Type-Images in Poetry, Religion, and Philosophy.* London: Oxford University Press, 1951.

Bodmer, Frederick. *The Loom of Language.* New York: W. W. Norton and Co., 1944.

Bogoslovsky, Boris B. *The Technique of Controversy.* London: Kegan Paul, 1928.

Bolinger, D. L. "Rime, Assonance, and Morpheme Analysis," *Word,* VI, No. 1 (April, 1950), 117–136.

Bond, Harold L. *The Literary Art of Edward Gibbon.* Oxford: The Clarendon Press, 1960.

Bongers, H. *The History and Principles of Vocabulary Control.* Holland, 1947.

Booth, Stephen. *Shakespeare's Sonnets.* Unpublished dissertation, Harvard University.

Bosanquet, Bernard. *History of Aesthetics,* 2nd ed. London: Allen & Unwin, 1904.

Boulding, Kenneth E. *The Image: Knowledge in Life and Society.* Ann Arbor: University of Michigan Press, 1956.

Boulton, James. *The Language of Politics in the Age of Wilkes and Burke.* London: Routledge & Kegan Paul, 1963.

Boulton, Marjorie. *The Anatomy of Prose.* London: Routledge & Kegan Paul, 1954.

Bowen, C. D. *Francis Bacon: The Temper of a Man.* Boston: Little, Brown and Co., 1963.

Bowra, C. M. *The Heritage of Symbolism.* London: Moche, 1943.

Bradbrook, Muriel. "Fifty Years of Criticism of Shakespeare's Style," *Shakespeare Survey,* Vol. VII (1954).

Brailsford, H. N. *Shelley, Godwin, and Their Circle,* 2nd ed. London: Oxford University Press, 1951.

Bram, Joseph. *Language and Society.* New York: Doubleday and Co., 1955.

Bray, J. W. *A History of English Critical Terms.* Boston, 1898.

Bréal, Michel. *Semantics: Studies in the Science of Meaning.* Trans. Mrs. H. Cust. London: W. Heinemann, 1900.

Brémond, Henri. *Prayer and Poetry: A Contribution to Poetical Theory.* Trans. Algar Thorold. London: Burns, Oates & Washbourne, Ltd., 1927.

Brenton, T. R. *An Essay on Poetics*. Oxford: Oxford University Press, 1932.

Brett, R. L. *Shaftesbury: A Study in Eighteenth Century Literary Theory*. London: Hutchinson's University Library, 1951.

Brewster, William. *Studies in Style*. New York, 1911.

Bridges, Robert. *Milton's Prosody*. Oxford: The Clarendon Press, 1893.

————. "Poetic Diction in English," in *Collected Essays, Papers*. London: Oxford University Press, 1928.

Brinkman, Friedrich. *Die Metaphern*. Bonn, 1878.

Britton, Karl. *Communication: A Philosophical Study of Language*. London: Kegan Paul, 1939.

Brody, Jules. *Boileau and Longinus*. Geneva: E. Droz, 1958.

Bronson, B. H. *Johnson and Boswell: Three Essays*. "University of California Publications in English," Vol. III, No. 9. Berkeley: University of California Press, 1944.

Brooke-Rose, Christine. *A Grammar of Metaphor*. London: Secker & Warburg, 1958.

Brooks, Cleanth. *Modern Poetry and Tradition*. Chapel Hill: University of North Carolina Press, 1939.

————, and Robert Penn Warren. *Understanding Poetry: An Anthology for College Students*. New York: Henry Holt and Co., 1938.

Brower, Reuben. *The Fields of Light*. London: Oxford University Press, 1951.

————, ed. *On Translation*. Cambridge, Mass.: Harvard University Press, 1959.

Brown, E. K. *Matthew Arnold: A Study in Conflict*. Chicago: University of Chicago Press, 1948.

Brown, Huntington. *Prose Styles*. Minneapolis: University of Minnesota Press, 1966.

Brown, James I. *Programed Vocabulary*. New York: Appleton-Century-Crofts, 1965.

Brown, Merle. *Neo-Idealistic Aesthetics*. Detroit, Mich.: Wayne State University Press, 1965.

Brown, Percy W. "Emerson's Philosophy of Aesthetics," *Journal of Aesthetics and Art Criticism*, XV, No. 3 (March, 1957), 350–354.

Brown, Roger. *Words and Things*. Glencoe, Ill.: Free Press, 1958.

Brown, Wallace Cable. *The Big Triumph of Form: A Study of the Later Masters of the Heroic Couplet*. Chapel Hill: University of North Carolina Press, 1948.

Brownell, William Crary. *The Genius of Style*. New York: Charles Scribner's Sons, 1924.

Brumbaugh, Robert S. *Plato on the One: The Hypotheses in the "Parmenides."* New Haven: Yale University Press, 1961.

Bruneau, Charles. "La Stylistique," *Romance Philology*, V (1951), 1–15.

Bruner, Jerome S. *The Process of Education*. Cambridge, Mass.: Harvard University Press, 1960.

————. *On Knowing*. Cambridge, Mass.: Belknap Press, 1962.

————, et al. *A Study of Thinking*. New York: John Wiley and Sons, 1956.

Bryant, D. C. *Edmund Burke and His Literary Friends*. St. Louis: "Washington University Studies," 1939.

Bryson, Gladys. *Man and Society*. Princeton, N.J.: Princeton University Press, 1945.

Bryson, Lyman, ed. *The Communication of Ideas*. New York: Harper and Brothers, 1948.

Buchanan, Scott. *Poetry and Mathematics*. New York: John Day Co., 1929.

Buchler, Justus. *The Philosophy of Peirce*. New York: Harcourt, Brace and Co., 1940.

Buck, Gertrude. *The Metaphor: A Study in the Psychology of Rhetoric*. "Contributions to Rhetorical Theory," No. 5. Ann Arbor: University of Michigan Press, 1899.

Buffon, George. *Discours sur le Style*. Paris: Librairie Hachette, 1921.

Bull, William E. "*Natural Frequency and Word Counts*," *The Classical Journal*, XLIV, No. 8 (May, 1949), 469–484.

———. "Spanish Word Counts: Theory and Practice," *The Modern Language Journal*, XXXIV, No. 1 (January, 1950), 18–26.

Bundy, Murray Wright. *The Theory of Imagination in Classical and Medieval Thought*. "University of Illinois Studies in Language and Literature," Vol. XII. Urbana: University of Illinois Press, 1927.

Bunge, Mario. *Causality*. Cambridge, Mass.: Harvard University Press, 1959.

Burke, Kenneth. *Counter-Statement*. New York: Harcourt, Brace and Co., 1931.

———. *A Grammar of Motives*. New York: Prentice-Hall, 1945.

———. *The Philosophy of Literary Form: Studies in Symbolic Action*. Baton Rouge: Louisiana State University Press, 1941.

———. *A Rhetoric of Motives*. New York: Prentice-Hall, 1950.

Burtt, E. A. *The Metaphysical Foundations of Modern Science*. New York: Doubleday and Co., 1954.

Bush, Douglas. *Mythology and the Romantic Tradition in English Poetry*. Cambridge, Mass.: Harvard University Press, 1927.

Butt, John, and George R. Potter. "Editing Donne and Pope." First Clark Library Seminar, University of California, Los Angeles, November 22, 1952.

Buxton, John. *Sir P. Sidney and the English Renaissance*. London: The Macmillan Co.; New York: St. Martin's Press, 1954.

Bysshe, Edward. *The Art of English Poetry*, 9th ed. London, 1762.

Calder, Grace J. *The Writing of Past and Present, A Study of Carlyle's Manuscripts*. New Haven: Yale University Press, 1949.

Cambon, Glauco. *The Inclusive Flame: Studies in Modern American Poetry*. Bloomington: University of Indiana Press, 1965.

Camp, W. H. "Biosystematy," *Brittonia*, VII, No. 3 (January, 1951), 113–127.

Campbell, George. *The Philosophy of Rhetoric*, rev. ed. Carbondale, Ill.: Southern University Press, 1963.

Campbell, Wm. Edward. *Erasmus, Tyndale, and More*. London: Eyre and Spottiswoode, 1949.

Caplan, Harry, ed. *Rhetorica ad Herennium*. Cambridge, Mass.: Harvard University Press, 1954.

Cargo, Robert T., ed. *A Concordance to Baudelaire's "Les Fleurs du Mal."* Chapel Hill: University of North Carolina Press, 1965.

Carnap, Rudolph. *Introduction to Semantics.* Cambridge, Mass.: Harvard University Press, 1942.

Carr, Lowell J. *Situational Analysis.* New York: Harper and Brothers, 1948.

Carritt, E. F. *A Calendar of British Taste, 1600–1800.* London: Routledge & Kegan Paul, 1949.

Carroll, John B. *A Factor Analysis of Verbal Abilities.* Dissertation. Minneapolis: University of Minnesota Press, 1941.

————. *The Study of Language: A Survey of Linguistics and Related Disciplines in America.* Cambridge, Mass.: Harvard University Press, 1953.

————. *Language and Thought.* Englewood Cliffs, N.J.: Prentice-Hall, 1964.

Cassirer, Ernst. *Determinism and Indeterminism in Modern Physics.* New Haven: Yale University Press, 1956.

————. *Essay on Man.* New Haven: Yale University Press, 1944.

————. *The Myth of the State.* New Haven: Yale University Press, 1946.

————. *Philosophy of Symbolic Forms.* Trans. Ralph Mannheim. 3 vols. New Haven: Yale University Press, 1953–1957.

Castro, Americo. *The Structure of Spanish History.* Trans. E. L. King. Princeton, N.J.: Princeton University Press, 1954.

Catlin, George E. G. *Thomas Hobbes as Philosopher, Publicist, and Man of Letters.* Oxford: Blackwell, 1922.

Cattell, Raymond B. *Personality and Motivation: Structure and Measurement.* Yonkers-on-Hudson: World Book Co., 1957.

Caudwell, Christopher. *Illusion and Reality: A Study of the Sources of Poetry.* London: Lawrence and Wishart, 1937.

Cecil, Lord D. *Walter Pater: The Scholar-Artist.* Cambridge, Eng.: The University Press, 1955.

Celières, André. *The Prose Style of Emerson.* Paris: Impressions Pierre Andris, 1936.

Chadwick, Hector Munro, and N. Kershaw. *The Growth of Literature.* Cambridge, Eng.: The University Press, 1932–1940.

Chambers, R. W. *On the Continuity of English Prose from Alfred to More and His School.* London: Oxford University Press, 1957.

Chandler, Albert. *Beauty and Human Nature.* New York: D. Appleton, 1934.

————, and Edward N. Barnhart. *A Bibliography of Psychological and Experimental Aesthetics, 1864–1937.* Berkeley: University of California Press, 1938.

Chandler, Zilpha. *An Analysis of the Stylistic Technique of Addison, Johnson, Hazlitt, and Pater.* "University of Iowa Humanistic Studies," Vol. IV, No. 3. Iowa City: University of Iowa Press, 1928.

Chappell, Vere Claiborne. *Ordinary Language.* Englewood Cliffs, N.J.: Prentice-Hall, 1964.

Charleston, Britta M. *Studies on the Emotional and Affective Means of Expression in Modern English.* Berne: Francke Verlag, 1960.

Charlton, H. B. *Castelvetro's Theory of Poetry.* Manchester, Eng.: Manchester University Press, 1913.

Charvat, William. *Origins of American Critical Thought, 1810–1835.* Philadelphia: University of Pennsylvania, 1936.

Chase, Stewart. *Roads to Agreement.* New York: Harper and Brothers, 1951.

Chatman, Seymour. *Metrics.* The Hague: Mouton & Co., 1965.

Chen, Shih-hsiang. "In Search of the Beginnings of Chinese Literary Criticism," *Semitic and Oriental Studies.* "University of California Publications in Semitic Philology," Vol. XI. Berkeley: University of California Press, 1951, pp. 45–63.

Cherry, Colin. *On Human Communication: A Review, a Survey, and a Criticism.* Cambridge, Mass.: Massachusetts Institute of Technology Press, 1957.

Chester, Allan G. *Hugh Latimer, Apostle to the English.* Philadelphia: University of Pennsylvania Press, 1954.

Chomsky, Noam. *Current Issues in Linguistic Theory.* The Hague: Mouton & Co., 1965.

————. *Syntactic Structures.* The Hague: Mouton & Co., 1957.

————. *Aspects of the Theory of Syntax.* Cambridge, Mass.: Massachusetts Institute of Technology Press, 1965.

Christensen, Francis. "A Generative Rhetoric of the Sentence," *College Composition and Communication,* Vol. XIV, No. 3 (October, 1963).

————. "A Generative Rhetoric of the Paragraph," *College Composition and Communication,* XVI, No. 3 (October, 1965), 144–150.

————. "John Wilkins and the Royal Society's Reform of Prose Style," *Modern Language Quarterly,* VII (1946), 178–188, 279–291.

Clark, A. F. B. *Boileau and the French Classical Critics in England, 1660–1830.* Paris: E. Champion, 1925.

Clark, Donald L. *John Milton at St. Paul's School: A Study of Ancient Rhetoric in English Renaissance Education.* New York: Columbia University Press, 1948.

————. *Rhetoric and Poetry in the Renaissance.* New York: Columbia University Press, 1922.

Cockeram, Henry. *The English Dictionarie of 1623.* New York: Huntington Press, 1930.

Coffin, C. M. *John Donne and the New Philosophy.* New York: Humanities Press, 1958.

Coffman, Stanley K., Jr. *Imagism: A Chapter for the History of Modern Poetry.* Norman: University of Oklahoma Press, 1951.

Cohen, Marcel. *Grammaire et Style.* Paris: Éditions Sociales, 1954.

Cohen, Morris R. *The Meaning of Human History.* La Salle, Ill.: Open Court Publishing Co., 1947.

————. *A Preface to Logic.* New York: Henry Holt and Co., 1944.

————. *Reason and Nature: An Essay on the Meaning of Scientific Method.* Glencoe, Ill.: Free Press, 1931, 1953.

Collingwood, R. G. *Idea of History.* London: Oxford University Press, 1946.

————. *Principles of Art.* Oxford: The Clarendon Press, 1938.

Colum, Mary M. *From These Roots: The Ideas That Have Made Modern Literature.* New York: Charles Scribner's Sons, 1937.

Congleton, J. E. *Theories of Pastoral Poetry in England, 1684–1798*. Gainesville: University of Florida Press, 1952.

Connell, W. *The Educational Thought and Influence of Matthew Arnold*. London: Routledge & Kegan Paul, 1950.

Connolly, Cyril. *Enemies of Promise*. Garden City, N.Y.: Doubleday and Co., 1960.

Constance, Lincoln. "The Versatile Taxonomist," *Brittonia*, VII, No. 4 (December, 1951), 225–231.

Cook, Albert S. *The Bible and English Prose Style*. Boston: D. C. Heath and Co., 1892.

Cope, Jackson. *Joseph Glanvill, Anglican Apologist*. St. Louis: Washington University Press, 1956.

Corder, James W. *Rhetoric*. New York: Random House, 1965.

Cornell, Kenneth. *The Symbolist Movement*. New Haven: Yale University Press, 1951.

Cowl, R. P., ed. *The Theory of Poetry in England*. London: The Macmillan Co., 1914.

Craigie, William A. *The Critique of Pure English from Caxton to Smollett*. "S.P.E. Tract LXV." Oxford: The Clarendon Press, 1946.

Craik, Henry. *English Prose Selections*. London, 1893.

Crane, Ronald S., ed. *Critics and Criticism, Ancient and Modern*. Chicago: University of Chicago Press, 1952.

Crane, Ronald S. *The Languages of Criticism and the Structure of Poetry*. Toronto: University of Toronto Press, 1953.

Croce, Benedetto. *Aesthetic as Science of Expression and General Linguistic*. Trans. Douglas Ainslie. New York: The Macmillan Co., 1922.

———. *Logic as the Science of the Pure Concept*. Trans. Douglas Ainslie. New York: The Macmillan Co., 1917.

Croll, Morris. "Baroque Style in Prose," *Studies in English Philology*. Ed. K. Malone. Minneapolis: University of Minnesota, 1929.

———. "Attic Prose in the Seventeenth Century," *Studies in Philology*, XVIII (April, 1921), 79–128.

———. "Muret and the History of Attic Prose," *PMLA*, XXXIX, No. 2, 254–309.

———. *Style, Rhetoric, and Rhythm*. Ed. J. M. Patrick, *et al*. Princeton, N.J.: Princeton University Press, 1965.

Crowther, J. G. *Francis Bacon, the First Statesman of Science*. London: Crescent Press, 1960.

Culler, A. Dwight. "Edward Bysshe and the Poet's Handbook," *PMLA*, LXIII, No. 3 (September, 1948), 858–886.

Cunningham, J. V. *Woe and Wonder*. Denver: University of Denver, 1951.

Curtius, Ernst Robert. *European Literature and the Latin Middle Ages*. Trans. Willard Trask. Bollingen Series, Vol. XXXVI. New York: Pantheon, 1953.

Daiches, David. *Milton*. London: Hutchinson University Library, 1961.

———. *Poetry in the Modern World: England 1900–1939*. Chicago: University of Chicago Press, 1940.

———. *The Place of Meaning in Poetry*. Edinburgh: Oliver & Boyd, 1935.

Dallas, E. S. *The Gay Science*. London, 1866.

Damon, Phillip. "Modes of Analogy in Ancient and Medieval Verse," "University of California Publications in Classical Philology," Vol. XV, No. 6. Berkeley: University of California Press, 1961, pp. 261–334.

Danby, I. F. *Poets on Fortune's Hill: Studies in Sidney, Shakespeare, Beaumont and Fletcher.* London: Faber & Faber, 1952.

Daniells, Roy. *Milton, Mannerism and Baroque.* Toronto: University of Toronto Press, 1963.

Daniels, Earl. *The Art of Reading Poetry.* New York: Farrar and Rinehart, 1941.

Davidson, Hugh M. *Audience, Words, and Art: Studies in Seventeenth-Century French Rhetoric.* Columbus: Ohio State University, 1965.

Davie, Donald. *Articulate Energy: An Inquiry into the Syntax of English Poetry.* London: Routledge & Kegan Paul, 1955.

———. *Poetics.* Warsaw: Naukowe, 1961.

———. *Purity of Diction in English Verse.* London: Chatto & Windus, 1952.

———. *The Language of Science and the Language of Literature.* London: Sheed & Ward, 1963.

Davies, H. S., Hugh Sykes, and George Watson, eds. *The English Mind.* Cambridge, Eng.: The University Press, 1964.

Davis, H. J. *The Satire of Jonathan Swift.* New York: The Macmillan Co., 1947.

Davis, Norman. "Styles in English Prose," in *La Langue et Littérature* ———, 165–181.

Davy, Charles. *Words in the Mind.* Cambridge, Mass.: Harvard University Press, 1965.

Delattre, Floris. *Ruskin et Bergson: De l'intuition esthétique à l'intuition métaphysique.* Oxford: The Clarendon Press, 1947.

Dennes, William Ray. "Conceptions of Descriptive and Normative," *Civilization,* "University of California Publications in Philosophy," Vol. XXIII. Berkeley: University of California Press, 1942, pp. 161–190.

———. "Conflict," *The Philosophical Review,* LV (July, 1946), 343–376.

———. *Some Dilemmas of Naturalism.* New York: Columbia University Press, 1960.

Denniston, J. D. *Greek Prose Style.* Oxford: The Clarendon Press, 1952.

DeQuincey, T. *Confessions of an E. Opium-eater.* London: MacDonald, 1956.

Deutsch, Babette. *This Modern Poetry.* New York: W. W. Norton and Co., 1935.

Devlin, Joseph. *A Dictionary of Synonyms and Antonyms.* New York: World Syndicate Publishers, 1938.

Dewey, Edward R., and Edwin F. Dakin. *Cycles: The Science of Prediction.* New York: Henry Holt and Co., 1947.

Dewey, Godfrey. *Relative Frequency of English Speech Sounds.* Cambridge, Mass.: Harvard University Press, 1943.

Dewey, John. *Art as Experience.* New York: Minton, Balch, 1934.

———, et al. *Art and Education.* Merion, Pa.: Barnes Foundation Press, 1947.

———. *Logic, The Theory of Inquiry.* New York: Henry Holt and Co., 1938.

————. "Ralph Waldo Emerson," *Characters and Events*. New York: Henry Holt and Co., 1929, I, 69–77.

————. "Theory of Valuation," *International Encyclopedia of Unified Science*, I and II: *Foundations of the Unity of Science*. Chicago: University of Chicago Press, 1939.

Dickoff, James and Patricia. *Symbolic Logic and Language*. New York: McGraw-Hill Book Co., 1965.

Diederich, Paul B. *The Frequency of Latin Words and Their Endings*. Chicago: University of Chicago Press, 1939.

Dilthey, Wilhelm. *The Essence of Philosophy*. Trans. S. A. and W. T. Emery. Chapel Hill: University of North Carolina Press, 1954.

Dion, Sister Clarice de Sainte Marie. *The Idea of "Pure Poetry" in English Criticism, 1900–1945*. Washington, D. C.: Catholic University of America Press, 1948.

Dixon, Robert. *Linguistic Science and Logic*. The Hague: Mouton & Co., 1963.

Dockhorn, Klaus. "Die Rhetorik als Quelle des vorromantischen Irrationalismus in der Literatur und Geistesgeschichte," *Nachrichten der Akademie der Wissenschaften in Göttingen*. "Philologisch-Historische Klasse," V. Göttingen: Gedr. in der Dieterichschen univ.-buchdr. 1949, 109–150.

Dockhorn, Klaus. "Wordsworth und die rhetorische Tradition in England," *Nachrichten der Akademie der Wissenschaften in Göttingen*. "Philologisch-Historische Klasse," Vol. XI. Göttingen: Vanderhoeck & Ruprecht, 1944.

Donne, John. *Complete Poetry and Selected Prose*, with an Introd. by Charles M. Coffin. New York: Modern Library, 1952.

————. *Sermons*. Ed. George R. Potter and Evelyn M. Simpson. Berkeley: University of California Press, 1953.

————. *Sermons on the Psalms and Gospels*. Ed. Evelyn M. Simpson. Berkeley: University of California Press, 1953.

Donnelly, Dorothy. *The Golden Well: An Anatomy of Symbols*. London: Sheed & Ward, 1950.

Donohue, James John. *Ancient Classifications of Literature*. Dubuque, Iowa: Loras College Press, 1943.

deDony, Yvonne. *Lexicon of Figurative Language*. New York, 1957.

Dowlin, C. M. *Sir William D'Avenant's Gondibert, Its Preface, and Hobbes' Answer: A Study in English Neo-Classicism*. Philadelphia: University of Pennsylvania Press, 1934.

Downey, June E. *Creative Imagination: Studies in the Psychology of Literature*. London: Kegan Paul, 1929.

Dray, William. *Laws and Explanation in History*. London: Oxford University Press, 1957.

Drew, Elizabeth. *Directions in Modern Poetry*. New York: W. W. Norton and Co., 1940.

————. *Discovering Poetry*. New York: W. W. Norton and Co., 1953.

Dryden, John. *Dryden Essays*. Ed. John Mahoney. Indianapolis, Ind.: Bobbs-Merrill Co., 1965.

Dudley, Louise and Austin Faricy. *The Humanities: Applied Aesthetics*. New York: McGraw-Hill Book Co., 1940.

Du Marsais, César. *Traité des Tropes*. Paris, 1775.

Duncan, Hugh Dalziel. *An Annotated Bibliography on the Sociology of Literature*. Chicago, 1947.

———. *Communication and Social Order*. New York, 1962.

Durham, W. H., ed. *Critical Essays, 1700–1725*. New Haven: Yale University Press, 1925.

Eaker, Jay G. *Walter Pater: A Study in Methods and Effects*. Iowa City: The University of Iowa Press, 1933.

Earle, John. *English Prose*. New York: G. P. Putnam's Sons, 1891.

Eastman, Max. *Enjoyment of Poetry with Other Essays in Aesthetics*. New York: Charles Scribner's Sons, 1939.

———. *The Literary Mind: Its Place in an Age of Science*. New York: Charles Scribner's Sons, 1932.

Eaton, Helen. *Semantic Frequency List for English, French, German, Spanish*. Chicago: University of Chicago Press, 1940.

Eaton, R. M. *Symbolism and Truth: An Introduction to the Theory of Knowledge*. Cambridge, Mass.: Harvard University Press, 1925.

Eells, John. *The Touchstones of Matthew Arnold*. New York: Bookman Associates, 1955.

Ehrenpreis, Irvin. *Swift: The Man, His Works, and the Age*. London: Methuen, 1962.

Ehrlich, Victor. *Russian Formalism*. The Hague: Mouton & Co., 1955.

Einstein, Albert, and Leopold Infeld. *The Evolution of Physics*. New York: Simon and Schuster, 1938.

Eiseley, Loren C. *Francis Bacon and the Modern Dilemma*. Lincoln: University of Nebraska, 1962.

Elioseff, Lee Andrew. *The Cultural Milieu of Addison's Literary Criticism*. Austin: University of Texas Press, 1963.

Eliot, T. S. *The Use of Poetry and the Use of Criticism: Studies in the Relation of Criticism to Poetry in England*. "Norton Lectures," 1932–1933. Cambridge, Mass.: Harvard University Press, 1933.

———. "The Borderline of Prose," *New Statesman*, IX (1917), 157–519.

Ellegård, Alvar. *Who Was Junius?* Uppsala, 1962.

Elliott, Robert C. *The Power of Satire, Magic, Ritual, Art*. Princeton, N.J.: Princeton University Press, 1960.

Ellis, A. Williams. *An Anatomy of Poetry*. New York: The Macmillan Co., 1922.

Ellmann, Richard. *James Joyce*. New York: Oxford University Press, 1959.

Emma, Ronald. *Milton's Grammar*. The Hague: Mouton & Co., 1964.

Empson, William. *Seven Types of Ambiguity*. London: Chatto & Windus, 1930.

———. *Some Versions of Pastoral*. London: Chatto & Windus, 1935.

———. *The Structure of Complex Words*. London: Chatto & Windus, 1951.

Enck, John J. *Jonson and the Comic Truth*. Madison: University of Wisconsin Press, 1957.

English Institute Essay, 1951. New York: Columbia University Press, 1952.

Enkvist, N. E. "On Defining Style," in *Linguistics in Style*. Ed. John Spencer. London: Oxford University Press, 1964.

Entwhistle, William J. *Aspects of Language*. London: Faber & Faber, 1953.

Estrich, Robert M., and Hans Sperber. *Three Keys to Language*. New York: Rinehart and Co., 1952.

Evans, Joan. *John Ruskin*. New York: Oxford University Press, 1954.

———. *Pattern: A Study of Ornament in Western Europe from 1180 to 1900*. Oxford: The Clarendon Press, 1931.

Faral, Edmond. *Les arts poétiques du XIIe et du XIIIe siècle*. Paris: É. Champion, 1924.

Farber, Hans. *Die Lyrik in der Kunsttheorie der Antike*. Munich, 1936.

Faris, Nabile Armin, ed. *The Arab Heritage*. Princeton, N.J.: Princeton University Press, 1944.

Fedelis, C. *Versuch über Alisons Ästhetik, Darstellung und Kritik; ein Beitrag zur Entwicklungsgeschichte der englishchen Ästhetik im XVIII Jahrhundert*. Munich: Dissertation, University of Munich, 1911.

Feibleman, James. *The Theory of Human Culture*. New York: Duell, Sloan and Pearce, 1946.

Fénelon, François. *Dialogues on Eloquence, 1718*. Trans. W. S. Howell. Princeton, N.J.: Princeton University Press, 1951.

Ferguson, Charles Wright. *Say It With Words*. New York: Alfred A. Knopf, 1959.

Festinger, L. and D. Katz, eds. *Research Methods in the Behavioral Sciences*. New York: Dryden Press, 1953.

Finney, Gretchen. *The Musical Background for English Literature*. New Brunswick, N.J.: Rutgers University Press, 1962.

Firth, J. R. *Papers in Linguistics, 1934–1951*. London: Oxford University Press, 1957 [1961].

Fisch, Harold. *Jerusalem and Albion*. London: Routledge & Kegan Paul, 1964.

Fish, Stanley. *John Skelton's Poetry*. New Haven: Yale University Press, 1965.

Fishman, Solomon. *The Interpretation of Art*. Berkeley: University of California Press, 1963.

Fiske, C. F. *A Study of a Feature of Sixteenth Century Conventionalism as It Reveals Itself in Holinshed's Chronicle*. Bloomington, Ill., 1950.

Fletcher, Angus. *Allegory*. Ithaca, N.Y.: Cornell University Press, 1964.

Fletcher, H. F. *The Intellectual Development of John Milton*. Urbana: University of Illinois Press, 1956.

———. *The Use of the Bible in Milton's Prose*. Urbana: University of Illinois Press, 1929.

Foakes, R. A. *The Romantic Assertion: A Study in the Language of Nineteenth-Century Poetry*. London: Methuen, 1958.

Fodor, J. A. and J. J. Katz, eds. *The Structure of Language: Readings in the Philosophy of Language*. Englewood Cliffs, N.J.: Prentice-Hall, 1964.

Fogarty, Daniel, S. J. *Roots for a New Rhetoric*. New York: Teachers' College, Columbia, 1959.

Fonágy, Ivan. "Communication in Poetry," *Word*, XVII, 1961.

Forster, E. M. *Two Cheers for Democracy*. New York: Harcourt, Brace and Co., 1951.

Fowler, H. W. and F. G. *The King's English*. Oxford: The Clarendon Press, 1922.

Fowlie, Wallace. *The Age of Surrealism*. Denver: Swallow Press, 1950.

Fraisse, P. *Les Structures Rythmiques: Étude Psychologique*. Louvain: Publications Universitaires de Louvain, 1956.

Francis, J. H. *From Caxton to Carlyle*. Cambridge, Eng.: Cambridge University Press, 1937.

Fraser, Russell. "Rationalism and the Discursive Style," *Hudson Review*, XVIII (Fall, 1965), 376–386.

Fraunce, Abraham. *The Arcadian Rhetoric*, 1588. Ed. Ethel Seaton. Oxford: Blackwell, 1950.

Freeman, Rosemary. *English Emblem Books*. London: Chatto & Windus, 1948.

Freimark, Vincent. "The Bible and Neo-Classical Views of Style," *Journal of English and Germanic Philology*, LI (1952), 517–526.

Frenz, Horst, and G. L. Anderson. *Indiana University Conference on Oriental-Western Literary Relations*. "University of North Carolina Studies in Comparative Literature," Vol. XIII. Chapel Hill: University of North Carolina Press, 1955.

Freud, Sigmund. *A General Introduction to Psychoanalysis*. Trans. G. Hall. New York: Boni and Liveright, 1920.

Friedman, Norman. *e. e. cummings, The Art of His Poetry*. Baltimore: Johns Hopkins University Press, 1960.

Friedrich, Carl J. "The Baroque Age," *Horizon*, II, No. 6 (July, 1960), 33–64.

Fries, C. C. *American English Grammar*. New York: D. Appleton-Century, 1940.

————. *The Structure of English*. New York: Harcourt, Brace and Co., 1952.

Frost, William. *Dryden and the Art of Translation*. New Haven: Yale University Press, 1955.

Frye, Northrop. *Anatomy of Criticism*. Princeton, N.J.: Princeton University Press, 1957.

————, ed. *Sound and Poetry*. "English Institute Essays," 1956. New York: Columbia University Press, 1957.

Fuchs, Wilhelm. "On Mathematical Analyses of Style," *Biometrika*, XXXIX, Nos. 1, 2 (May, 1952), 122–129.

Furniss, W. Todd. *Three Studies in the Renaissance: Ben Jonson's Masques*. New Haven: Yale University Press, 1958.

Fussell, Paul, Jr. *Poetic Meter and Poetic Form*. New York: Random House, 1965.

————. *Theory of Prosody in Eighteenth Century England*. New London: Connecticut College, 1954.

Gardner, Helen L. ed. *John Donne: A Collection of Critical Essays*. Englewood Cliffs, N.J.: Prentice-Hall, 1962.

Gardner, Martin. *The Ambidextrous Universe*. New York: Basic Books, 1964.

Garvin, Paul L. *On Linguistic Method: Selected Papers*. The Hague: Mouton & Co., 1964.

Gellner, Ernest. *Words and Things*. London: V. Gollancz, 1959.

Gibson, James. *The Perception of the Visual World*. Boston: Houghton Mifflin Co., 1950.

Gibson, Walter. *Poems in the Making*. Boston: Houghton Mifflin Co., 1963.

Gilbert, Allan H. *The Symbolic Persons in the Masques of Ben Jonson*. Durham, N.C.: Duke University Press, 1948.

Gilbert, Katherine E., and Helmut Kuhn. *A History of Aesthetics*. New York: Mosher, 1939.

Gilchrist, Marie. *Writing Poetry: Suggestions for Young Writers with Poems by Members of the Stevenson Room Poetry Group of the Cleveland Public Library*. New York: Houghton Mifflin Co., 1932.

Gildon, Charles. *The Complete Art of Poetry*. 2 vols. London, 1718.

Gilman, Margaret. *The Idea of Poetry in France*. Cambridge, Mass.: Harvard University Press, 1958.

Gilman, W. E. *Milton's Rhetoric: Studies in His Defense of Liberty*. Columbia: University of Missouri Press, 1939.

Gilson, Étienne. *The Arts of the Beautiful*. New York: Charles Scribner's Sons, 1965.

Givens, Sean, ed. *James Joyce: Two Decades of Criticism*. New York: Vanguard Press, 1963.

Gleason, H. A. *Introduction to Descriptive Linguistics*, rev. ed. New York: Henry Holt and Co., 1961.

Goldberg, Isaac. *The Wonder of Words*. New York: D. Appleton, 1938.

Goldschmidt, Walter. *Man's Way: A Preface to the Understanding of Human Society*. New York: Henry Holt and Co., 1959.

Gombrich, E. H. *Art and Illusion: A Study in the Psychology of Pictorial Representation*. New York: Pantheon, 1960.

Goodman, Paul. "The Human Uses of Science," *Commentary*, XXX, No. 6 (December, 1960), 461–472.

———. *The Structure of Literature*. Chicago: University of Chicago Press, 1954.

Gordon, Kate. *Esthetics*. New York: Henry Holt and Co., 1927.

Gowers, Sir Ernest. *Plain Words: Their ABC*. New York: Alfred A. Knopf, 1954.

Grabo, Norman S. "The Veiled Vision: The Role of Aesthetics in Early American Intellectual History," *William and Mary Quarterly*, 3rd Series, XIX, No. 8 (October, 1962), 493–510.

———. *Edward Taylor*. New York: Twayne, 1962.

Graves, Robert. *Contemporary Techniques of Poetry: A Political Analogy*. London: L. & Virginia Woolf, 1925.

———. *The Reader Over Your Shoulder*. New York: The Macmillan Co., 1943.

Gray, Charles Montgomery. *Hugh Latimer and the Sixteenth Century: An Essay in Interpretation*. Cambridge, Mass.: Harvard University Press, 1950.

Gray, Floyd Francis. *Le Style de Montaigne*. Paris: Nizet, 1958.

Greenough, J. B., and G. S. Kittredge. *Words and Their Ways in English Speech*. New York: The Macmillan Co., 1920.

Greenslade, Rev. A. L. *The Work of William Tyndale*, with an Essay on Tyndale and the English Language by G. D. Bone. London: Blackie & Son, 1938.

Gregg, John R. *The Language of Taxonomy*. New York: Columbia University Press, 1954.

Grey, Lennox, and Consultants. "What Communication Means Today." Chicago: National Council of Teachers of English, 1944.

Grierson, Sir Herbert J. C., ed. *Essays and Studies by Members of the English Association*, XVI. London: Oxford University Press, 1931.

Grimes, N. G. *et al. Sweet Smoke of Rhetoric*. Coral Gables, Fla.: University of Miami Press, 1964.

Grindon, Leo. *Figurative Language: Its Origin and Constitution*. London, 1879.

Groom, Bernard. *The Diction of Poetry from Spenser to Bridges*. Toronto: University of Toronto Press, 1955.

———. *On the Diction of Tennyson, Browning, and Arnold*. "Society for Pure English," Tract LIII. Oxford: The Clarendon Press, 1939.

Gross, Llewellyn. *Symposium on Sociological Theory*. Evanston, Ill.: Row, Peterson, 1959.

Grube, G. M. A. *The Greek and Roman Critics*. London: Methuen, 1965.

Grudin, Louis. *A Primer of Aesthetics: Logical Approaches to a Philosophy of Art*. New York: Covici, Friede, 1930.

Grylls, R. G. *William Godwin and His World*. London: Odham Press, 1953.

Guérard, Albert. *Art for Art's Sake*. Boston: Lothrop, Lee and Shepard, 1936.

Guiraud, Pierre. *Les Caractères Statistiques du Vocabulaire*. Paris: Presses Universitaires de France, 1954.

Gumperz, John. "Language," *Biennial Review of Anthropology*. Ed. Bernard Siegal. Stanford: Stanford University Press, 1965.

———. *Language et Versification d'après l'oeuvre de Paul Valéry*. Paris: Klincksieck, 1953.

Hagstolz, H. B. *The Educational Theories of Ruskin*. Lincoln: University of Nebraska Press, 1942.

Hagstrum, Jean H. *S. Johnson's Literary Criticism*. Minneapolis: University of Minnesota Press, 1952.

———. *The Sister Arts: The Tradition of Literary Pictorialism and English Poetry from Dryden to Gray*. Chicago: University of Chicago Press, 1958.

Hale, William B. *The Story of a Style*. New York: B. W. Huebsch, 1920.

Hall, Stuart, and Paddy Whannel. *The Popular Arts*. London: Hutchinson Educational Library, 1964.

Hall, Vernon, Jr. *Renaissance Literary Criticism: A Study of Its Social Content*. New York: Columbia University Press, 1945.

Haller, William. *Liberty and Reformation in the Puritan Revolution*. New York: Columbia University Press, 1955.

Halliday, M. A. K., Angus McIntosh and Peter Stevens. *The Linguistic Sciences and Language Teaching*. London: Longmans, Green, 1964.

Halpern, Martin. "The Two Chief Metrical Modes in English," *PMLA* (June, 1962).

Hamer, Enid. *The Metres of English Poetry*. London: Methuen, 1930.

Hamilton, G. Rostrevor. *Poetry and Contemplation: A New Preface to Poetics*. Cambridge, Eng.: The University Press, 1937.

————. *The Tell-Tale Article: A Critical Approach to Modern Poetry*. New York: Oxford University Press, 1950.

Hamilton, Kenneth. *The Two Harmonies: Poetry and Prose in the 19th Century*. New York: Oxford University Press, 1963.

Hamm, V. M. "Meter and Meaning," *PMLA*, LXIX (1954), 695–710.

Handlin, Oscar. *Chance or Destiny*. Boston: Little, Brown and Co., 1955.

Hanley, Miles Lawrence. *Word Index to James Joyce's "Ulysses."* Madison: University of Wisconsin Press, 1937.

Hardison, O. B., Jr., ed. *Modern Continental Literary Criticism*. New York: Appleton-Century-Crofts, 1965.

Harding, D. P. *Milton and the Renaissance Ovid*. Urbana: University of Illinois Press, 1946.

Harpsfield, Nicholas. *The Life and Death of Sir Thomas More*. With an Introd. on the Continuity of English Prose from Alfred to More by R. W. Chambers. London: Oxford University Press, 1932.

Harris, Zellig S. "Distributional Structure," *Linguistics Today*. Ed. A. Martinet and U. Weinreich. New York: Linguistic Circle of New York, 1954, pp. 26–42.

————. *Methods in Structural Linguistics*. Chicago: University of Chicago Press, 1947–1951.

Harrold, C. F. *Carlyle and German Thought*. New Haven: Yale University Press, 1934.

Hartman, Geoffrey H. *The Unmediated Vision*. New Haven: Yale University Press, 1954.

————. *Wordsworth's Poetry*. New Haven: Yale University Press, 1964.

Harvey, John. *The Gothic World, 1100–1600: A Survey of Art and Architecture*. London: Bateford, 1950.

Hathaway, Baxter. *The Age of Criticism*. Ithaca, N.Y.: Cornell University Press, 1962.

Hatzfeld, Helmut. *A Critical Bibliography of the New Stylistics Applied to the Romance Literatures, 1900–1952*. Chapel Hill: University of North Carolina Press, 1953.

Haugen, Einar. *Norwegian Word Studies*. Madison: University of Wisconsin Press, 1942.

Heidbreder, Edna. *Seven Psychologies*. New York: D. Appleton-Century Co., 1935.

Hegel, G. W. F. *The Philosophy of Fine Art*. Trans. F. P. B. Osmaston. London: G. Biel & Sons, 1920.

Hempel, Carl G. "Fundamentals of Concept Formation in Empirical Science," *Foundations of the Unity of Science*, II, No. 7, "International Encyclopedia of Unified Science." Chicago: University of Chicago Press, 1952.

Henle, Paul. *Language, Thought, and Culture.* Ann Arbor: University of Michigan Press, 1958.

Henn, T. R. *Longinus and English Criticism.* Cambridge, Eng.: The University Press, 1934.

Herdan, Gustav. *The Calculus of Linguistic Observations.* The Hague: Mouton & Co., 1962.

————. *Language as Choice and Chance.* Groningen: P. Noordhoff, 1956.

Heron, Patrick. *The Changing Forms of Art.* New York: The Macmillan Co., 1950.

Herrick, Marvin Theodore. *The Poetics of Aristotle in England.* "Cornell Studies in English," XVII. New Haven: Yale University Press, 1930.

Herskovitz, Melville J. *Man and His Works.* New York: Alfred A. Knopf, 1948.

————, and Frances S. *Dahomean Narrative: A Cross-Cultural Analysis.* Evanston, Ill.: Northwestern University Press, 1958.

Herzog, G. "Some Linguistic Aspects of American Indian Poetry," *Word,* II (1946), 82.

Heyl, Bernard C. *New Bearings in Esthetics and Art Criticism: A Study in Semantics and Evaluation.* New Haven: Yale University Press, 1943.

Hick, John, E. Sandeen, and Alvan Ryan. *Critical Studies in Arnold, Emerson, and Newman.* Iowa City: Iowa University Press, 1942.

Higgons, Bevil. *Historical and Critical Remarks on Bp. Burnet's History of His Own Time.* London: Printed for P. Meighan, 1725.

Highet, Gilbert. *The Classical Tradition.* London: Oxford University Press, 1949.

Hill, Archibald A. *Introduction to Linguistic Structure: From Sound to Sentence in English.* New York: Harcourt, Brace and Co., 1958.

Hjelmslev, Louis. *Prologomena to a Theory of Language.* Trans. Francis Whitfield. "Indiana University Publications in Anthropology and Linguistics," No. 7. Bloomington: Indiana University Press, 1953.

Hoenigswald, Henry. *Language, Change, and Linguistic Reconstruction.* Chicago: University of Chicago Press, 1960.

Hoffman, Arthur W. *John Dryden's Imagery.* Gainesville: University of Florida Press, 1962.

Hoffman, Frederick J. *Freudianism and the Literary Mind.* Baton Rouge: Louisiana State University Press, 1945.

Hogrefe, Pearl. *The Sir Thomas More Circle: A Program of Ideas and Their Impact on Secular Drama.* Urbana: University of Illinois Press, 1959.

Hollander, John. *The Untuning of the Sky: Ideas of Music in English Poetry, 1500–1700.* Princeton, N.J.: Princeton University Press, 1961.

Hollis, Christopher. *A Study of George Orwell: The Man and His Works.* London: Hollis & Carter, 1956.

Holloway, John. *The Victorian Sage: Studies in Argument.* London: The Macmillan Co., 1953.

Holmes, John. *The Poet's Work.* New York: Oxford University Press, 1939.

Holmes, Roger W. *The Rhyme of Reason: An Invitation to Accurate and Mature Thinking.* New York: D. Appleton, 1939.

Holthusen, Hans Egon. "German Lyric Poetry since 1945," *Poetry, A Magazine of Verse*, LXXXVIII, No. 4 (July, 1956), 257–266.

Homans, George C. *The Human Group*. New York: Harcourt, Brace and Co., 1950.

Home, Henry, Lord Kames. *Elements of Criticism*. New York, 1830.

Honig, Edwin. *Garcia Lorca: The Makers of Modern Literature*. Norfolk, Conn.: New Directions, 1944.

———. *Dark Conceit: The Making of Allegory*. Evanston, Ill.: Northwestern University Press, 1959.

Hopkins, Gerard Manley. *Letters*. Ed. C. C. Abbott. 2 vols. New York: Oxford University Press, 1955.

———. *Notebooks and Papers*. Ed. Humphrey House. London: Oxford University Press, 1937.

Hopkins, Vivian C. *Spires of Form: A Study of Emerson's Aesthetic Theory*. Cambridge, Mass.: Harvard University Press, 1951.

Hospers, John. *Meaning and Truth in the Arts*. Chapel Hill: University of North Carolina Press, 1946.

Hough, Graham. *Reflections on a Literary Revolution*. Washington, D.C.: Catholic University Press, 1960.

Housman, A. E. *The Name and Nature of Poetry*. New York: The Macmillan Co., 1933.

Howell, A. C. "Res et Verba," *Journal of English History* (1946) 131–142.

Howell, Wilbur Samuel. *Logic and Rhetoric in England, 1500–1700*. Princeton, N.J.: Princeton University Press, 1956.

Howes, Raymond F., ed. *Historical Studies of Rhetoric and Rhetoricians*. Ithaca, N.Y.: Cornell University Press, 1960.

Hubbell, G. S. *A Concordance to the Poems of Ralph Waldo Emerson*. New York: The H. W. Wilson Co., 1932.

Hubbell, Harry Mortimer. *The Influence of Isocrates on Cicero, Dionysius and Aristides*. New Haven: Yale University Press, 1913.

Hughes, John. *Science of Language*. New York: Random House, 1962.

Hughes, Richard. "The Contemporaneity of Classic Rhetoric," *College Composition and Communication*, XVI, No. 3 (October, 1965), 144–150.

Hoijer, Harry, ed. "Language in Culture," *The American Anthropologist*, Vol. LVI, No. 6, Part 2 (December, 1954).

Horton, Philip. *Hart Crane*. New York: W. W. Norton and Co., 1937.

Hulme, T. E. *Speculations*. Ed. Herbert Read. London: Kegan Paul, 1924.

———. *Further Speculations*. Ed. Sam Hynes. Minneapolis: University of Minnesota Press, 1955.

Humphreys, A. R. *Steele, Addison and Their Periodical Essays*. London: Longmans, Green, 1959.

Hunt, M. L. *Thomas Dekker: A Study*. New York: Columbia University Press, 1911.

Hunter, G. J. *Lyly: The Humanist as Courtier*. Cambridge, Mass.: Harvard University Press, 1962.

Huntley, F. *Sir Thomas Browne: A Biographical and Critical Study*. Ann Arbor: University of Michigan Press, 1962.

Hussey, Christopher. *The Picturesque: Studies in a Point of View*. London: G. P. Putnam, 1929.

Huxley, Aldous. *Ends and Means: An Inquiry into the Nature of Ideals and into the Methods Employed for Their Realization*. New York: Harper and Brothers, 1937.

Huyghe, Rene. *Ideas and Images in World Art*. New York: Abrams, 1959.

Hyman, Herbert. *Survey Design and Analysis*. Glencoe, Ill.: Free Press, 1955.

Hyman, Stanley Edgar. *The Tangled Bank: Darwin, Marx, Frazer, and Freud as Imaginative Writers*. New York: Atheneum, 1962.

Hymes, Dell. *Language in Culture and Society: A Reader in Linguistics and Anthropology*. New York: Harper and Brothers, 1964.

———. "Phonological Aspects of Style: Some English Sonnets," in *Style in Language*. Ed. Thomas Sebeck. New York: John Wiley and Sons, 1960.

———. "Some North Pacific Coast Poems: A Problem in Anthropological Philology," *American Anthropologist*, LXVII, No. 2.

Ingarden, Roman. *Das Literarische Kunstwerk*. Halle, Germany: Niemeyer, 1931.

Jackson, Holbrook. *Dreamers of Dreams: The Rise and Fall of Nineteenth Century Idealism*. London: Faber & Faber, 1948.

Jackson, R. W. *Swift and His Circle: A Book of Essays*. Dublin: Talbot Press, 1945.

Jacobi, Johan. *Psychology of C. G. Jung*. Trans. K. W. Bash. London: Kegan Paul, 1942–1943.

Jacobs, M. *Jonathan Swift*. Berlin: Wedding Verlag, 1948.

Jacobsen, Josephine, and William R. Mueller. *The Testament of Samuel Beckett*. New York: Hill and Wang, 1964.

Jacobsson, Beugt. *Inversion in English*. Uppsala: Almquist & Wiksell, 1951.

Jaeger, Werner. *Paideia: The Ideals of Greek Culture*. Trans. Gilbert Highet. New York: Oxford University Press, 1939.

Jakobson, Roman. "Linguistics and Communication Theory," *Structure of Language and Its Mathematical Aspects*, "Proceedings of Symposia in Applied Mathematics," XII (1961), 245–252.

———. "The Metaphoric and Metonymic Poles," *Fundamentals of Language*. The Hague: Mouton & Co., 1956, pp. 76–82.

———, and Morris Halle. *Fundamentals of Language*. The Hague: Mouton & Co., 1956.

———, et al. *Preliminaries to Speech Analysis: The Distinctive Features and Their Correlates*. Report No. 13. Cambridge, Mass.: Massachusetts Institute of Technology Press, 1952.

James, D. G. *Matthew Arnold and the Decline of English Romanticism*. Oxford: The Clarendon Press, 1961.

———. *Skepticism and Poetry: An Essay on the Poetic Imagination*. London: Allen & Unwin, 1937.

———. *The Dream of Learning: An Essay on the Advancement of Learning, Hamlet, and King Lear*. Oxford: The Clarendon Press, 1951.

Jameson, R. D. *A Comparison of Literature*. London: Kegan Paul, 1935.

Jameson, T. H. *Francis Bacon: Criticism and the Modern World*. New York: F. A. Praeger, 1954.

Jantz, Harold. *The First Century of New England Verse*. New Haven: Yale University Press, 1944.

Jenkins, J. J. "Associative Processes in Verbal Behavior," Report of the Minnesota Conference, mimeographed. Minneapolis, 1959.

———. "The Change in Some American Word Association Norms in the Twentieth Century." Paper presented at the Fifteenth International Congress of Psychology. Brussels, 1957.

Jennings, J. G. *Metaphor in Poetry*. London: Blackie & Son, 1915.

Jespersen, Otto. *Essentials of English Grammar*. London: Allen & Unwin, 1933.

———. *Growth and Structure of the English Language*. New York: G. E. Stechert, 1905.

———. *Selected Writings*. London: Allen & Unwin, 1962.

———. *Language: Its Nature, Development, and Origin*. New York: Henry Holt and Co., 1922.

———. *Mankind, Nations, and Individuals from a Linguistic Point of View*. Cambridge, Mass.: Harvard University Press, 1925.

———. *Philosophy of Grammar*. New York: Henry Holt and Co., 1924.

Jessop, T. E. *Thomas Hobbes*. London: Longmans, Green, 1960.

Johnson, Alexander Byron. *A Treatise on Language*. Ed. David Rynin. Berkeley: University of California Press, 1947.

Johnson, R. *Walter Pater: A Study of His Critical Outlook and Achievement*. Melbourne: The University Press, 1961.

Johnson, Samuel. *The Age of Johnson: Essays Presented to C. B. Tinker*. New Haven: Yale University Press, 1949.

———. *The Lives of the English Poets*. Ed. George Birback Hill. Oxford: The Clarendon Press, 1905.

Johnson, W. S. *The Voices of Matthew Arnold: An Essay in Criticism*. New Haven: Yale University Press, 1961.

Jones, Ebenezer. *Studies of Sensation and Event*. London, 1879.

Jones, John. *The Egotistical Sublime: A History of Wordsworth's Imagination*. London: Chatto & Windus, 1954.

Jones, P. M. *The Background of Modern French Poetry*. Cambridge, Eng.: The University Press, 1951.

Jones, Richard Foster. *The Seventeenth Century: Studies in the History of Thought and Literature from Bacon to Pope*. Stanford, Calif.: Stanford University Press, 1951.

———. *The Triumph of the English Language*. Stanford, Calif.: Stanford University Press, 1951.

Jonson, Ben. *Timber*, with an Introduction by Ralph S. Walker. Syracuse, N.Y.: Syracuse University Press, 1953.

———. *The English Grammar: Made by Ben Jonson for the Benefit of All Strangers, Out of His Observations of the English Language Now Spoken and in Use*. London: Lanston Monotype Corp., 1928.

Joos, Martin. *The English Verb: Form and Meaning*. Madison: University of Wisconsin Press, 1964.

Jordan, J. E. *Thomas De Quincey, Literary Critic, His Method and Achievement.* Berkeley: University of California Press, 1952.

Joseph, Sister Miriam. *Shakespeare's Use of the Arts of Language.* New York: Columbia University Press, 1947.

Jung, C. G. *Psychology of the Unconscious: A Study of the Transformations and Symbolisms of the Libido. A Contribution to the History of the Evolution of Thought.* Trans. Beatrice M. Hinkle. New York: Dodd, Mead, 1925.

———, ed. *Studies in Word-Association.* Trans. Dr. M. D. Eder. London: W. Heinemann, 1918.

Kadish, Mortimer R. "Sin, Science, and the Dry, Hard Style," *Philosophy and Phenomenological Research*, XIX, No. 2 (December, 1958), 212–225.

Kahn, Sholom J. *Science and Aesthetic Judgment: A Study in Taine's Critical Method.* New York: Columbia University Press, 1953.

Kallen, Horace. *Art and Freedom.* New York: Duell, Sloan and Pearce, 1942.

Kalstone, David. *Sidney's Poetry: Contexts and Interpretations.* Cambridge, Mass.: Harvard University Press, 1965.

Kane, Elisha K. *Gongorism and the Golden Age.* Chapel Hill: University of North Carolina Press, 1928.

Kantor, J. R. *An Objective Psychology of Grammar.* Bloomington: Indiana University Press, 1952.

Kaplan, Abraham, and Ernst Kris. "Aesthetic Ambiguity," *Philosophy and Phenomenological Research*, VIII, No. 3 (March, 1948), 415–435.

Kardiner, Abram. *The Individual and His Society.* New York: Columbia University Press, 1939.

———, Ralph Linton, Cora de Bois, and James West. *The Psychological Frontier of Society.* New York: Columbia University Press, 1945.

Karlsen, Rolf. *Studies in the Connectives of Clauses.* Bergen, 1959.

Kasanin, J. B. *Language and Thought in Schizophrenia.* Berkeley: University of California Press, 1944.

Katz, J. J., and P. M. Portal. *An Integrated Theory of Linguistic Descriptions,* Research Monograph No. 26. Cambridge, Mass.: Massachusetts Institute of Technology Press, 1964.

Kaufmann, Walter. *Hegel Reinterpretation: Texts and Commentary.* Garden City, N.Y: Doubleday and Co., 1965.

Kaye, J. B. *George Bernard Shaw and the Nineteenth Century Tradition.* Norman: University of Oklahoma Press, 1958.

Kazin, Alfred. *On Native Grounds: An Interpretation of Modern American Prose Literature.* New York: Reynal and Hitchcock, 1942.

Keats, John. *Letters.* Ed. M. Buxton Forman. 2 vols. London: Oxford University Press, 1931.

Keesing, Felix. *Cultural Change: An Analysis and Bibliography of Anthropological Sources to 1952.* Stanford, Calif.: Stanford University Press, 1953.

Kempt, R., ed. *The American Joe Miller.* London, 1865.

Ker, W. P. *Form and Style in Poetry.* Ed. R. W. Chambers. New York: The Macmillan Co., 1928.

Kenner, Hugh. *Flaubert, Joyce, and Beckett: The Store Comedians.* Boston: Beacon Press, 1962.

Kermode, Frank. *John Donne.* London: Longmans, Green, 1961.

————. *The Romantic Image.* London: Kegan Paul, 1957.

————. *The Living Milton: Essays by Various Hands.* London: Routledge & Kegan Paul, 1960.

Kindilien, Carlin T. *American Poetry in the 1890's.* Providence, R.I.: Brown University Press, 1956.

King, Arthur H. *The Language of Satirized Characters in Poetaster: A Sociostylistic Analysis, 1597–1602.* Lund, Sweden: C. W. K. Gleerup, 1941.

Kinneavy, Brother James Leo. *A Study of Three Contemporary Theories of Lyric Poetry.* Washington, D.C.: Catholic University of America Press, 1956.

Kirkconnel, Watson. *The Celestial Cycle: The Theme of "Paradise Lost" in World Literature, with Translations of the Major Analogues.* Toronto: University of Toronto Press, 1952.

Kliger, Samuel. *The Goths in England: A Study of Seventeenth and Eighteenth Century Thought.* Cambridge, Mass.: Harvard University Press, 1952.

Knickerbocker, William S., ed. *Twentieth Century English.* New York: Philosophical Library, 1946.

Knight, G. Wilson. *The Burning Oracle: Studies in the Poetry of Action.* London: Oxford University Press, 1939.

————. *The Starlit Dome: Studies in the Poetry of Vision.* London: Oxford University Press, 1941.

Knight, Richard Payne. *The Symbolist Language of Ancient Art and Mythology,* new edition. New York, 1892.

Knights, L. C. "Elizabethan Prose," *Scrutiny,* II (1934).

Kobayashi, Shozo. *Rhythm in the Prose of Thomas De Quincey.* Tokyo: Dainippon Printing Co., 1956.

Korzybski, Alfred. *Science and Sanity: An Introduction to Non-Aristotelean Systems and General Semantics.* New York: International Non-Aristotelean Library Publishing Co., 1933.

Kretzmann, Norman, trans. *William of Sherwood's Introduction to Logic.* Minneapolis: University of Minnesota Press, 1965.

Krieger, Murray. *The New Apologists for Poetry.* Minneapolis: University of Minnesota Press, 1956.

Kristeller, Paul O. *Studies in Renaissance Thought and Letters.* Rome: Edizioni di Storia e Letteratura, 1956.

Kroeber, A. L. *Anthropology.* New York: Harcourt, Brace and Co., 1923.

————. *Configurations of Culture Growth.* Berkeley: University of California Press, 1944.

————. *Style and Civilizations.* Ithaca, N.Y.: Cornell University Press, 1957.

————. "Parts of Speech in Periods of Poetry," *PMLA,* LXIII, No. 4 (September, 1958), 309–314.

Krutch, Joseph Wood. *Experience and Art: Some Aspects of the Esthetics of Literature.* New York: Harrison Smith and Robert Haas, 1932.

Kurth, Burton O. *Milton and the English Traditions of Biblical Heroic Narrative.* Berkeley: University of California Press, 1955.

188

LaBarre, Weston. *The Human Animal*. Chicago: University of Chicago Press, 1954.

Ladd, Henry. *The Victorian Morality of Art*. New York: Long and Smith, 1932.

Lambert, Mildred. "Studies in Stylistics," *American Speech*, III (1928), in 3 parts.

Lamprecht, Sterling P. *Nature and History*. New York: Columbia University Press, 1950.

Landar, Herbert. *Language and Culture*. New York: Oxford University Press, 1965.

Langbaum, Robert. *The Poetry of Experience: The Dramatic Monologue in Modern Literary Tradition*. London: Chatto & Windus, 1957.

Langer, Suzanne. *Feeling and Form: A Theory of Art Developed from "Philosophy in a New Key."* New York: Charles Scribner's Sons, 1953.

———. *Philosophy in a New Key: A Study in the Symbolism of Person, Rite, and Art*. Cambridge, Mass.: Harvard University Press, 1942.

———, ed. *Reflections on Art*. Baltimore, Md.: Johns Hopkins University Press, 1958.

Lanier, Sidney. *The Science of English Verse*. New York: Charles Scribner's Sons, 1880.

Lannering, Jan. *Studies in the Prose Style of Joseph Addison*. Cambridge: Harvard University Press, 1951.

Lasswell, Harold D., Nathan Leites, *et al. Language of Politics: Studies in Quantitative Semantics*. New York: George Stewart, 1949.

Lawton, George. *John Wesley's English: A Study of His Literary Style*. London: Allen & Unwin, 1962.

Lazarsfeld, Paul, and Morris Rosenberg. *The Language of Social Research*. Glencoe, Ill.: Free Press, 1955.

Leavis, E. R. *New Bearings in English Poetry: A Study of the Contemporary Situation*. London: Chatto & Windus, 1932.

———. *Revaluation: Tradition and Development in English Poetry*. London: Chatto & Windus, 1936.

LeComte, E. S. *Yet Once More: Verbal and Psychological Pattern in Milton*. New York: Liberal Arts Press, 1953.

———. *A Milton Dictionary*. New York: Philosophical Library, 1961.

Lee, Dorothy. "Lineal and Nonlineal Codifications of Reality," *Psychosomatic Medicine*, XII, No. 2 (March–April, 1950), 89–97.

Lee, Irving J., ed. *The Language of Wisdom and Folly*. New York: Harper and Brothers, 1949.

Lee, Vernon. *The Handling of Words, and Other Studies in Literary Psychology*. London: John Lane, 1923.

Leed, Jacob, ed. *Computers and Literary Analysis*. Kent, Ohio: Kent State University Press, 1966.

Lees, R. B. *The Grammar of English Nominalization, International Journal of American Linguistics*, 26, suppl. (1964).

LeFevre, Carl. *Linguistics and Reading*. New York: McGraw-Hill Book Co., 1964.

————, and Helen. *Writing by Patterns*. New York: Alfred A. Knopf, 1963.

Le Hir, Yves. *Esthétique et Structure du Vers Français d'Après les Théoriciens du XVIᵉ Siècle à Nos Jours*. Paris: Presses Universitaires de France, 1956.

Lehmann, A. G. *The Symbolist Aesthetic in France, 1885–1895*. Oxford: Blackwell, 1950.

Lemaitre, Georges. *From Cubism to Surrealism in French Literature*. Cambridge, Mass.: Harvard University Press, 1951.

Lemmi, C. W. *The Classic Deities in Bacon: A Study in Mythological Symbolism*. Baltimore: Johns Hopkins University Press, 1933.

Lemon, Lee T. *The Partial Critics*. Lincoln: University of Nebraska, 1965.

Lennering, Jan. *Studies in the Prose Style of Joseph Addison*. "Essays in English Language and Literature," Vol. IX. Uppsala, 1951.

Leonard, Sterling Andrus. *The Doctrine of Correctness in English Usage, 1700–1800*. "University of Wisconsin Studies in Language and Literature," No. 25. Madison, 1929.

Leroy, Oliver. *Le Chevalier Thomas Browne: Médicin, Styliste et Métaphysicien*. Paris: Librairie J. Gamber, 1931.

Levin, Harry. *James Joyce: A Critical Introduction*, rev. and augmented ed. Norfolk, Conn.: New Directions, 1960.

————, ed. *Perspectives of Criticism*. Cambridge, Mass.: Harvard University Press, 1950.

————. *The Power of Blackness*. New York: Alfred A. Knopf, 1958.

Levin, Kurt. *Field Theory in Social Science*. New York: Harper and Brothers, 1951.

Levin, Samuel R. *Linguistic Structures in Poetry*. The Hague: Mouton & Co., 1962.

————. "Two Grammatical Approaches to Poetic Analysis," *College Composition and Communication*, Vol. XVI (December, 1965).

Levi-Straus, C., R. Jakobson, C. F. Voegelin, and T. A. Sebeok. *Results of the Conference of Anthropologists and Linguistics*. Baltimore: Johns Hopkins University Press, 1953.

Lewis, B. Roland. *Creative Poetry: A Study of its Organic Principles*. London: Oxford University Press, 1931.

Lewis, C. Day. *The Poetic Image*. New York: Oxford University Press, 1948.

Lewis, C. S. *The Allegory of Love: A Study in Medieval Tradition*. London: Oxford University Press, 1936.

————. *Psycho-Analysis and Literary Criticism*. "Essays and Studies by Members of the English Association," XXVII. Collected by Nowell C. Smith. London: Oxford University Press, 1942.

————. *Studies in Words*. Cambridge, Eng.: The University Press, 1960.

Lewis, Edwin Herbert. *The History of the English Paragraph*. Chicago: University of Chicago Press, 1894.

Lewis, Gilbert N. *Anatomy of Science*. New Haven: Yale University Press, 1926.

Lewis, R. W. B. *The American Adam: Innocence, Tragedy, and Tradition in the Nineteenth Century*. Chicago: University of Chicago Press, 1955.

Lewis, Wyndham. *Time and Western Man*. Boston: Beacon Press, 1957.

Leyburn, Ellen Douglas. *Satiric Allegory: Mirror of Man*. New Haven: Yale University Press, 1956.

Lily, William. *A Shorte Introduction of Grammar*. New York: Scholars' Facsimiles, 1945.

Linton, Ralph, ed. *The Science of Man — The World Crisis*. New York: Columbia University Press, 1945.

Litz, A. Walton. *The Art of James Joyce: Method and Design in "Ulysses" and "Finnegan's Wake."* London: Oxford University Press, 1961.

Long, Ralph B. *The Sentence and Its Parts*. Chicago: University of Chicago Press, 1961.

Longinus on the Sublime and Sir Joshua Reynold's Discourses. Trans. Benedict Einarsson, with an Introd. by Elder Olson. Chicago: Packard, 1945.

Lovejoy, Arthur. *Essays in the History of Ideas*. Baltimore: Johns Hopkins University Press, 1948.

————. *The Great Chain of Being: A Study of the History of an Idea*. Cambridge, Mass.: Harvard University Press, 1936.

Lowell, James Russell. "Emerson the Lecturer," *From My Study Window*. Boston: Houghton Mifflin Co., 1895, 152–160.

Lowenthal, Leo. *Literature, Popular Culture, and Society*. Englewood Cliffs, N.J.: Prentice-Hall, 1961.

Lowes, John Livingston. *Convention and Revolt in Poetry*. Boston: Houghton Mifflin Co., 1924.

————. *The Road to Xanadu*. Boston: Houghton Mifflin Co., 1930.

Lowie, Robert H. *An Introduction to Cultural Anthropology*. New York: Farrar and Rinehart, 1934.

Lowth, Robert. *A Short Introduction to Grammar*. London, 1762, 1775.

————. *Lectures on the Sacred Poetry of the Hebrews*, 2nd ed. London, 1816.

Lucas, Frank L. *The Art of Living. Four Eighteenth Century Minds: Hume, Walpole, Burke, Franklin*. London: Cassell, 1959.

————. *Style*. New York: Collier, 1962.

Lunt, H. G., ed. *Proceedings of the Ninth International Congress of Linguists, Cambridge, Mass., 1962*. The Hague: Mouton & Co., 1964.

Lyly, John. *Euphues: The Anatomy of Wit. Euphues & His England*. Ed. Morris William Croll and Harry Clemons. New York: E. P. Dutton Co., 1916.

Lynch, J. J. "The Tonality of Lyric Poetry: An Experiment in Method," *Word*, IX (1953), 211–224.

Lynch, Kathleen. *Roger Boyle: First Earl of Orrery*. Knoxville: University of Tennessee Press, 1965.

Lyons, John. *Structural Semantics*. London: Oxford University Press, 1963.

Mackin, Ronald and P. D. Strevens, eds. *Language and Language Learning*. Oxford: Oxford University Press, 1965.

McGrath, Earl J., ed. *Communication in General Education*. Dubuque, Iowa: W. C. Brown Co., 1949.

McKee, Paul G. *Language in the Elementary School*. Boston: Houghton Mifflin Co., 1939.

MacKenzie, Donald A. *The Migration of Symbols and Their Relation to Beliefs and Customs*. New York: Alfred A. Knopf, 1926.

McKeon, Richard. "The Philosophic Bases of Art and Criticism," *Modern Philology*, XLI, No. 3 (February, 1944), 129–171.

———. *Thought, Action, and Passion*. Chicago: University of Chicago Press, 1954.

McKnight, George H. *English Words and Their Backgrounds*. New York: D. Appleton, 1923.

MacLean, Kenneth. *John Locke and English Literature of the Eighteenth Century*. New Haven: Yale University Press, 1936.

MacLeish, Archibald. *The Irresponsibles*. New York: Duell, Sloan and Pearce, 1940.

MacLuhan, Marshall. *Understanding Media*. New York: McGraw-Hill Book Co., 1965.

Madden, John F., and F. P. Magoun. *A Grouped Frequency Word-List of Anglo-Saxon Poetry*. Cambridge, Mass.: Harvard University Press, 1957.

Maier, N. R. F., and H. Willard Reininger. *A Psychological Approach to Literary Criticism*. New York: D. Appleton, 1933.

Malinowski, Bronislaw. *A Scientific Theory of Culture and Other Essays*. Chapel Hill: University of North Carolina Press, 1944.

———, and Phyllis M. Kaberry, eds. *The Dynamics of Culture Change: An Inquiry into Race Relations in Africa*. New Haven: Yale University Press, 1935.

Malkiel, Yakov. "Etymology and General Linguistics," *Word*, XVIII, Nos. 1 and 2 (April–August, 1962), 198–219.

———. "A Tentative Typology of Romance Historical Grammars," *Lingua*, IX, No. 4 (1960), 321–416.

Mannheim, Karl. *Essays on the Sociology of Knowledge*. London: Kegan Paul, 1952.

Markey, John F. *The Symbolic Process and Its Integration in Children: A Study in Social Psychology*. London: Kegan Paul, 1928.

Marsh, George P. *Lectures on the English Language*. New York: Columbia Lectures, 1859.

Marsh, Robert. *Four Dialectical Theories of Poetry*. Chicago: University of Chicago Press, 1965.

Martin, Harold, ed. *Style in Prose Fiction*. "English Institute Essays," 1958. New York: Columbia University Press, 1959.

Martinet, André. *Elements of General Linguistics*. Trans. Elisabeth Palmer. London: Faber & Faber, 1960.

Massey, B. W. A. *The Compound Epithets of Keats and Shelley*. Poznan, Poland, 1923.

Matthews, William, ed. *Later Medieval English Prose*. New York: D. Appleton, 1965.

Matsuura, Kaichi. *A Study of Donne's Imagery: A Revelation of His Outlook on the World and His Vision of a Universal Christian Monarchy*. Tokyo: Kenkyuska, 1953.

Matthiessen, F. O. *The Achievement of T. S. Eliot: An Essay on the Nature of Poetry*. Boston: Houghton Mifflin Co., 1935.

————. *American Renaissance*. New York: Oxford University Press, 1941.

Maxim, Hudson. *The Science of Poetry and the Philosophy of Language*. New York: Funk and Wagnalls, 1910.

May, Rollo, ed. *Symbolism in Religion and Literature*. New York: Braziller, 1960.

Mazzeo, J. A. *Reason and Imagination, 1600–1800*. New York: Columbia University Press, 1962.

Mead, George. *Movements of Thought in the Nineteenth Century*. Chicago: University of Chicago Press, 1936.

Medewar, P. B. *The Future of Man*. New York: Basic Books, 1960.

Mendenhall, John Cooper. *Aureate Terms*. Philadelphia: University of Pennsylvania Press, 1919.

Mentré, François. *Les Générations Sociales*. Paris: Editions Bossard, 1920.

Merton, E. S. *Science and Imagination in Sir Thomas Browne*. New York: King's Crown Press, 1949.

Meyerhoff, Hans. *Time in Literature*. Berkeley: University of California Press, 1955.

Miles, Josephine. *Continuity of Poetic Language: Studies in English Poetry from 1640's to 1940's*. Berkeley: University of California Press, 1951; New York: Octagon Press, 1966.

————. *Emerson*. Minneapolis: University of Minnesota Press, 1964.

————. "American Poetry, 1965," *Massachusetts Review*, VII (Spring, 1966), 2.

————. "English: A Colloquy: or, How What's What in the Language," *California English Journal*, II (Winter, 1966).

————. "Review of Concordances," *Victorian Studies* (March, 1965), 290–292.

————. "Emerson's Wise Universe," *University of Minnesota Review*, II, No. 3 (Spring, 1962), 305–313.

————. "A Poet Looks at Graphs," *Michigan Quarterly Review*, IV, No. 3 (Summer, 1965), 185–188.

————. *Eras and Modes in English Poetry*, 2nd rev. ed. Berkeley: University of California Press, 1964.

————. "Language of Lycidas," *Lycidas*. Ed. Dean Patrides. New York: Oxford University Press, 1961.

————. *Pathetic Fallacy in the Nineteenth Century: Study of Changing Relation Between Object and Emotion*. Berkeley: University of California Press, 1942; "University of California Publications in English," Vol. XII, No. 2. New York: Octagon Press, 1965.

————. "Poetry of Praise," *Kenyon Review*, XXIII, No. 1 (Winter, 1961), 104–125.

————. "Reading Poems," *English Journal*, Vol. LII, Nos. 3, 4 (March–April, 1963).

————. *Renaissance, Eighteenth-Century and Modern Language in English Poetry*. Berkeley: University of California Press, 1960.

————. "What We Compose," *College Composition and Communication,* Vol. XV (October, 1964).

————. "Wordsworth and Glitter," *Studies in Philology,* XL, No. 4 (October, 1943), 552–559.

————. *Wordsworth and the Vocabulary of Emotion.* Berkeley: University of California Press, 1942. "University of California Publications in English," Vol. XII, No. 1. New York: Octagon Press, 1965.

Milic, Louis. *The Style of Swift.* New York: W. W. Norton and Co., 1966.

Miller, George A. *Language and Communication.* New York: McGraw-Hill Book Co., 1951.

Miller, J. Hillis. *Poets of Reality.* Cambridge, Mass.: Harvard University Press, 1965.

Miller, James E. *A Critical Guide to "Leaves of Grass."* Chicago: University of Chicago Press, 1957.

Miller, Perry. *The New England Mind.* Cambridge, Mass.: Harvard University Press, 1953.

————. *The Transcendentalists.* Cambridge, Mass.: Harvard University Press, 1950.

Mills, Ralph I., Jr. *Contemporary American Poetry.* New York: Random House, 1965.

Milton, John. *Areopagitica and Other Prose Works,* with an Introd. by K. M. Burton. New York: E. P. Dutton Co., 1955.

————. *Areopagitica,* with an introd. by John W. Hales. London: Oxford University Press, 1961.

————. *Areopagitica,* with a Commentary by Sir Richard C. Jebb. Cambridge, Eng.: The University Press, 1933.

Minto, William. *A Manual of English Prose Literature.* Boston: Ginn and Co., 1895.

Modern European Poetry. New York: Bantam Books, 1965.

Moloney, Michael F. *John Donne: His Flight from Medievalism.* Urbana: University of Illinois Press, 1944.

Mollenauer, Robert, ed. *Introduction to Modernity: A Symposium on Eighteenth-Century Thought.* Austin: University of Texas Press, 1965.

Monk, Samuel. *The Sublime: A Study of Critical Theories in Eighteenth Century England.* New York: Modern Language Association, 1935; new ed., Ann Arbor: University of Michigan Press, 1961.

Monroe, Harriet. *A Poet's Life.* New York: The Macmillan Co., 1938.

Montgomery, Robert L. *Symmetry and Sense: The Poetry of Sir Philip Sidney.* Austin: University of Texas Press, 1961.

Moore, Cecil. *Backgrounds of English Literature,* 1700–1760. Minneapolis: University of Minnesota Press, 1953.

Moore, George, ed. *Anthology of Pure Poetry.* New York: Boni and Liveright, 1925.

Moore, H. T. *D. H. Lawrence, His Life and Work,* rev. ed. New York: Twayne Publishers, 1964.

More, Thomas. *The Apology,* with an introd. and notes by Arthur Irving Taft. London: Oxford University Press, 1930.

―――. *A Dialogue of Comfort Against Tribulation.* Ed. Leland Miles. Bloomington: University of Indiana Press, 1965.

Morgenstern, Sam, ed. *Composers on Music.* New York: Pantheon, 1956.

Morris, Bertram. *The Aesthetic Process.* "Northwestern University Studies in Humanities," No. 8. Evanston, Ill.: Northwestern University Press, 1943.

Morris, C. W. *Foundation of Theory of Signs.* Chicago: University of Chicago Press, 1938.

―――. *Varieties of Human Value.* Chicago: University of Chicago Press, 1956.

Mosteller, Frederick, and David Wallace, eds. *Inference and Disputed Authorship: The Federalist.* Reading, Mass.: Addison-Wesley, 1964.

Muir, Edwin. *An Autobiography.* New York: W. Sloane, 1954.

―――. *The Structure of the Novel.* London: Hogarth Press, 1957.

Muir, Kenneth. *John Milton.* London: Longmans, Green, 1960.

―――. *An Autobiography.* New York: W. Sloane, 1954.

―――. *Sir Philip Sidney.* London: Longmans, Green, 1960.

Müller-Freienfels, Richard. *Evolution of Modern Psychology.* Trans. W. Burton Wolfe. New Haven: Yale University Press, 1935.

Muller, Herbert J. *Science and Criticism: The Humanities Tradition in Contemporary Thought.* New Haven: Yale University Press, 1943.

Mumford, Lewis. *The Conditions of Man.* New York: Harcourt, Brace and Co., 1944.

―――. *The Culture of Cities.* New York: Harcourt, Brace and Co., 1938.

Munro, Thomas. "The Marxist Theory of Art History," *Journal of Aesthetics and Art Criticism,* XVIII (June, 1960), 430–445.

―――. *Scientific Method in Aesthetics.* New York: W. W. Norton and Co., 1928.

Munz, Peter. *The Place of Hooker in the History of Thought.* London: Routledge & Kegan Paul, 1952.

Murchison, Carl, ed. *Handbook of Social Psychology.* London: Oxford University Press, 1935.

Murphy, Gardner. *Human Potentialities.* New York: Basic Books, 1958.

Murray, Gilbert. *The Classical Tradition in Poetry.* Cambridge, Mass.: Harvard University Press, 1927.

Murray, Henry, ed. "Myth and Myth Making," *Daedalus,* Vol. LXXXVIII, No. 2 (Spring, 1959).

Murry, J. Middleton. *The Problem of Style.* London: Oxford University Press, 1936.

―――. *Swift.* London: Longmans, Green, 1955.

Nascimento, Braulio de. "Literary Criticism as an Applied Science," *Revista Branca,* VI, No. 30 (1954), 135–160.

Nathan, Leonard. *The Tragic Drama of W. B. Yeats.* New York: Columbia University Press, 1964.

Neal, John. *American Writers: A Series Contributed to Blackwood's Magazine, 1824–1825.* Ed. F. L. Pattee. Durham, N.C.: Duke University Press, 1937.

Nelson, Lowry, Jr. *Baroque Lyric Poetry.* New Haven: Yale University Press, 1961.

Newman, John B. "Writing and Speaking," *College Composition and Communication*, XVI, No. 3 (October, 1965), 157–160.

Nicolson, Marjorie Hope. *The Breaking of the Circle*. Evanston, Ill.: Northwestern University Press, 1950.

Nida, Eugene A. *Morphology*, 2nd ed. Ann Arbor: University of Michigan Press, 1949.

———. *Mountain Gloom and Mountain Glory: The Development of the Aesthetics of the Infinite*. Ithaca, N.Y.: Cornell University Press, 1959.

———. *A Synopsis of English Syntax*. Norman: University of Oklahoma Press, 1960.

Niebuhr, Reinhold. *The Self and the Drama of History*. New York: Charles Scribner's Sons, 1955.

Nietzsche, Friedrich. *Birth of Tragedy and Genealogy of Morals*. New York: Doubleday and Co., 1956.

Nitchie, Elizabeth. *The Criticism of Literature*. New York: The Macmillan Co., 1928.

Nowottny, Winifred. *The Language Poets Use*. London: University of London Press, 1962.

O'Conner, William Van. *Sense and Sensibility in Modern Poetry*. Chicago: University of Chicago Press, 1948.

Obertello, Alfredo. *Carlyle's Critical Theories*. Geneva, Switzerland: Edizioni L.U.P.A., 1948.

Oertel, Hans Joachim. *George Berkeley und die Englische Literatur*. Halle, Germany: Niemeyer, 1934.

Ogden, C. K. *Bentham's Theory of Fictions*. London: Kegan Paul, 1932.

Ogden, C. K., I. A. Richards, and James Wood. *The Foundation of Aesthetics*. London: Allen & Unwin, 1922.

Ogden, C. K., and I. A. Richards. *Meaning of Meaning: Study of Influence of Language on Thought and of Science of Symbolism*. London: Kegan Paul, 1926; with Supplementary Essays by B. Malinowski and F. G. Crookshank, 2nd rev. ed. New York: Harcourt, Brace and Co., 1927.

Ohmann, Richard M. *Shaw: The Style and the Man*. Middletown, Conn.: Wesleyan University Press, 1962.

Omond, T. S. *English Metrists*. Tunbridge Wells, Eng.: R. Pelton, 1903.

Osborn, Louise Brown. *The Life, Letters, and Writings of John Hoskins*. "Yale Studies in English," LXXXVII. New Haven: Yale University Press, 1937.

Osgood, Charles, George J. Suci, and Percy Tannenbaum. *The Measurement of Meaning*. Urbana: University of Illinois Press, 1957.

Oxenhandler, Neal. "Ontological Criticism in America and France," *Modern Language Review*, LV, No. 1 (January, 1960), 17–23.

Panofsky, Erwin. *Meaning in the Visual Arts*. New York: Doubleday and Co., 1955.

———. *Studies in Iconology*. New York: Oxford University Press, 1939.

Parkes, Henry Barnford. *The Pragmatic Test: Essays in the History of Ideas*. San Francisco: Colt, 1941.

Parkinson, Thomas. *W. B. Yeats: Self-Critic*. Berkeley: University of California Press, 1951.

———. *W. B. Yeats: The Later Poetry*. Berkeley: University of California Press, 1964.

Parrington, Vernon Lewis. *Main Currents in American Thought*. New York: Harcourt, Brace and Co., 1927.

Partridge, A. C. *The Accidence of Ben Jonson's Plays, Masques and Entertainments*. Cambridge, Eng.: Bowes & Bowes, 1953.

———. *Studies in the Syntax of Ben Jonson's Plays*. Cambridge, Eng.: Bowes & Bowes, 1953.

Partridge, B. *The Broken Compass: A Study of the Major Comedies of Ben Jonson*. New York: Columbia University Press, 1958.

Pater, Walter. *Appreciations: With an Essay on Style*. London: The Macmillan Co., 1920.

Paulson, Ronald. *Theme and Structure in Swift's "Tale of a Tub."* Yale Studies in English," Vol. CXLIII. New Haven: Yale University Press, 1960.

Payne, Stanley. *The Art of Asking Questions*. Princeton, N.J.: Princeton University Press, 1951.

Pearson, Karl. *The Grammar of Science*, 1st ed. New York: Charles Scribner's Sons, 1892.

Peirce, Charles Sanders. *Collected Papers*. Ed. Charles Hartshorne and Paul Weiss. Cambridge, Mass.: Harvard University Press, 1931–1935.

———. *Philosophical Writings*. Selected and edited by Justus Buchler. New York: Dover, 1955.

Peltola, Niilo. *The Compound Epithet and Its Use in American Poetry from Broadstreet through Whitman*. Helsinki, 1956.

Pepper, Stephen C. *The Basis of Criticism in the Arts*. Cambridge, Mass.: Harvard University Press, 1945, 1949.

———. *Principles of Art Appreciation*. New York: Harcourt, Brace and Co., 1949.

———. *World Hypotheses*. Berkeley: University of California Press, 1942.

Peters, Richard. *Hobbes*. Middlesex, Eng.: Penguin Books, 1956.

Petitjean, Armand M. *Présentation de Swift*. Paris: Gallimard, 1939.

Pevsner, Nikolaus. *The Englishness of English Art*. New York: F. A. Praeger, 1956.

Peyre, Henri. *Writers and Their Critics: A Study of Misunderstanding*. Ithaca, N.Y.: Cornell University Press, 1944.

Philostratus, Imagines. *Callistratus, Descriptiones*. Trans. Arthur Fairbanks. "Loeb Classic Library." New York: G. P. Putnam's Sons, 1931.

Piaget, Jean. *The Language and Thought of the Child*. Trans. M. Worden. New York: Harcourt, Brace and Co., 1926.

Pike, K. L. *The Intonation of American English*. Ann Arbor: University of Michigan Press, 1945.

———. *Language in Relation to a Unified Theory of the Structure of Human Behavior*. 2 vols. Glendale, Calif.: Summer Institute of Linguistics, 1954–1955.

Platt, Joan. "Development of English Colloquial Idiom During the Eighteenth Century," *Review of English Studies*, II, No. 5 (January, 1926), 70–81; II, No. 6 (April, 1926), 189–196.

Poirier, Michel. *Sir Philip Sidney, Le Chevalier Poète Élizabéthain.* Lille, France: Bibliothèque Universitaire, 1948.

Pollock, Thomas Clarke. *The Nature of Literature: Its Relation to Science, Language, and Human Experience.* Princeton, N.J.: Princeton University Press, 1942.

Pool, I. de Sola, ed. *Trends in Content Analysis.* Urbana: University of Illinois Press, 1959.

Pope, Alexander. *The Art of Sinking in Poetry.* Ed. Edna Steeves. New York: King's Crown Press, 1952.

Potter, G. R. *Editing Donne and Pope.* Los Angeles: University of California Press, 1953.

Potter, Simeon. *Our Language.* London: Pelican Books, 1950.

Potter, Stephen. *The Muse in Chains: A Study in Education.* London: J. Cape, 1937.

Pottle, Frederick A. *The Idiom of Poetry.* Ithaca, N.Y.: Cornell University Press, 1941.

Poulett, J. M. *Jonathan Swift and the Anatomy of Satire: A Study of Satiric Technique.* Cambridge: Harvard University Press, 1953.

Pound, Ezra. *Letters.* Ed. D. D. Page. New York: Hartcourt, Brace and Co., 1950.

————. *The ABC of Reading.* Norfolk, Conn.: New Directions, 1951.

————. *Instigations.* New York: Boni and Liveright, 1920.

————. *Spirit of Romance.* London: J. M. Dent & Sons, 1910.

Powell, A. E. *The Romantic Theory of Poetry, in Light of Croce's "Aesthetic."* London: J. M. Dent & Sons, 1926.

Prall, D. W. *Aesthetic Analysis.* New York: T. Y. Crowell, 1936.

————. *Aesthetic Judgment.* New York: T. Y. Crowell, 1929.

Pratt, Alice Edwards. *The Use of Color in the Verse of the English Romantic Poets.* Chicago: University of Chicago Press, 1898.

Prescott, Frederick Clarke. *The Poetic Mind.* New York: The Macmillan Co., 1922.

Press, John. *The Chequer'd Shade: Reflections on Obscurity in Poetry.* London: Oxford University Press, 1958.

Price, Martin. *Swift's Rhetorical Art: A Study in Structure and Meaning.* New Haven: Yale University Press, 1953.

Priestley, John B. *William Hazlitt.* London: Longmans, Green, 1960.

Proctor, S. K. *Thomas De Quincey's Theory of Literature.* Ann Arbor: University of Michigan Press, 1943.

Progoff, Iva. *Jung's Psychology and Its Social Meaning.* New York: Doubleday and Co., 1953.

Puttenham, George. *The Arte of English Poesie.* Ed. Gladys Willock and Alice Walker. Cambridge, Eng.: The University Press, 1936.

Pyles, Thomas. *The Origins and Development of the English Language.* New York: Harcourt, Brace and Co., 1964.

Quantity and Quality. Ed. Gerald Holton, *Daedalus,* Vol. LXXX, No. 4 (Fall, 1959).

Quayle, Thomas. *Poetic Diction: A Study of Eighteenth Century Verse.* London: University of Liverpool Press, 1924.

Quennell, Peter. *The Profane Virtues: Four Studies of the Eighteenth Century (Boswell, Gibbon, Sterne, Wilkes).* New York: Viking Press, 1945.

Quine, Willard. *From a Logical Point of View.* Cambridge, Mass.: Harvard University Press, 1953.

————. *Word and Object.* Cambridge: Massachusetts Institute of Technology Press, 1960.

Quintana, Ricardo. *The Mind and Art of Swift.* London: Methuen, 1953.

Radcliffe-Brown, A. A. *Structure and Function in Primitive Society.* Glencoe, Ill.: Free Press, 1952.

Radin, Mats. *Word-Order in English Verse from Pope to Sassoon.* Uppsala, 1925.

Rainolde, Richard. *The Foundacion of Rhetorike.* New York: Scholars' Facsimile and Reprints, 1945.

Raleigh, J. H. *Matthew Arnold and American Culture.* Berkeley: University of California Press, 1957.

Randall, Henry John. *The Creative Centuries: A Study in Historical Development.* New York: Longmans, Green, 1945.

Ransom, John Crowe. *The New Criticism.* Norfolk, Conn.: New Directions, 1941.

————. *The World's Body.* New York: Charles Scribner's Sons, 1938.

Rapoport, Anatol. *Science and the Goals of Man.* New York: Harper and Brothers, 1950.

Raymond, George Lansing. *Poetry as a Representative Art: An Essay in Comparative Aesthetics,* 7th rev. ed. New York: G. P. Putnam's Sons, 1899.

Read, Herbert. *Form in Modern Poetry.* London: Sheed & Ward, 1932.

————. *The Innocent Eye.* New York: Henry Holt and Co., 1947.

————. *Phases of English Poetry.* London: Leonard and Virginia Woolf, 1928.

Reed, Robert Burns. *Evolution of Didacticism in the English Lyric: Preface to a Critical Aesthetic.* Portland, Ore.: Reed College Press, 1938.

Rehder, Helmut, ed. *Literary Symbolism: A Symposium.* Austin: University of Texas, 1965.

Reichenbach, Hans. *Experience and Prediction: An Analysis of the Foundations and Structure of Knowledge.* Chicago: University of Chicago Press, 1938.

————. *The Rise of Scientific Philosophy.* Berkeley: University of California Press, 1951.

Reid, John R. "The Apotheosis of Intelligence," *Journal of Philosophy,* XXXII, No. 14 (July, 1935), 375–385.

————. *A Theory of Value.* New York: Charles Scribner's Sons, 1938.

Reynolds, W. V. "The Reception of Samuel Johnson's Prose Style," *Review of English Studies,* XI (1935), 145–162.

Richards, I. A. *Coleridge on Imagination.* London: Routledge & Kegan Paul, 1934.

―――. *Interpretation in Teaching*. New York: Harcourt, Brace and Co., 1938.

―――. *The Philosophy of Rhetoric*. London: Oxford University Press, 1936.

―――. *Practical Criticism*. New York: Harcourt, Brace and Co., 1930.

―――. *Principles of Literary Criticism*, 4th ed. London: Kegan Paul, 1925.

―――. *Science and Poetry*. London: Kegan Paul, 1926.

―――. *Speculative Instruments*. Chicago: University of Chicago Press, 1955.

Richardson, Charles F. *A Study of English Rhyme*. Hanover, N.J.: 1909.

Rickert, Edith. *New Methods for the Study of Literature*. Chicago: University of Chicago Press, 1927.

Ridenour, George M. *The Style of "Don Juan."* New Haven: Yale University Press, 1960.

Rieser, Max. "Analysis of the Poetic Simile," *Journal of Philosophy*, XXXVII, No. 8 (April 11, 1940), 209–217.

Ritchie, A. D. *The Natural History of Mind*. New York: Longmans, Green, 1936.

Roberts, Michael. *The Modern Mind*. New York: The Macmillan Co., 1937.

Roberts, Paul. *English Syntax*. New York: Harcourt, Brace and Co., 1964.

Robins, R. H. *Ancient and Medieval Grammatical Theory in Europe*. London: Bell, 1951.

Rodway, A. *Godwin and the Age of Transition*. London: G. H. Harrap, 1952.

Rohrer, John, ed. *Social Psychology at the Crossroads*. New York: Harper and Brothers, 1951.

Romanell, Patrick. *Toward a Critical Naturalism*. New York: The Macmillan Co., 1958.

Rosenberg, Alfred. *Longinus in England*. Berlin: Mayer & Müller, 1917.

Rosenberg, John D. *The Darkening Glass: A Portrait of Ruskin's Genius*. New York: Columbia University Press, 1961.

Rosenheim, Edward W. *Swift and the Satirist's Art*. Chicago: University of Chicago Press, 1963.

Rosenzweig, Mark R. "Comparison Among Word-Association Responses in English, French, German, and Italian," *American Journal of Psychology*, LXXIV, No. 3 (September, 1961), 347–360.

Ross, A. S. C. *Etymology*. Fair Lawn, N.J.: Essential Books, 1958.

Rossi, Marco. *A Plea for Man*. Edinburgh: University Press, 1956.

Røstvig, Maren Sofie. *The Background of English Neo-Classicism, with Comments on Swift and Pope*. Oslo: Universitetsprag, 1961.

―――. *The Happy Man: Studies in the Metamorphoses of a Classical Ideal*. 2 vols. Oslo, 1954; Oxford: Blackwell, 1958.

Roston, Murray. *Prophet and Poet*. Evanston, Ill.: Northwestern University Press, 1965.

Rougemont, Denis de. *The Devil's Share*. Trans. Haakon Chevalier. New York: Pantheon Press, 1944.

Rubel, Veré L. *Poetic Diction in the English Renaissance*. New York: Modern Language Association of America, 1941.

Ruesch, Jurgen and Weldon Kees. *Non-Verbal Communication. Notes on the Visual Perception of Human Relations*. Berkeley: University of California Press, 1956.

Runes, Dagobert, ed. *Twentieth-Century Philosophy: Living Schools of Thought.* New York: Philosophical Library, 1943.

Ruskin, John. *Modern Painters.* "Everyman's Library." New York: E. P. Dutton Co., 1929–1935.

Russell, Bertrand. *A History of Western Philosophy: Its Connection with Political and Social Circumstances from the Earliest Times to the Present Day.* New York: Simon and Schuster, 1945.

———. *An Inquiry into Meaning and Truth.* New York: W. W. Norton and Co., 1940.

———. *Introduction to Mathematical Philosophy,* 2nd ed. New York: The Macmillan Co., 1920.

Ruwet, Nicolas. "L'Analyse structurale de la poésie," *Linguistics,* No. 2. The Hague: Mouton & Co., 1963.

Ryan, Lawrence V. *Roger Ascham.* Stanford, Calif.: Stanford University Press, 1963.

Rylands, George. "English Poetry and the Abstract Word," *Essays and Studies,* Vol. XVI. Ed. H. J. C. Grierson. London: Oxford University Press, 1931.

———. *Words and Poetry.* New York: Payson and Clarke, 1928.

Ryle, Gilbert. *The Concept of Mind.* New York: Barnes and Noble, 1949.

Sachs, Curt. *The Commonwealth of Art.* New York: W. W. Norton and Co., 1946.

———. *Rhythm and Tempo.* New York: W. W. Norton and Co., 1953.

Sackton, A. H. *Rhetoric as a Dramatic Language in Ben Jonson.* New York: Columbia University Press, 1948.

Saintsbury, George. *History of Criticism and Literary Taste in Europe from Earliest Texts to the Present Day.* Edinburgh: W. Blackwood, 1902–1906.

———. *A History of English Prose Rhythm.* London: The Macmillan Co., 1912.

———. *A History of English Prosody.* 3 vols. London: The Macmillan Co., 1906, 1908, 1910.

Salisbury, John of. *The Metalogican: A Twelfth Century Defense of the Verbal and Logical Arts of the Trivium.* Trans. with introd. by D. G. McGarry. Berkeley: University of California Press, 1955.

Sampson, H. *The Language of Poetry.* London: Cranton, 1925.

Samuel, Irene. *Plato and Milton.* Ithaca, N.Y.: Cornell University Press, 1947.

Santayana, George. *Scepticism and Animal Faith.* New York: Charles Scribner's Sons, 1923.

———. *The Sense of Beauty: Outlines of Aesthetic Theory.* New York: Charles Scribner's Sons, 1896.

Sapir, Edward. *Language, An Introduction to the Study of Speech.* New York: Harcourt, Brace and Co., 1921.

———. *Culture, Language, and Personality: Selected Essays.* Berkeley: University of California Press, 1956.

Sartre, Jean-Paul. *L'Être et le Néant.* 13th ed. Paris: Gallimard, 1943.

de Saussure, F. *Cours de Linguistique Générale.* Ed. Charles Bally. Paris, 1922;

2nd ed., Paris: Payot, 1949. Trans. Wade Baskin. New York: Philosophical Library, 1959.

Sayce, R. A. *Style in French Prose: A Method of Analysis*. Oxford: The Clarendon Press, 1953.

Scarfe, Francis. *Auden and After: The Liberation of Poetry, 1930–1941*. London: Routledge & Kegan Paul, 1945.

Scheer, Cecil. *The Search for Order*. New York: Harper and Brothers, 1960.

Scheuerwegs, Gustave. *Present Day English Syntax: A Survey of Sentence Patterns*. New York: Longmans, Green, 1959.

Schiller, Andrew. "Gnomic Structure in Emerson's Poetry." "Papers of the Michigan Academy of Science, Arts and Letters," Vol. XL. Ann Arbor: University of Michigan Press, 1955, 313–320.

Schilling, B. N., ed. *Dryden: A Collection of Critical Essays*. Englewood Cliffs, N.J.: Prentice-Hall, 1963.

Schlauch, Margaret. *The Gift of Language*. New York: Dover Publications, Inc., 1955.

———. "Language and Poetic Creation," *The Gift of Tongues*. New York: Modern Age Books, 1942, pp. 227–259.

Schmezer, Guido. *Das Poetische Genus in den Gedichten von Matthew Arnold und Arthur Hugh Clough*. Dissertation, Berne, Switzerland, 1952.

Schneider, Elizabeth. *Aesthetic Motive*. New York: The Macmillan Co., 1939.

Schneider, Wilhelm. *Ausdruckswerte der deutschen Sprache: Eine Stilkunde*. Berlin: B. G. Teubner, 1931.

Schucking, Levin L. *The Sociology of Literary Taste*. Trans. E. W. Dickes. New York: Oxford University Press, 1944.

Schultz, Howard. *Milton and Forbidden Knowledge*. New York: Modern Language Association of America, 1955.

Schopenhauer, Arthur. *The Art of Literature*. Trans. T. Bailey Saunders. London: Swan Sonnenschein & Co., 1891.

Schwartz, Joseph, and John Rycenga, eds. *The Province of Rhetoric*. New York: Ronald Press Co., 1965.

Scott, F. N., and J. V. Denney. *Paragraph Writing*. Boston: Allyn and Bacon, 1909.

———. "The Scansion of Prose Rhythm," *PMLA*, Vol. XX (1908).

Sebeok, Thomas A., ed. *Myth: A Symposium*. Bloomington: Indiana University Press, 1958.

———, ed. *Style in Language*. Cambridge, Mass.: Massachusetts Institute of Technology Press, 1960.

de Selincourt, Ernest. *On Poetry: An Inaugural Lecture*. . . . Oxford: The Clarendon Press, 1929.

Selvin, Hanon Charles. *Effects of Leadership*. Glencoe, Ill.: Free Press, 1960.

Seward, Barbara. *The Symbolic Rose*. New York: Columbia University Press, 1960.

Sewell, Elizabeth. *The Orphic Voice: Poetry and Natural History*. New Haven: Yale University Press, 1960.

Shaftesbury, Anthony Ashley Cooper. *Characteristics of Men, Manners, Opin-*

ions, *Times*, with an Introduction by Stanley Green. Indianapolis, Ind.: Bobbs-Merrill Co., 1964.

Shapiro, Karl. *A Bibliography of Modern Prosody*. Baltimore: Johns Hopkins University Press, 1948.

Shapiro, Karl, and R. Beum. *Prosody Handbook*. New York: Harper and Brothers, 1965.

Sheldon, W. H. *Process and Polarity*. New York: Columbia University Press, 1944.

———. *The Varieties of Temperament: A Psychology of Constitutional Differences*. New York: Harper and Brothers, 1942.

Sherman, L. A. *Analytics of Literature*. Boston: Ginn and Co., 1893.

Shoemaker, Francis. *Aesthetic Experience and the Humanities*. New York: Columbia University Press, 1943.

Shumaker, Wayne. *Literature and the Irrational*. Englewood Cliffs, N.J.: Prentice-Hall, 1960.

Simpson, E. M. *A Study of the Prose Works of John Donne*, 2nd ed. Oxford: The Clarendon Press, 1948.

Sitwell, Edith. *Aspects of Modern Poetry*. London: Duckworth, 1934.

Skard, Sigmund. "The Use of Color in Literature," *Proceedings of the American Philosophical Society*, Vol. XC, No. 3 (July, 1946).

Skinner, B. F. *Verbal Behavior*. New York: D. Appleton, 1957.

Smith, Adam. *Lectures on Rhetoric and Belles Lettres*. Ed. John Lothian. New York: T. Nelson, 1963.

Smith, Arnold. *Grammar and the Use of Words*. London: Methuen, 1923.

Smith, Bernard. *Forces in American Criticism*. New York: Harcourt, Brace and Co., 1939.

Smith, Chard Powers. *Pattern and Variation in Poetry*. New York: Charles Scribner's Sons, 1932.

Smith, Gregory, ed. *Elizabethan Critical Essays*. 2 vols. Oxford: The Clarendon Press, 1904.

Söderlind, Johannes. *Verb Syntax in John Dryden's Prose*. Cambridge, Mass.: Harvard University Press, 1951–1958.

Sparrow, John. *Sense and Poetry: Essays on the Place of Meaning in Contemporary Verse*. London: Constable & Co., 1934.

Spence, Joseph. *Anecdotes, Observations, and Characters of Books and Men*, 2nd ed. Ed. S. W. Singer. London, 1858.

Spevack-Husmann, Helga. *The Mighty Pan: Milton's Mythologische Vergleiche*. Münster: Aschendorff, 1963.

Spingarn, J. E. *Critical Essays of the Seventeenth Century*. Oxford: The Clarendon Press, 1908.

———. *A History of Literary Criticism in the Renaissance*. New York: Harcourt, Brace and Co., 1963.

———. *The New Criticism*. New York: Columbia University Press, 1911.

Spitzer, Leo. *Classic and Christian Ideas of World Harmony*. Baltimore: Johns Hopkins University Press, 1962.

———. *Linguistics and Literary History: Essays in Stylistics*. Princeton, N.J.: Princeton University Press, 1948.

————. *Stilstudien*. Munich: Max Hueber, 1928.

Sprat, Thomas. *The History of the Royal Society of London*, 3rd ed. London: Samuel Chapman, 1722.

Spratt, S. E. "Cicero's Theory of Prose Style," *Philological Quarterly*, XXXIX (1955), 1–17.

————. *Milton's Art of Prosody*. Oxford: Blackwell, 1953.

Stanlis, Peter J. *Edmund Burke and the Natural Law*. Ann Arbor: University of Michigan Press, 1965.

Starkman, M. K. *Swift's Satire on Learning in "A Tale of a Tub."* Princeton, N.J.: Princeton University Press, 1950.

Staton, Walter, Jr. "The Characters of Style in Elizabethan Prose," *Journal of English and Germanic Philology*, LVII (1958), 197–207.

Stauffer, Donald, ed. *The Intent of the Critic*. Princeton, N.J.: Princeton University Press, 1941.

————. *The Nature of Poetry*. New York: W. W. Norton and Co., 1946.

Stebbing, L. S. *Logic in Practice*. London: Methuen, 1934.

Stebbing, William. *Some Verdicts of History Renewed*. London, 1887.

Stein, Gertrude. *Lectures in America*. New York: Random House, 1935.

Stein, Leo. *The ABC of Aesthetics*. New York: Boni and Liveright, 1927.

Stephen, Leslie. *English Thought in the Eighteenth Century*. London, 1876.

Stevenson, Charles L. *Ethics and Language*. New Haven: Yale University Press, 1944.

Steward, Julian H. *Theory of Culture Change*. Champagne: University of Illinois Press, 1955.

Stewart, George R. *Modern Metrical Technique as Illustrated by Ballad Meter, 1700–1920*. New York, 1922.

————. *The Technique of English Verse*. New York: Henry Holt and Co., 1930.

Stoehr, Taylor. *Dickens: The Dreamer's Stance*. Ithaca, N.Y.: Cornell University Press, 1965.

Stouffer, S. A., L. Guttman, *et al. Measurement and Prediction*. Princeton, N.J.: Princeton University Press, 1950.

Strachey, John. *Literature and Dialectical Materialism*. New York: Covici, Friede, 1934.

Strang, Barbara. *Modern English Structure*. New York: St. Martin's Press, 1962.

Strawson, P. F. *Individuals: An Essay in Descriptive Metaphysics*. London: Methuen, 1961.

Stutterheim, C. F. P. "Modern Stylistics," *Lingua*, III, No. 1 (1952), 52–68.

Sullivan, M. W. *Programmed English*. New York: The Macmillan Co., 1963.

Sutcliffe, Emerson Grant. *Emerson's Theories of Literary Expression*. "University of Illinois Studies in Language and Literature," VIII, No. 1 (February, 1923), 9–143.

Sutherland, James R. *On English Prose*. Toronto: University of Toronto Press, 1957.

————, and Ian Watt. *Restoration & Augustan Prose*. "Papers delivered at the Third Clark Library Seminar, William Andrews Clark Memorial Library." Los Angeles: University of California Press, 1956.

Svartengren, T. Hilding. *Intensifying Similes in English*. Dissertation. Lund, Sweden, 1915.

Sweeting, Elizabeth J. *Early Tudor Criticism, Linguistic and Literary*. Oxford: Blackwell, 1940.

Swedenberg, H. T. *The Theory of the Epic in England, 1650–1800*. "University of California Publications in English," Vol. XV. Berkeley: University of California Press, 1944.

Swift, Jonathan. *A Tale of a Tub*, 2nd ed., with an Introduction by A. C. Guthkilch and D. N. Smith. Oxford: The Clarendon Press, 1958.

———. *The Works of the Rev. Jonathan Swift, D.D.*, Vol. V (19 vols.). Arranged by Thomas Sheridan; corrected and revised by John Nichols. London: J. Johnson, 1801.

Symons, Arthur. *The Symbolist Movement in Literature*, rev. ed. New York: E. P. Dutton Co., 1919.

Sypher, Wylie. *Four Stages of Renaissance Style Transformations in Art and Literature, 1400–1700*. New York: Doubleday and Co., 1955.

———. *Rococo to Cubism in Art*. New York: Random House, 1960.

Tarski, Alfred. *Introduction to Logic and to the Methodology of the Deductive Sciences*. London: Oxford University Press, 1941.

Tasker, R. V. G. "The General Epistle of James: An Introduction and Commentary." *The Tyndale N. T. Commentaries*, Grand Rapids, Mich.: Eerdmans, 1957.

———. "The Gospel According to St. John." *The Tyndale N. T. Commentaries*, Grand Rapids, Mich.: Eerdmans, 1960.

Tate, Allen, ed., Phillip Wheelright, Cleanth Brooks, I. A. Richards, and Wallace Stevens. *The Language of Poetry*. Princeton, N.J.: Princeton University Press, 1942.

Tate, Allen. *On the Limits of Poetry: Selected Essays, 1928–1948*. New York: Swallow and Morrow, 1948.

———. *Reactionary Essays on Poetry and Ideas*. New York: Charles Scribner's Sons, 1936.

———. *Reason in Madness: Critical Essays*. New York: G. P. Putnam, 1941.

Taylor, Archer. *Proverbial Comparisons and Similes from California*. Berkeley: University of California Press, 1954.

Taylor, Henry. "Poetical Essays on Poetry," *Works*, Vol. V. London: Kegan Paul, 1878.

Teeter, Louis. *The Dramatic Use of Hobbes' Political Ideas: A Chapter from Political Themes in Restoration Tragedy*. Dissertation, Baltimore: Johns Hopkins University, 1936.

Teggart, F. J. "Causation in Historical Events," *Journal of History*, Vol. III, No. 1 (January, 1942).

———. *Processes of History*. New Haven: Yale University Press, 1918.

———. *Prolegomena to History*. "University of California Publications in History," Vol. IV, No. 3. Berkeley: University of California Press, 1916.

Tempest, Norton R. *The Rhythm of English Prose*. Cambridge: Eng.: The University Press, 1930.

Temple, Ruth Zabriskie. *The Critics' Alchemy: A Study of the Introduction of French Symbolism into England*. New York: Twayne Publishers, 1953.

Thaler, A. *Shakespeare and Sir Philip Sidney: The Influence of the Defense of Poesy*. Cambridge, Mass.: Harvard University Press, 1947.

Thayer, C. G. *Ben Jonson: Studies in the Plays*. Norman: University of Oklahoma Press, 1963.

Theory and Practice in Historical Study. "A Report of the Committee on Historiography," Bulletin No. 54. New York: Social Research Council, 1946.

Thompson, Craig R. *The Translations of Lucian by Erasmus and St. Thomas More*. Binghamton, N.Y.: The Vail-Ballou Press, 1940.

Thompson, John. *The Founding of English Metre*. London: Routledge & Kegan Paul, 1961.

Thomson, J. A. K. *Classical Influences on English Prose*. New York: Collier, 1962.

Thorndike, Edward L. *The Teacher's Word Book*. New York: Columbia University Press, 1921.

Thorpe, Clarence DeWitt. *The Aesthetic Theory of Thomas Hobbes*. Ann Arbor: University of Michigan Press, 1940.

Thorpe, James E. *Milton Criticism: Selections from Four Centuries*. New York: Rinehart and Co., 1950.

Thurstone, L. L. *Vectors of Mind: Multiple-Factor Analysis for the Isolation of Primary Traits*. Chicago: University of Chicago Press, 1935.

Tillotson, Geoffrey. *Essays in Criticism and Research*. New York: Columbia University Press, 1942.

Tillyard, E. M. *Milton*. London: Longmans, Green, 1962.

Tobin, James. *A Bibliography of Eighteenth Century English Literature and Its Cultural Background*. New York: Fordham University Press, 1939.

Toliver, Harold E. *Marvell's Ironic Vision*. New Haven: Yale University Press, 1965.

Tooke, John Horne. *The Diversions of Purley*, new ed. London, 1840.

Townsend, F. G. *Ruskin and the Landscape Feeling: A Critical Analysis of His Thought During the Crucial Years of His Life*. Urbana: University of Illinois Press, 1951.

Townsend, Freda. *Apologie for Bartholomew Fayre: The Art of Jonson's Comedies*. New York: Modern Language Association of America; London: Oxford University Press, 1947.

Trager, George L., and Henry Lee Smith. *An Outline of English Structure*. Norman: University of Oklahoma Press, 1951.

Trapp, Joseph. *Praelectiones Poeticae*, 2 vols. Oxford, 1711–1715.

Treece, Henry, ed. *Herbert Read: An Introduction to His Work by Various Hands*. London: Faber & Faber, 1944.

Trench, Archbishop Richard Chenevix, D.D. *On the Study of Words*. Ed. A. S. Palmer. London: Routledge, 1913.

Trend, J. B. *Lorca and the Spanish Poetic Tradition*. Oxford: Blackwell, 1956.

Trilling, Lionel. *Matthew Arnold*, 2nd ed. New York: Columbia University Press, 1949.

Trimpi, Wesley. *Ben Jonson's Poems: A Study of the Plain Style*. Stanford, Calif.: Stanford University Press, 1962.

Trowbridge, Hugh. "Aristotle and the New Criticism," *Sewanee Review*, LII, No. 4 (Autumn, 1944), 537–556.

Tucker, Susie. *English Examined: Two Centuries of Comment*. Cambridge, Eng.: The University Press, 1961.

Turbayne, Colin. *The Myth of Metaphor*. New Haven: Yale University Press, 1962.

Turnbull, Eleanor L., trans. *Contemporary Spanish Poets*. Baltimore: Johns Hopkins University Press, 1945.

Tuve, Rosemond. *Seasons and Months: Studies in a Tradition of Middle English Poetry*. Paris: Librairie Universitaire, 1933.

Tuveson, Ernest. *Millennium and Utopia*. Berkeley: University of California Press, 1949.

———. *The Imagination as a Means of Grace: Locke and the Aesthetics of Romanticism*. Berkeley: University of California Press, 1960.

Tyler, L. *Psychology of Human Differences*. New York: Appleton-Century-Crofts, 1956.

Ullmann, Stephen. *The Principles of Semantics*, 2nd ed. New York: Philosophical Library, 1957.

Upton, Albert. *Design for Thinking: A First Book in Orthology*. Whittier, California: 1945–1946.

Urban, Wilbur M. *Language and Reality: The Philosophy of Language and the Principles of Symbolism*. London: Allen & Unwin, 1939.

Ushenko, Andrew Paul. *The Field Theory of Meaning*. Ann Arbor: University of Michigan Press, 1958.

Ussher, A. *Three Great Irishmen: Shaw, Yeats, Joyce*. London: Gollancz, 1952.

Utley, Thomas E. *Edward Burke*. London: Longmans, Green, 1957.

Valentine, C. W. *Introduction to Experimental Psychology of Beauty*. London: E. C. Joch, no date.

Valéry, Paul. *The Art of Poetry*. "Bollingen Series," Vol. XLV. New York: Pantheon, 1958.

Vallins, G. H. *The Pattern of English*. London: Deutsch, 1956.

Van der Vat, Daniel. *The Fabulous Opera: A Study of Continuity in French and English Poetry of the Nineteenth Century*. Groningen, Batavia: J. B. Wolter, 1936.

Vartamian, Aram. *Diderot and Descartes: A Study of Scientific Naturalism in the Enlightenment*. Princeton, N.J.: Princeton University Press, 1953.

Vendryes, J. *Language: A Linguistic Introduction to History*. Trans. Paul Rodin. New York: Alfred A. Knopf, 1925.

Véron, Eugène. *Aesthetics*. Trans. W. H. Armstrong. London: Chapman & Hull, 1879.

Vico, Giambattista. *Autobiography of Giambattista Vico*. Trans. Max Fisch and Thomas Bergin. Ithaca, N.Y.: Cornell University Press, 1944.

Visser, F. Th. *An Historical Syntax of the English Language, Pt. 1: Syntactical Units with One Verb.* Leiden: E. J. Brill, 1963.

———. *A Syntax of the English Language of St. Thomas More.* Louvain: C. Uystpruyst, 1946–1956.

The Visual Arts Today. Daedalus, Vol. LXXXIX, No. 1 (Winter, 1960).

Vivante, Leone. "The Misleading Comparison between Art and Drams." Trans. Prof. Brodrick-Bulloch, *New Criterion,* IV, No. 3 (July, 1926), 436–453.

Voegelin, C. F., and J. Yegerlehner. "Toward a Definition of Formal Style, with Examples from Shawnee," in W. E. Richmond, ed. *Studies in Folklore.* Bloomington: University of Indiana Press, 1957, pp. 141–150.

Voigt, Milton. *Swift and the Twentieth Century.* Detroit: Wayne State University Press, 1964.

Vossler, Karl. *The Spirit of Language in Civilization.* Trans. Oscar Oeser. London: Kegan Paul, 1932.

Voorhees, Richard J. *The Paradox of George Orwell.* Lafayette, Ind.: Purdue University Press, 1961.

Wackwitz, Beate. *Die Theorie des Prosastils im England des 18. Jahrhunderts.* "Brittannica et Americana," Vol. X. Hamburg: Cram, de Gruyter & Co., 1962.

Waddell, Robert. *Grammar and Style.* New York: Duell, Sloane and Pearce, 1951.

Wain, John. *Essays on Literature and Ideas.* London: The Macmillan Co., 1963.

Walcutt, Charles. *Anatomy of Prose.* New York: The Macmillan Co., 1962.

Wallace, K. R. *Francis Bacon on Communication and Rhetoric.* Chapel Hill: University of North Carolina Press, 1943.

Wallerstein, Ruth. "The Development of the Rhetoric and Metric of the Heroic Couplet, Especially in 1625–1645," *PMLA,* L, No. 1 (March, 1935), 166–209.

———. *Studies in Seventeenth Century Poetic.* Madison: University of Wisconsin Press, 1961.

Walpole, Hugh R. *Semantics: The Nature of Words and Their Meanings.* New York: W. W. Norton and Co., 1941.

Warren, Alba H. *English Poetic Theory, 1825–1865.* Princeton, N. J.: Princeton University Press, 1950.

Warren, Austin. *Rage for Order: Essays in Criticism.* Chicago: University of Chicago Press, 1948.

Wasserman, Earl. *The Subtler Language: Critical Readings of Neoclassic and Romantic Poems.* Baltimore: Johns Hopkins University Press, 1959.

Waterman, J. T. *Perspectives in Linguistics.* Chicago: University of Chicago Press, 1963.

Watts, A. G. *The Language and Mental Development of Children.* London: Harrap, 1944.

Weaver, Richard. *The Ethics of Rhetoric.* Chicago: Regnery, 1953.

Weaver, W. "Probability, Rarity, Interest and Surprise," *Scientific Monthly,* XIV, No. 2 (1948), 390–392.

Webber, Joan. *Contrary Music: The Prose Style of John Donne*. Madison: University of Wisconsin Press, 1963.

Webster, Noah. *Dissertation on the English Language*. Boston, 1789.

Wedgwood, C. V. *Edward Gibbon*. London: Longmans, Green, 1955.

Welby, V. *What is Meaning? Studies in the Development of Significance*. London: Kegan Paul, 1903.

Wellek, René. "Concepts of Form and Structure in Twentieth-Century Criticism," *Neophilologus*, IV, No. 2 (1958), 2–11.

———. *A History of Modern Criticism, 1750–1850*. New Haven: Yale University Press, 1955.

———. "Periods and Movements in Literary History," *English Institute Journal*, 1940; New York: Columbia University Press, 1941, pp. 73–93.

———. *The Rise of English Literary History*. Chapel Hill: University of North Carolina Press, 1941.

Wells, Henry W. *Poetic Imagery*. New York: Columbia University Press, 1924.

Werner, Heinz. *Die Ursprünge der Lyrik: Eine entwicklungspsychologische Untersuchung*. Munich: E. Reinhardt, 1924.

West, James. *Plainville, USA*. New York: Columbia University Press, 1945.

Weyl, Herman. *Symmetry*. Princeton, N.J.: Princeton University Press, 1952.

Whately, Richard. *Elements of Rhetoric*. New York: Harper and Brothers, 1860.

Whatmough, Joshua. *Language: A Modern Synthesis*. New York: St. Martin's Press, 1956.

Wheat, Leonard B. *Free Associations to Common Words*. New York: Bureau of Publications, Teachers College, Columbia University Press, 1931.

Wheelwright, Philip. *The Burning Fountain: A Study in the Language of Symbolism*. Bloomington: Indiana University Press, 1954.

———. *Metaphor and Reality*. Bloomington: Indiana University Press, 1962.

White, Lancellot Law, ed. *Aspects of Form*. London: Humphries, 1951.

White, Leslie. *The Science of Culture*. New York: Farrar, Strauss, 1959.

White, Lynn. *Frontiers of Knowledge in the Study of Man*. New York: Harper and Brothers, 1956.

White, William. *John Donne Since 1900: a Bibliography of Periodical Articles*. Boston: F. W. Faxon, 1942.

Whitehall, H. "From Linguistics to Criticism," *Kenyon Review*, XVIII, No. 3 (1956), 411–421.

———. *Structural Essentials of English*. Cambridge, Mass.: Harvard University Press, 1951, 1956.

Whitehead, Alfred North. *Science and the Modern World*, "Lowell Lectures, 1925." New York: New American Library, 1948.

———. *Symbolism: Its Meaning and Effect*, "Lectures at the University of Virginia, 1927." New York: The Macmillan Co., 1927.

Whorf, Benjamin Lee. *Four Articles on Metalinguistics*. Washington, D.C.: Department of State, 1950.

———. *Language, Thought and Reality: Selected Writings*. Ed. John B. Carroll, Cambridge, Mass.: Massachusetts Institute of Technology Press, 1956.

Wilhelm, Helmut. *Change*. Trans. Cary Baynes. New York: Pantheon, 1960.

Wilkins, Ernest A., and Thomas Bergin, eds. *A Concordance to the Divine Comedy of Dante*. Cambridge, Mass.: Harvard University Press, 1965.

Wilkinson, L. P. *Golden Latin Artistry*. Cambridge, Eng.: The University Press, 1963.

Willey, Basil. *The Eighteenth Century Background*. London: Chatto & Windus, 1940.

———. *The Seventeenth Century Background*. London: Chatto & Windus, 1934.

Williams, Ralph M. *Poet, Painter, and Parson: The Life of John Dyer*. New York: Bookman Associates, 1956.

Williams, William Carlos. *Selected Letters*. New York: McDowell, Obolensky, 1957.

———. *Autobiography*. New York: Random House, 1951.

Williamson, A. *Bernard Shaw: Man and Writer*. New York: T. Y. Crowell, 1963.

Williamson, George. *The Proper Wit of Poetry*. Chicago: University of Chicago Press, 1961.

———. *The Senecan Amble: A Study in Prose from Bacon to Collier*. Chicago: University of Chicago Press, 1951.

Wilson, Edmund. *Axel's Castle: A Study in the Imaginative Literature of 1870–1930*. New York: Charles Scribner's Sons, 1931.

Wilson, F. P. *Seventeenth Century Prose*. Berkeley: University of California Press, 1960.

Wilson, Katharine. *Sound and Meaning in English Poetry*. London: Jonathan Cope, 1930.

Wilson, Thomas. *Arte of Rhetorique*, 1560. Ed. C. H. Mair. Oxford: The Clarendon Press, 1919

Wilstach, Frank Jenners. *Dictionary of Similes*. Boston: Little, Brown, and Co., 1916.

Wimsatt, W. K., Jr. *The Verbal Icon*. Lexington: University of Kentucky Press, 1954.

Wimsatt, William Kurtz. *Philosophic Words: A Study of Style and Meaning in "The Rambler" and "Dictionary of Samuel Johnson."* New Haven: Yale University Press, 1948.

———. *The Prose Style of Samuel Johnson*. New Haven: Yale University Press, 1941.

Winchester, C. J. *Some Principles of Literary Criticism*. New York: The Macmillan Co., 1899.

Winters, Yvor. *Anatomy of Nonsense*. Norfolk, Conn.: New Directions, 1943.

———. *Maule's Curse*. Norfolk, Conn.: New Directions, 1948.

———. *Primitivism and Decadence: A Study of American Experimental Poetry*. New York: Arrow Editions, 1939.

Wirth, Louis, ed. *Contemporary Social Problems*. Chicago: University of Chicago Press, 1939.

Wisdom, J. O. *Foundations of Inference in Natural Science*. London: Methuen, 1952.

Wittgenstein, Ludwig. *Philosophical Investigations.* Trans. G. E. M. Anscombe. New York: The Macmillan Co., 1960.

Wolff, Erwin. *Shaftesbury und seine Bedeutung für die englische Literatur des 18 Jahrhunderts: der Moralist und die literarische Form.* Tübingen: Niemeyer, 1960.

Wölfflin, Heinrich. *Principles of Art History.* Trans. M. D. Hottinger. New York: Dover Publications, 1932.

Woods, Margaret L., ed. *Essays by Divers Hands.* "Transactions of the Royal Society of the United Kingdom," New Series, Vol. VII. London: Royal Society of Literature in the United Kingdom, 1927.

Woodworth, Robert. *Dynamics of Behavior.* New York: Henry Holt and Co., 1958.

Wordsworth, William. *The Letters of William and Dorothy Wordsworth: The Middle Years.* Ed. E. de Selincourt. Oxford: The Clarendon Press, 1937; *The Later Years,* 1939.

————. *Poems and Extracts Presented to Lady Mary Lowther, 1819.* (Printed literally from the original album with facsimiles.) London: Oxford University Press, 1905.

Wormald, B. H. G. *Clarendon: Politics, History and Religion, 1640–60.* Cambridge, Eng.: The University Press, 1951.

Wright, George T. *The Poet in the Poem.* Berkeley: University of California Press, 1958.

Wright, Louis B. *Middle Class Culture in Elizabethan England.* Chapel Hill: University of North Carolina Press, 1935.

Wyld, Henry Cecil. *Some Aspects of the Diction of English Poetry: Three Lectures.* Oxford: University of London Press, 1933.

Wyler, Siegfried. *Die Adjektive des mittelenglischen Schoenheitsfeld.* Zurich, 1944.

Yeats, W. E. *Autobiographies.* New York: The Macmillan Co., 1927.

————. *Essays and Introductions.* London: The Macmillan Co., 1961.

————. *A Vision.* New York: The Macmillan Co., 1961.

Young, Agnes Brooks. *Recurring Cycles of Fashion, 1760–1937.* New York: Harper and Brothers, 1937.

Young, Charles L. *Emerson's Montaigne.* New York: The Macmillan Co., 1941.

Young, R. B. "English Petrarke: A Study of Sidney's Astrophel and Stella," in *Three Studies in the Renaissance.* New Haven: Yale University Press, 1958.

Yule, G. Udny. *The Statistical Study of Literary Vocabulary.* Cambridge, Eng.: The University Press, 1944.

Zabel, Morton Dauwen, ed. *Literary Opinion in America: Essays Illustrating the Sections, Methods, and Problems of Criticism in the United States Since the War.* New York: Harper and Brothers, 1937.

Zahner, Louis C. *Language in General Education.* New York: Progressive Education Association, 1940.

Ziegler, D. W. *In Divided and Distinguished Worlds: Religion and Rhetoric in the Writings of Thomas Browne.* Cambridge, Mass.: Harvard University Press, 1943.

Zimmer, Heinrich. *Myths and Symbols in Judean Art and Civilization*. Ed. Joseph Campbell. New York: Pantheon Books, 1946.

Zipf, George Kingsley. *Human Behavior and the Principle of Least Effort*. Cambridge, Mass.: Addison-Wesley, 1949.

———. *The Psycho-Biology of Language*. Boston: Houghton Mifflin Co., 1935.

Zwerdling, Alex. *Yeats and the Heroic Ideal*. New York: New York University Press, 1965.